Delphi Nuts &
For Experienced
Programmers,
Second Edition

About the Author...

Gary Cornell is a computer programmer and professor of mathematics at the University of Connecticut. He has written or coauthored several acclaimed books, including *The Visual Basic 4 for Windows 95 Handbook* and the first editon of *Delphi Nuts & Bolts: For Experienced Programmers.*

He can be reached at 75720.1524@compuserve.com.

Delphi Nuts & Bolts:
For Experienced Programmers,
Second Edition

Gary Cornell

Osborne **McGraw-Hill**

Berkeley New York St. Louis San Francisco
Auckland Bogotá Hamburg London Madrid
Mexico City Milan Montreal New Delhi Panama City
Paris São Paulo Singapore Sydney
Tokyo Toronto

Osborne **McGraw-Hill**
2600 Tenth Street
Berkeley, California 94710
U.S.A.

For information on translations or book distributors outside the U.S.A., or to arrange bulk purchase discounts for sales promotions, premiums, or fundraisers, please contact Osborne **McGraw-Hill** at the above address.

Delphi Nuts & Bolts: For Experienced Programmers, Second Edition

1234567890 DOC 99876

ISBN 0-07-882203-3

Acquisitions Editor
Wendy Rinaldi

Senior Editorial Assistant
Daniela Dell'Orco

Technical Editor
Todd Miller

Project Editor
Janet Walden

Copy Editor
Jan Jue

Proofreader
Pat Mannion

Indexer
David Heiret

Computer Designer
Peter F. Hancik

Series Design
Marcela V. Hancik

Quality Control Specialist
Joe Scuderi

Cover Design
Ted Mader Associates

For

Shara Claire
Rebecca Ann
Alyssa Jane
Deborah Rae
Emma Esther

who are my chief delight, both collectively and individually.

—Uncle Gary

Contents at a Glance

Table of Contents

Acknowledgments

One of the best parts of writing a book is when the authors get to thank those who have helped them, for rarely (and certainly not in this case) is a book truly the product of the authors' work alone. First and foremost, I have to thank the team at Osborne/McGraw-Hill. Their patience, dedication, help, cheerfulness—you name it—made this project both possible and tolerable. To Wendy Rinaldi, Janet Walden, Daniela Dell'Orco, and Marcela and Peter Hancik: Thanks!

Next, I would like to thank Todd Miller who did an outstanding job on the tech review, far beyond what an author can expect, or hope for. I really can't thank him enough—almost every page in this edition benefitted from his suggestions.

I want to thank Cay Horstmann, who is not only a good friend, but also the best programmer I know. He has taught me an immense amount, both through conversation and through his well-written books.

Thanks also to Troy Strain, my coauthor on the previous edition of this book. His graciousness and friendship are much appreciated.

I also want to thank those people at Borland (whose names I unfortunately don't know) who created Delphi and improved it dramatically in the 32-bit version. It's a truly great product. Nan Borreson is the author liaison at Borland. Her patience with strange requests and her general all-around helpfulness went way beyond the call of duty. Without the information she supplied, this book could never have been completed.

Finally, I would like to thank all my friends who put up with my strange ways and occasionally short temper for lo, so many months. In particular, thanks to Bruce, Caroline, and Kurt; without their special friendship and help, this book would have been impossible to write.

Introduction

Delphi is the most exciting language product to hit the market in quite a while. The press has rarely been so excited by a product. So what is all the hype about? Exactly what is Delphi and what can it do for you? Well, it's an easy-to-use, yet extraordinarily powerful tool for developing Windows applications. Moreover, it uses modern compiler technology to produce incredibly fast executables. It even has the ability to do true object-oriented programming and client-server database development.

If this doesn't seem like enough to justify all the hoopla, remember that with Delphi, C and C++ expertise will rarely if ever be required even for developing the most sophisticated applications. No longer will you have to be an expert C programmer and keep about 20 pounds of documentation around in order to develop lightning-fast Windows applications.

About This Book

This book is a short guide to *both* versions of Delphi for experienced programmers. I tried to make this book useful to developers for both Windows 3.X and Windows 95, and for users of both versions of Delphi. I am assuming you have some programming experience (what language really doesn't matter), and that concepts like loops and decision structures are familiar to you. In sum, what I want to do in this book is show you why Delphi is so useful and what you need to know to make Delphi part of your programming tool chest.

More precisely, the idea I had in writing this book was to distill out the essence of both versions of Delphi and present it to you clearly and concisely. I've tried hard to stress the new ways of thinking needed to master Delphi programming, so even experts in more traditional programming languages can benefit from this book. I've taken this approach because trying to force Delphi into the framework of older programming languages is ultimately self-defeating—you can't take advantage of its power if you continue to think within an older paradigm.

I assume that after you know what makes Delphi "tick" you can use the online help and the manuals supplied with Delphi as needed. I don't burden you with a lot of examples, I assume that you have written lots of code before. I feel that once you are well grounded in the ways of thinking in Delphi you can look at the many pieces of sample code supplied with the product if you need more examples than I give in this book.

How This Book Is Organized

This book can be used in a variety of ways, depending on your background and needs. People familiar with Visual Basic might want to skim the early chapters and spend more time on the later chapters where I cover the underlying language in Delphi. Those who are familiar with Pascal or C, but not an event-driven language like Visual Basic, might want to spend more time on the early chapters and skim the chapters that cover the underlying language. (In any case, I do suggest looking at all the chapters, because no matter what your language background, there is information specific to Delphi to be found in them all.)

Here are brief descriptions of the 14 chapters:

- ♦ Chapter 1 gives you an introduction to Delphi and shows you two simple programs.
- ♦ Chapter 2 shows you the environment for using Delphi 32.
- ♦ Chapter 3 shows you the environment for using Delphi 16.
- ♦ Chapter 4 starts you right off with the notion of a customizable window (called a form) that is the heart of every Microsoft Windows (and, thus, Delphi) application. You'll see how to add and manipulate the basic Delphi objects such as push buttons, places to enter text, labels, timers, and grids to your forms.
- ♦ Chapters 5 and 6 survey the version of Object Pascal used in Delphi.
- ♦ Chapter 7 is a brief introduction to object-oriented programming.
- ♦ Chapter 8 covers ***exceptions***, which is Delphi's very sophisticated way of handling run-time errors.
- ♦ Chapter 9 discusses debugging techniques.
- ♦ Chapter 10 covers techniques for handling files.

♦ Chapter 11 introduces you to the world of dynamic data exchange (DDE) and object linking and embedding (OLE).

♦ Chapter 12 introduces you to the world of graphics. Since Microsoft Windows is a graphical environment, the powers of Delphi in this arena are pretty spectacular.

♦ Chapter 13 covers more advanced user interface features such as techniques for working with a mouse.

♦ Chapter 14 is a brief introduction to Delphi's basic database features.

 Note: This book does not cover how to use Delphi to develop client-server applications.

Conventions Used in This Book

First off, I call the 32-bit version of Delphi by the more common "street name" of Delphi 32, rather than the official (seldom used) name of Delphi 2.0. Similarly, I use Delphi 16 rather than the official name of Delphi 1.0. Windows versions prior to Windows 95 are referred to as Windows 3.X.

Keys are set in small capital letters in the text. For example, keys such as CTRL and ALT appear as shown here. Arrow and other direction keys are spelled out and also appear in small capital letters. For example, if you need to press the right arrow key, you'll see, "Press RIGHT ARROW."

When you need to use a combination of keys to activate a menu item, the keys will be separated by hyphens and the entire key combination will appear in small capital letters. For example, "Press CTRL-A-B" indicates that you should hold down the key marked "Ctrl" on your keyboard while pressing first an "A" and then a "B." On the other hand, "ALT-F, P" means press the "ALT" and "F" keys, and then the "P" key—you don't have to hold down the "ALT" key.

DOS commands, filenames, and file extensions appear in full capital letters: COMMAND.COM, .TXT, and so on. I try to follow Delphi's own documentation conventions. Menu choices are indicated with a bar between them, e.g., "Choose Run | Run." Keywords appear in the text in lowercase boldface, as in "**try/finally**." Built-in functions and procedures follow Delphi's own naming convention and so usually appear with the first letter of each word capitalized, such as Font, TextOut, and so on.

The syntax for a command in Delphi is most often set as regular text in an inline list. Items in the syntax that the programmer can change appear in italics. For example, the Rename command used to rename a file would appear as

Rename (*OldFileName, NewFileName*)

Finally, programs are set in a monospace font, as shown here:

```
procedure TForm1.FormClick(Sender: TObject);
begin
  ShowMessage('Hello world!');
end;
```

(Even though Delphi boldfaces keywords in code listings, I only do so in Chapter 1, or when I am presenting a template to you.)

Finally, I have numerous notes and tips that are indicated by various icons. For example, a note is something like this:

 Note: Most of the screen shots for this book were done in Delphi 32 under Windows 95. The screen shots under Delphi 16 will be similar.

A general tip might be something like this:

 Tip: Don't try to install both versions of Delphi in the same directory.

There are also tips that are of primary interest to Visual Basic programmers. They are indicated as shown here:

 Visual Basic Tip: Delphi 16 comes with a file called DELPHI2VB.TXT in its DOC directory that should be studied once you are more familiar with Delphi.

Finally, there are tips for people moving from the earlier version of Borland's Pascal language. They look like this:

Pascal Tip: You should not try to combine a program using Borland's Object Vision with Delphi's Visual Component Library.

Chapter

1

Getting Started

This chapter gives you an overview of the ideas behind programming both the 16- and 32-bit versions of Delphi. You'll also see how easy it is to create simple Delphi programs. The two programs described later in this chapter introduce the event-driven, object-oriented model that makes both versions of Delphi so powerful. What this chapter (and book) does not do is show you how to install either version of Delphi, start it, manipulate windows within a Windows environment, and so on—we are assuming that you know this. However, we are *not* assuming any expertise in Delphi or Windows programming—just a general level of programming sophistication that may have come from working in any environment.

Why Windows and Why Delphi?

Graphical user interfaces, or *GUIs* (pronounced "gooies"), have revolutionized the microcomputer industry. They demonstrate that the proverb "a picture is worth a thousand words" hasn't lost its truth. Instead of the cryptic C:> prompt that DOS users have long seen (and that some have long feared), users are presented with a desktop filled with icons and with programs that use mice and menus. Perhaps even more important in the long run than the *look* of Microsoft Windows applications is the *feel* of applications developed for it. Regardless of which version of Windows you use, Windows applications generally have a consistent user interface. (At least there is an attempt at consistency—Windows 95 programs, of course, look different than Windows 3.X programs.) The idea is that users can spend more time mastering the application and less time worrying about which keystrokes do what within menus and dialog boxes.

While programmers have long had mixed feelings about GUIs, beginning users seem to like them, so all Windows programs are expected to be based on the GUI model (and to have the right look and feel). Therefore, if you need to develop programs for Windows, you'll want a tool to develop GUI-based applications efficiently.

For a long time there were *no* such tools. Before Visual Basic was introduced in 1991, developing Windows applications was much harder than developing DOS applications. Programmers had to worry about too much, such as what the mouse was doing, where the user was inside a menu, and whether he or she was clicking or double-clicking at a given place. Developing a Windows application required expert C programmers and hundreds of lines of code for the simplest task. Even the experts had trouble. (The Microsoft Windows Software Development Kit that was required in addition to a C compiler weighed in at $9\frac{1}{2}$ pounds.)

Visual Basic in its first three versions started changing this process; the 16-bit version of Delphi revolutionized it. The new 32-bit version of Delphi (commonly called Delphi 32, although officially named Delphi 2.0) brings the same features to Windows 95 and Windows NT development that the 16-bit version of Delphi (commonly called Delphi 16, officially Delphi 1.0) brought to Windows 3.X development—and a lot more. Sophisticated Windows applications can now be developed in a fraction of the time previously needed. Programming errors (bugs) don't happen as often and, if they do, they're a lot easier to detect and fix. Simply put: *with Delphi, programming for all versions of Windows has become not only more efficient, but also fun* (most of the time).

Regardless of which version of Delphi you are working with, you will have the following advantages over the first four versions of Visual Basic:

♦ Applications developed with Delphi are essentially as fast as those developed in C or C++.

♦ With Delphi you can build true executables including DLLs. (*DLLs* stands for *dynamic link libraries*—the cornerstone of Windows programming.)

♦ You can build reusable objects following the paradigms of object-oriented programming (see Chapter 7).

Of course, the 32-bit version of Delphi adds far more: for example, it allows you to handle essentially unlimited-length strings with the ease of Visual Basic, building completely OLE-compliant applications, such as a financial functions package. It even has a new compiler whose error messages are often helpful—unlike Delphi 1.0's compiler.

Note: Although the client/server versions of Delphi are not covered in this book, both the 16- and 32-bit versions of Delphi Client/Server make developing such applications much easier as well.

How You Develop a Delphi Application

The first step in developing a Delphi application is to plan what the user will see—in other words, to design the screens. What menus do you want? How large a window should the application use? How many windows should there be? Should the user be able to resize the windows? Where will you place the push buttons that the user will click on to activate the applications? Will the applications have places (*edit boxes* and *memo fields*) to enter text?

In Delphi, the objects a programmer places on the windows he or she is designing are called *components.* Depending on which version of Delphi you have, you start with more than 70 (for the 16-bit version) or more than 100 (for the 32-bit version) components at your disposal, and then you can add components by buying them or creating them. See Chapter 4 for a survey of the components supplied with Delphi.

Note: If you have some familiarity with object-oriented programming (OOP), then you should be aware that Delphi components are indeed objects in the sense of OOP. (Please see Chapter 7 for more on object-oriented programming and how Delphi's components fit in with the tenets of OOP.)

Delphi shares with Visual Basic the ease with which you can design the screen. You literally draw the user interface, almost as though you were using a paint program. In addition, when you're done drawing the interface, the command buttons and other components that you have placed in a blank window will automatically recognize user actions such as mouse movements and button clicks. Delphi also comes with a menu design feature that makes creating both ordinary and pop-up menus a snap—and *unlike* Visual Basic, Delphi makes it easy to reuse any interface features you created in previous applications.

Only after you design the interface does anything like traditional programming occur. Components in Delphi will recognize events like mouse clicks; how the objects respond to them depends on the code you write. You will almost always need to write code in order to make components respond to events. This makes Delphi programming fundamentally different from conventional procedural-oriented programming as in early versions of Turbo Pascal.

Programs in conventional programming languages run from the top down. For older programming languages, execution starts from the first line and moves with the flow of the program to different parts as needed. A Delphi program usually works completely differently. The core of a Delphi program is a set of independent pieces of code that are *activated* by, and so *respond* to, only the events they have been told to recognize. This is a fundamental shift. Now, instead of a programmer designing a program to do what the programmer thinks should happen, the user is in control.

The programming code in Delphi that tells your program how to respond to events like mouse clicks begins inside what Delphi calls *event procedures*. An event procedure is a body of code that is only executed in response to an external event. In almost all cases, everything executable in a Delphi program is either in an event procedure or is used by an event procedure to help the procedure carry out its job. In fact, to stress that Delphi is fundamentally different from ordinary programming languages, the documentation uses the term *project*, rather than *program*, to refer to the combination of programming code and user interface that goes into making a Delphi application possible.

Here is a summary of the steps you take to design a Delphi application:

1. Customize the windows that the user sees.
2. Decide what events the components on the window should recognize.
3. Write the event procedures for those events (and the subsidiary procedures and objects that make those event procedures work).

Here is what happens when the application is running:

1. Delphi monitors the windows and the components in each window for *all* the events that each control can recognize (mouse movements, clicks, keystrokes, and so on).
2. When Delphi detects an event, if there isn't an internal built-in response to the event, Delphi examines the application to see if you've written an event procedure for that event.
3. If you have written an event procedure, Delphi executes the code that makes up that event procedure and goes back to step 1.
4. If you have not written an event procedure, Delphi waits for the next event and goes back to step 1.

These steps cycle continuously until the application ends. Usually, an event must happen before Delphi will do anything. Thus, event-driven programs are *reactive* more than *active*—and that makes them more user-friendly.

Since Delphi's programming language is based on Object Pascal, it's easy to build large programs by using modern modular and object-oriented techniques. Delphi also provides sophisticated error handling for the all-too-common task of preventing end users from bombing an application. The Delphi compiler is incredibly fast—this means that correcting the routine programming and typographical errors that are so common when you begin building an application is a snap. It also has an extensive online help system for quick reference while you're developing an application.

What You Need to Run Delphi
Delphi is a sophisticated program. To work with the 16-bit version of Delphi, you'll need at least the following:

♦ At least a 386 CPU with 6 MB of RAM. (Realistically, you'll want a fast 486 or Pentium, and at least 8 MB of RAM.)

♦ A hard disk with at least 27 MB free. (A full installation of the client/server edition can require 90 MB!)

♦ A mouse or a pointing device compatible with a mouse.

♦ Microsoft Windows 3.X or later, running in enhanced mode.

 Note: Although Delphi 16 (Delphi 1.0) runs under Windows NT or Windows 95, it does so only as a 16-bit application and only creates 16-bit applications.

To work with the 32-bit version of Delphi, you'll need at least the following:

♦ Microsoft Windows 95 or Windows NT 3.51 or later.

♦ At least a fast 486 or Pentium and at least 16 MB of RAM.

♦ A hard disk with at least 40 MB free. (A full installation of the client/server edition can require 90 MB!)

♦ A mouse or a pointing device compatible with a mouse.

Working with Delphi

In this section you'll see a step-by-step process that uses Delphi to build two programs. The steps are essentially the same in both versions of Delphi. The first program is a modification of the traditional "Hello World" program, the other is a bitmap viewer. The viewer particularly shows off how efficient Delphi is at developing Windows applications—it uses only two lines of code! In C or C++ the same amount of functionality would take a few hundred lines.

When you start up Delphi, your initial screen will look something like Figure 1-1 in the 16-bit version and Figure 1-2 in the 32-bit version. You'll see a lot more about the Delphi environment in the next two chapters, but for now it is probably easier if you just follow the steps without worrying too much about the environment.

Note the blank window in the center of the screen, which has a grid of dots. This is the *form* that you will customize. You use the grid to align components such as command buttons and list boxes on the screen (you'll

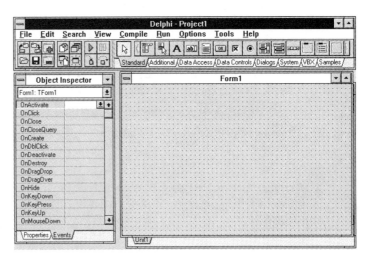

The initial Delphi screen in the 16-bit version

Figure 1-1.

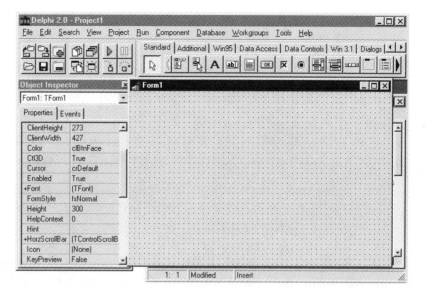

The initial
Delphi screen
in the 32-bit
version

Figure 1-2.

learn more about this in Chapter 4). When you run your project (or compile
it so that it can be run independently of the Delphi development
environment), forms become the windows that users see.

At the top of the blank form is the title bar with its caption. (*Caption* is the
Delphi term for what appears in the title bar of the form.) Currently, this
form is titled Form1, which is the default caption that Delphi gives to a form
when you start working on a new project.

To the left of the Form1 window is the Object Inspector. (If you do not see it,
press F11 or ALT-V-O to reveal it.) The Object Inspector is what you use to
customize the form and the various components you'll place on it.

For now, concentrate on Form1. You should be completely comfortable with
the methods for changing the size and location of this form before you
move on. In many Delphi applications, the size, shape, and location of the
form at the time you finish the design (usually called *design time*) are the
same that the user sees at *run time.* This is not to say that Delphi doesn't let
you change the size and location of forms as a project runs (see Chapter 4);
in fact, an essential property of Delphi is its ability to make dynamic changes
in response to user events.

One way, common to all Microsoft Windows applications, to resize a form is
to first click inside the form so it is active. (You can always tell when a
window is active because the title bar is highlighted.) Then move the mouse
to one of the *hot spots* of the form. In a form, the hot spots are the sides or
corners of the form. The mouse pointer changes to a double-headed arrow

when you're at a hot spot. At this point, you can drag the form to change its size or shape. Similarly, to move the form, you can click anywhere in the title bar, and then drag the form to a new location. The size and location of a form are examples of what Delphi calls *properties* of the form.

To start developing the first sample application, do the following:

1. Change the form's default size, shape, and location by manipulating it at some of the hot spots or by dragging it around the screen.
2. Run the project by choosing Run from the Run menu.

Notice that what you see is an ordinary looking Windows window with the same size, shape, and location that you left the form in at design time.

Next, notice that when you run this new project, the window that pops up has standard Windows features like resizable borders, a control box (in the upper-left corner), and maximum and minimum buttons in the upper-right corner. (Under Windows 95 it will also have the exit button in the far-right corner.) This shows one of the most important features of Delphi: your forms become windows that already behave in the way they should under the various versions of Windows, without your having to do anything.

Return to the development environment by pressing ALT-F4 or double-clicking on the control box. Notice that your application automatically responds to these standard ways of closing a Windows application. (You also could have clicked on the Exit button if you were working with the 32-bit version of Delphi.) This illustrates the important point that, in many cases, without your needing to do anything, Delphi applications behave the way Windows users expect.)

A "Hello World"-type Program

Now we'll show you how to write a project that displays "Hello new user" in the title bar of a blank window in response to a user clicking the mouse. We'll complicate it a little by making the title bar of this window start out with the words "Waiting for a click!"

Here are the necessary steps to do this (they will work in both versions of Delphi):

1. Move to the Object Inspector, click on the Properties tab (if necessary), and then click on the item marked "Caption" as shown in the following illustration. (It will look similar in both versions of Delphi.) The word "Form1" should be highlighted after the click.

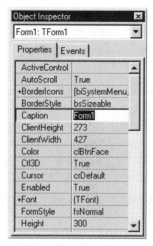

2. Type the sentence **Waiting for a click!** in the right column of the Caption item in the Object Inspector.

What you have just done is called *setting a property of the form.* If you run the project (remember that's what Delphi calls an application in the development stage) by pressing F9 or choosing Run | Run, what you'll see will look like Figure 1-3 under Windows 95. (The Windows 3.X version will be similar, except it will lack the Windows 95 interface elements such as an exit button.)

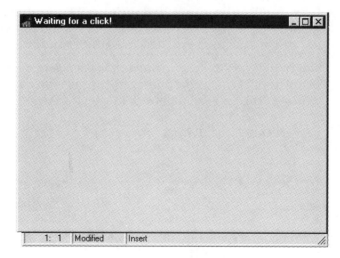

First step in the "Hello new user" project

Figure 1-3.

Note: It is possible that your version of Delphi will ask you to save your work before it compiles the program. If this happens, just except the default names that Delphi proposes.

Notice that this window is fairly inert: whether you click or double-click, nothing happens. Notice again, however, that if you use the standard ALT-F4 shortcut for closing a Windows application, the project ends and you are placed back in the development environment.

Since the essence of a Microsoft Windows program (and, therefore, of Delphi projects) is to make your forms responsive to user actions, now let's make the caption change in response to a user click inside the form. To do this, you'll need to write varying amounts of code. For the example, as you'll soon see, a single line of code will suffice.

A First Event Procedure

To illustrate using an event procedure, make sure you have ended the previous program—by using ALT-F4, for example. Now click on the Events tab in the Object Inspector. (As you can see in Figures 1-1 and 1-2, the tab is on the top under Windows 95 and on the bottom under Windows 3.X.) Double-click in the right column of the item marked "OnClick." Double-clicking in the right column for an event brings the *Code Editor window* to the top of the screen. Regardless of which version of Delphi you are using, your screen should look similar to Figure 1-4. Notice in Figure 1-4 that the form is obscured but still visible. If you click on any part of the form, you'll go back to it, and the Code Editor window will be hidden—although a tab marks its place behind the form. (You can also click on the Unit tab to reveal the Code Editor window.)

Notice in Figure 1-4 the *event procedure template* shown here. (As with any template, an event procedure template gives you a framework in which to work—in this case, a framework in which to write your code.)

```
procedure TForm1.FormClick(Sender: TObject);
begin

end;

end.
```

Although the syntax used for event procedures may seem obscure, don't worry about it now. It will be explained in Chapters 5 and 7. For now, move

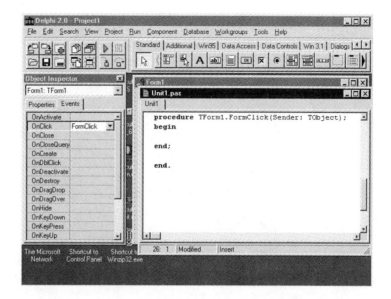

Figure 1-4.

the cursor to the blank line right after the word "begin" and type the
following line of code:

Form1.Caption := 'Hello new user';

Your screen will look like Figure 1-5. (Visual Basic programmers should note
that Delphi uses single quotes rather than double quotes for strings.) Now
run the project (by pressing F9) and click inside the form. Notice the caption
changes.

End the project and return to the design environment by using ALT-F4 or by
double-clicking on the control box.

Adding a Component
So far our application uses no components. Let's modify the project by
introducing a command button that changes the caption after a click. Also,
let's change the project so that if you click anywhere but on the command
button, a message box pops up, telling you to click on the button. To do this:

1. Go to the line of code that you typed, and select it using ordinary
   Windows techniques (a mouse drag or SHIFT-ARROW keys).

(If the form is visible but the code isn't, click on the visible part of the Unit
to go back to the Code Editor window. Another possibility is to press F12.)

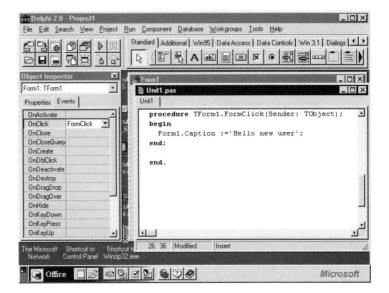

First event
procedure
coded
Figure 1-5.

2. Replace the line of code by typing with the following over the highlighted text:

ShowMessage('Please click on the button');

If you decide to run the project at this point and click inside the form, a little message box pops up that looks like the following. Click on the OK button to make the message box disappear.

Of course, you haven't added the command button yet. To do that, return to the development environment by using ALT-F4. (Click on the form if it is not visible.) Move to the Component palette (shown here), and double-click on the icon for the Button component that the cursor is pointing to in this illustration:

Under Windows 3.X your Component palette will look like this:

1

(Note that in either case the icon for the Button component looks the same and is always located in the standard page of the Component palette. This is another example of how the 16-bit and 32-bit versions of Delphi are mostly compatible.)

This adds a command button to the center of the screen in the default size and shape. (Chapter 4 will show you how to move and size components as well as more about the properties of command buttons.) For now, double-click on the command button to open up an event procedure template for the OnClick event for the button as shown here:

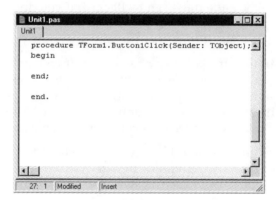

Type the line **Form1.Caption := 'Hello new user';**
after the word "begin," as shown here:

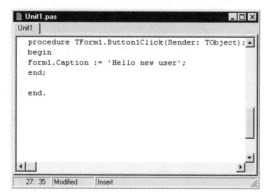

If you run the project, you'll see that the application behaves as previously described. A click on the button changes the caption, a click anywhere else gives the message box.

A More Powerful Project

The previous section showed you three essential steps in Delphi development: adding components to a form, setting properties of Delphi objects, and writing (simple) event procedures. Now let's write a far more sophisticated project—which, surprisingly enough, needs essentially no more code. I hope this project will whet your appetite for Delphi and demonstrate how powerful the components supplied with Delphi really are.

My aim is to show you the first steps you would take to build a graphics file viewer. Using a few components and a few lines of code, you can have a Windows application that will display any bitmap. Of course, this application will be quite fragile and will crash if you don't follow the steps I outline exactly. But after all, you don't yet know how to save the project, bulletproof it, or make it truly user-friendly—it's only the first chapter, after all!

So first off, start up a new project. If you are working with Delphi 32, all you need do is select File | New Application and respond to any message boxes about saving your work with a click on the No button. If you are working in the 16-bit version of Delphi, choose File | New and again answer any questions about saving your work by clicking on No.

This time let's add two components to the blank form: an *image* component for displaying graphics and an *OpenDialog* component for displaying the file/directory structure. Regardless of which version of Delphi you are using, to get an image component onto the form, click on the Additional tab of the Component palette, and then double-click on the Image component icon (it looks like a landscape). It will always look like the icon that the cursor is pointing to here:

Next, add an OpenDialog component by clicking on the Dialogs tab of the Component palette and then double-clicking on the OpenDialog component icon as shown here. (Again, regardless of which version of Delphi you are using, you will have these standard components available to you.)

Your screen will look something like Figure 1-6. Notice there's an icon of a folder opening, surrounded by a dotted box.

You now need to set the *Filter* properties of the OpenDialog component so that only files with the .BMP extension, which indicates a bitmap, will be shown. Make sure the Object Inspector shows that you are working with the properties of the OpenDialog1 component as shown here:

If it doesn't look like this, click on the OpenDialog icon, as shown in Figure 1-6, and then click on the Properties tab in order to work with the properties of the OpenDialog1 component. Move through the Object Inspector until

Initial screen for bitmap viewer

Figure 1-6.

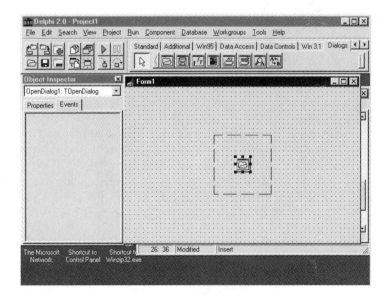

you get to the Filter property of this component. Click in the right column and type: ***.bmp**. This will tell the OpenDialog box to display only files that end in *bmp* (the convention for bitmaps). Next enter the text **Choose bitmap** in the right column of the Title property.

By the way, if you try to run the project now, nothing will happen. The OpenDialog box needs to be activated in order to be displayed. To activate the OpenDialog box, you need to use a new Delphi tool: a *method*. Roughly speaking, in Delphi, properties determine what components *are,* methods determine what they *do,* and events are, usually, user-triggered actions.

The method we need is called the Execute method, and we will put it together with the other line of code we need inside the OnActivate event procedure for the form. The OnActivate event procedure is a little unusual in that Delphi calls it whenever a form becomes active—which certainly happens when the project starts running.

To get to the event procedure template for OnActivate:

1. Click on any blank area in the form. (This is one way to shift the Object Inspector to work with the form; later chapters will show you other methods.)
2. Click on the Events tab in the Object Inspector.
3. Double-click in the right column of the OnActivate event.

This will open up the event procedure template for the OnActivate event. Now enter the following two lines of code so that your event procedure template looks like this:

```
Procedure TForm1.Activate(Sender: TObject);
begin
  OpenDialog1.Execute;
  Image1.Picture.LoadFromFile(OpenDialog1.FileName);
end;
end.
```

That's it. If you run this project, you'll be presented with an ordinary Windows dialog box (with the caption "Choose Bitmap") that will be restricted to displaying only files with the .BMP extension. You can navigate among the directories on your drives by clicking and double-clicking as is usual with an OpenDialog box in Windows. Find a bitmap, click on OK, and Delphi will display the bitmap on the form.

Tip: You'll find a large number of bitmaps in the directories in the IMAGES subdirectory below where your version of Delphi is stored.

1

Of course, this is by no means a foolproof application: if you click on OK without selecting a bitmap (or even click on Cancel without selecting a bitmap file), the application will crash. (If you do crash the project, close any message boxes and then use ALT-F4 or Run | Program Reset in order to get back to the development environment.)

Note: Making this application essentially bulletproof needs only a few more lines of code. You will see this code in Chapter 13.

In spite of its fragility, this application shows you various techniques for developing a Delphi application that will occur again and again. The interfaces and code will get more sophisticated, but the ideas of

♦ Customizing components by changing their properties

♦ Customizing their behavior by using methods

will never change. Moreover, components in Delphi have a lot of built-in functionality. This will become even more obvious as you work with other components.

Chapter 2

The Delphi 32 Programming Environment

In this chapter, you'll see how to use the menus and windows that make up the Delphi 32 (Delphi 2.0) environment. (In this chapter "Delphi" will always mean Delphi 32—and "Windows" will always mean Windows 95, although Delphi 32, of course, runs under Windows NT 3.51 or later.) If you are not completely comfortable with the look and feel of Microsoft Windows 95 applications, then this chapter will help. After all, Delphi is itself a very well-designed Windows 95 application, and the way its elements respond is typical of Windows 95 programs. Experienced Windows users may want to skim much of this material. Remember, though, that until you are familiar with how a Windows application should look and feel, you can't take full advantage of the power of Delphi. When you're finished with this chapter, you'll be comfortable with the online help, the editing tools, and the file-handling utilities built into Delphi.

If you are developing an application with Delphi for your personal use, then conforming to the Windows standard is not essential. However, if others will be using your application, following the Windows standard essentially eliminates the learning curve for using your application. For example, since Windows users expect a single click with a mouse to select an item and a double-click to activate the item, you must ensure that your application follows this standard.

Note: The most complete guidelines for a Windows 95 application can be found in Microsoft's publication, *The Windows Interface Guidelines for Software Design,* ISBN 1-55615-679-0. Contact Microsoft or your local bookstore for price and availability.

The default settings built into the design process of a Delphi application make it easy to conform to the Microsoft Windows guidelines. As you saw in the last chapter, windows default to the proper shape, have the proper elements, and can be moved and resized as users expect. Similarly, menus respond the way users are accustomed to. Of course, Delphi doesn't lock you into these defaults, but it is not a good idea to make changes casually.

Given Delphi's richness of tools and detailed menus, it's easy to be overwhelmed at first. To help reduce any confusion, this chapter gives you a detailed description of what the environment has to offer.

An Overview of the Main Screen

When you start Delphi, you are presented with a splash screen indicating which version of Delphi you have. After a short pause, you are automatically dropped into the Delphi environment, which is shown in Figure 2-1. You can see the four parts of the standard Delphi environment: the menu bar, Object Inspector, form window, and the Code Editor window, although the Code Editor window is partially obscured. Other windows that provide more specialized features, such as the one for debugging, are also available to you when you need to work with them.

Note: Delphi can remember how you arranged the screens the previous time and reuses that arrangement. For this reason, your screen may look different from Figure 2-1.

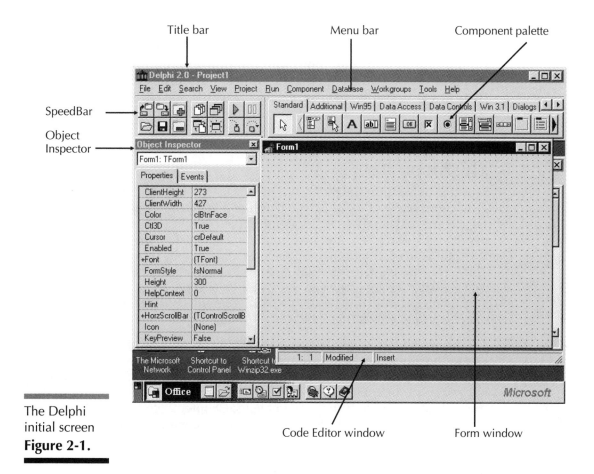

The Delphi
initial screen
Figure 2-1.

The following is a description of the most commonly used parts of the main screen. Subsequent sections of this chapter cover the help system and the most commonly used parts of the menus.

The Caption Bar

The *caption,* or title, *bar* is the horizontal bar located at the top of the screen; it tells you the name of the application and is common to all Microsoft Windows applications. Interactions between the user and the caption bar are handled by Windows, not by the application. Everything except the bottom and side borders below the caption and menu bars in a Windows application is called the *client area.* Your application is completely responsible for the look, feel, and response of the objects you place in the client area.

In Delphi, the caption bar starts out by displaying **Delphi 2.0 - Project1**. This is typical of Microsoft Windows applications. In sophisticated programs (like Delphi) that have multiple states, the caption bar changes to indicate the different states. For example, when you are running a project within the Delphi environment, the caption bar switches to **Delphi 2.0 - Project1 [Running]**. And when you are debugging (correcting errors in a project's code) and have temporarily stopped the project, the caption bar reads **Delphi 2.0 - Project1 [Stopped]**.

The Menu Bar

Selecting items from the pull-down menus listed on a menu bar is one of the most common ways to utilize the power of a Windows application. The same is true of Delphi itself. For Delphi, the menu bar gives you the tools needed to develop, test, and save your application. The File menu contains the commands for working with the files that compile into your application. The Edit menu contains the editing tools to make it easier to write the code that activates the interface you design for your application. This includes the alignment and placement tools. The Search menu contains the search-and-replace editing tools.

The View menu gives you fast access to the different parts of your project and to the different windows that make up the Delphi environment. The Project menu contains compile and syntax checking tools. The Run menu lets you test your application while developing it, and it gives you access to the tools used to correct (debug) problems. Chapter 9 offers a detailed discussion of debugging techniques. The Component menu lets you work with the component library in Delphi. For example, this is where you go to install new components that you build or buy. The Database menu contains tools, like the Database Form Expert, that make it easier to work with databases. The Tools menu contains the important Options menu item, which gives you a tabbed dialog box that lets you control the Delphi's environment, and useful tools such as the Database Desktop. Finally, the Help menu gives you access to the very detailed online help system provided with Delphi.

As with any Windows application, you can open a menu by pressing ALT and the underlined letter, which is called an *accelerator key* (or an access or hot key). If you press ALT alone to activate the menu bar, you can move around the bar with the LEFT ARROW and RIGHT ARROW keys and then press ENTER or DOWN ARROW to open a menu. Once a menu is open, all you need to press is an accelerator key to select a menu option. For example, if the Help menu is open, pressing A brings up the About box. Accelerator keys are not case sensitive.

Tip: When the About box is on the screen, you can get the version number by holding down the ALT key and typing **version**. Also, ALT and **team** shows a list of the Delphi Team at Borland. ALT and **developers** shows a list of the Delphi Developer Team at Borland, and ALT and **and** gives you a picture of Anders Hejlsberg, who is the lead architect of Delphi.

2

Some menu items have shortcut keys. A *shortcut key* is usually a combination of keys the user can press to perform an action without opening a menu. For example, as is common in Windows applications, pressing ALT-F4 exits Delphi without going through the File menu.

The SpeedBar

The SpeedBar, shown in the following illustration, is immediately below the menu bar. As is common in Windows applications, Borland added SpeedBar icons to let you activate common tasks without using the menus. Since every item on the SpeedBar has a keyboard equivalent for the same task, which method you choose is a matter of taste. To make it easier to remember what each icon does, when you move the cursor over an icon, what Borland calls a "help hint" pops up, providing text that tells you what the icon does. Table 2-1 shows and describes each SpeedBar icon.

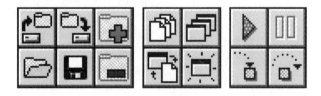

Note: The icons shown in Table 2-1 are the default SpeedBar buttons. You can customize the SpeedBar to suit your needs by clicking on the right mouse button anywhere within the SpeedBar, then selecting Properties from the pop-up menu, and following the onscreen instructions to drag and drop the buttons you want to be on the SpeedBar.

Icon	Name	Purpose
	Open Project	Opens an existing project (see the section "Loading and Running Programs" in this chapter). Same as Open on the File menu.
	Save All	Lets you save your Delphi project. Same as Save All on the File menu. If the project is new, it will prompt for new filenames.
	Add File to Project	Lets you add an existing form (customizable window) or Unit (source code) file to a project. Same as Add to Project on the File menu.
	Select Unit from List	Brings up the View Unit dialog box. Same as Units on the View menu.
	Select Form from List	Brings up the View Form dialog box. Same as Forms on the View menu.
	Run	Runs the application. Same as choosing Run from the Run menu (F9 is the shortcut).
	Pause	Pauses a running project. (Programs can usually be continued by choosing Run from the Run menu, or by pressing F9.) Same as Program Pause on the Run menu.
	Open File	Opens an existing Form file or Unit file (although any file can be opened). Same as Open File on the File menu. Note: if a form's DFM file (form properties) is opened, it is converted from its binary state into a text format and then resaved in its binary state.
	Save File	Lets you save the selected file, form, or Unit file. Same as Save on the File menu.
	Remove File from Project	Removes a form or Unit file from the project. Same as Remove from Project on the File menu.
	Toggle Form/Unit	Switches focus from a form to its Unit. Same as Toggle Form/Unit on the View menu (F12 is the shortcut).
	New Form	Lets you add a new form (customizable window) to a project. Same as New Form on the File menu. See Chapter 5 for more information on using multiple forms in your applications.

The Default SpeedBar Icons
Table 2-1.

Icon	Name	Purpose
	Trace Into	Moves through your project's code one line at a time. It is also a debugging tool and is discussed further in Chapter 9. Same as Trace Into on the Run menu (F7 is the shortcut).
	Step Over	Moves through your project's code one line at a time while executing procedures as a single step. Like Trace Into, it is also a debugging tool and is discussed in Chapter 9. Same as Step Over on the Run menu (F8 is the shortcut).

The Default
SpeedBar
Icons
(continued)
Table 2-1.

2

The Component Palette

Located near the top right of the screen in Figure 2-1, just to the right of the SpeedBar, the tabbed Component palette contains the around 100 basic tools you use for developing your application. In the last chapter you saw some of these components at work. Chapter 4 will cover more about the various components that are available.

The Initial Form Window

The initial Form window takes up much of the center of the screen. As you saw in the last chapter, this is where you customize the window that users will see. The code for the forms that make up the visual part of your application is usually stored in a binary format that is not readable by other applications. Form files always have the extension .DFM. See Chapter 4 for more details on forms and the Form window.

Note: Delphi allows you to save your Form files (.DFM) as ASCII text files (see Chapter 4).

Visual **Basic Tip:**   It is not too difficult to change the ASCII representation of a Visual Basic form to the ASCII representation of a Delphi form. If you have many forms to create, EarthTrek (617) 273-0308 sells a program that will do some of the conversion for you.

The Object Inspector Window

The Object Inspector window is where you set the properties that define your application's initial appearance. It also is where you go to set up the code that responds to events such as user actions. The Object Inspector has two pages: Properties and Events. You access these by clicking on the tabs. You use the Properties page to set design time properties of the form and its components. You use the Events page to specify the code to associate with predefined event procedures. For more details about the Object Inspector, see Chapters 4, 5, and 6.

 Visual Basic Tip: The Properties tab on the Object Inspector is similar to the Visual Basic Properties window.

Many people like to have the Object Inspector visible at all times. To do this:

1. Move to the Object Inspector and click the right mouse button to open the speedmenu.
2. Choose Stay on Top from this menu.

The Code Editor Window

The Code Editor window is just behind and slightly below the Form window. You can see the bottom edge of the Code Editor window below the Form window. The Code Editor is the place where you write the code that tells Delphi how to handle events. An *event handler,* as mentioned in Chapter 1, is what you use to make Delphi respond to the user's actions. The event handlers for a form are kept separate from the visual part of your form. They are kept in a type of file called a *Unit* file. Unit files always have a .PAS extension to indicate that they contain code written in Object Pascal, the language used in Delphi. Unlike Form files, Unit files are always stored in ASCII format. (For more on units, please see Chapter 6.)

 Visual Basic Tip: Unit files are similar to Visual Basic Code Modules. One difference from Visual Basic is that a Delphi form does not also contain the code that handles the form's events.

Pascal Tip: You can usually reuse units created with earlier versions of Pascal, and you almost certainly can use units created with Delphi 16. (Delphi supports the WinCrt unit from Turbo Pascal 7.0, for example.) Of course, you may need to rethink the interface, but any code that just processes data should port relatively easily. However, unlike with Delphi 16, the OWL library from Turbo Pascal 7 was not ported to Delphi 32.)

2

The Project Manager Window

Since it is quite common for Delphi applications to share code or previously customized forms, Delphi organizes applications into what it calls *projects*. A project is made up of the visual interface along with the code that activates the interface. Each project can have multiple forms, allowing you to build applications that have multiple windows. The code that is needed for a form in your project (for example, the code to respond to events) is stored in a separate Unit file that Delphi automatically associates to that form. General programming code that you will want shared by all the forms in your application is placed in Unit files as well. Unit files containing general code can be stored separately and added to your project as needed—maximizing reusability.

What this means is that each project then is made up of one or more *Form files* (files with a .DFM extension) and one or more Unit files (files with a .PAS extension). To see which files make up your project, you need to use the Project Manager window. You activate the Project Manager window from the View menu. The Project Manager window contains a list of the forms and units that make up your project. Here's what the initial Project Manager window looks like:

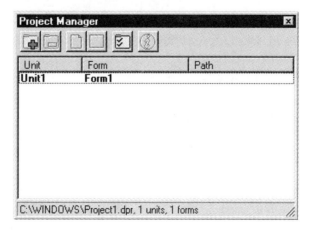

Notice that the first line in the Project Manager lists the initial form and its associated unit.

Although Delphi separately stores the files that go into making up your project, it does need to keep track of where they are. It creates a file, called the *Project file,* that tells it (and you, if you look at the file) where the individual files that make up a project are located. Delphi creates the Project file whenever you choose Save Project As from the File menu (or use the equivalent Save Project tool from the SpeedBar). Project files always have a .DPR extension in their filename. Moreover, anytime you choose Save Project As, Delphi pops up a dialog box that lets you create a different Project file.

Tip: If you use a separate directory for the files that make up each project, you will find it much easier to make backups. (Copy the directory using xcopy.)

The Alignment Palette Window

Sometimes, it can be tricky to line up components on a form. If you select the Alignment Palette option from the View menu, you will pop up the Align window. You can use this to align components to each other or to the form. Here's what it looks like:

You'll learn more about the Alignment Palette option in Chapter 4.

The Help System

The Setup program that installs Delphi automatically installs the help information that comes with it. The online help system contains far more information than the manuals supplied with Delphi. In addition, there are example programs and dozens of useful tables. The Setup program creates icons to launch the various help files.

The online help system contains a very useful feature: it is context sensitive for help. This means that you can press F1 whenever you need help with something, and you bypass the help system's Search dialog box in order to go directly to the relevant information. You can get information about any keyword in the Delphi programming language, about an error message, or about the parts of the Delphi environment. Once you start up the help system, you can move the Help window anywhere you want. You can resize it or minimize it to an icon as necessary.

More on the File Menu

2

You use the main File menu to work with the files that make up your project. This menu includes commands for creating, saving, loading, and printing files. They are covered briefly here. The File menu also lets you exit Delphi. As mentioned earlier, another way to exit Delphi when the focus is on the main menu bar is to use ALT-F4. As with any Windows application, you can also double-click on, or open up, the System menu on the menu bar and choose Close.

Most of the items on the main File menu are useful only when you've started developing your own applications and will be discussed in the later chapters of this book. What follows is a brief discussion of each item, which should help you to orient yourself.

New The New option brings up the important New Items dialog box shown here:

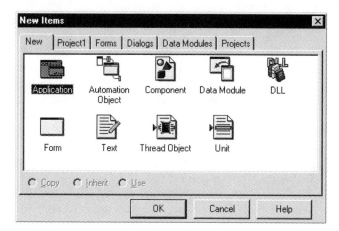

If you click on Application, you unload the current project and start a new one. If you've made any changes to a project since you last saved it, a dialog box pops up, asking you if you want to save your work. If you answer Yes, you are led to another dialog box for saving files. The other items let you add new things to your project, such as additional forms and units (see Chapter 5). The following table gives brief descriptions of the pages on this dialog box:

New	This is the front page that gives you visual clues to each of the new items you can create by clicking on the various icons.
Project	This lets you create new forms based on existing forms in your project through object-oriented techniques (via inheritance—see Chapter 7). This lets you resuse the properties of your current form.
Forms	This gives you access to a gallery of prebuilt forms that you can add to your projects.
Dialogs	This gives you access to a gallery of prebuilt forms for various kinds of dialog boxes.
Data Modules	This gives you access to prebuilt data form forms that can be used in database development.
Projects	This lets you build an MDI (multiple document interface) project or SDI (single document interface) project (see Chapter 13).

New Application   This is another way to start up a new application. It is obviously a little quicker to use this, rather than using New and then choosing New Application in the New Items dialog box.

New Form   This item is another way to add another form to your project. (See Chapter 5 for more on multiform projects.)

New Data Module   This brings up a blank form that you can add data access controls to (see Chapter 14). A Data Module is a form that contains database relationships that can be used in other data aware forms in your project.

Open   This brings up a dialog box that lets you add an existing file to your project. For example, if you open an existing Form (.PAS) file, Delphi adds that form to your project.

Reopen   This contains a list of the most recently used projects.

Save   The Save item saves the current file. The first time you use it, a dialog box pops up to allow you to give the file its initial name.

Save As   This item pops up a dialog box that lets you save the current item you are working with under a new name. It's useful for backups, for example, although the project then uses the newly saved file and not the old one.

Save Project As   The Save Project As option pops up a dialog box that lets you save all the files that make up the current project with a new name. It does this by creating a new Project file and saving the files with their current names. (You would presumably have used Save As to create new file names for the parts of your project if you intended to do a true backup.) You can also use this option to keep backup copies of the project on a different disk or to save different versions of the project, but again, the project uses the newly saved files rather than the original ones.

Save All   This option saves all the files in the current project and creates the initial Project file if one doesn't exist already. (Recall that a Project file is a list of all the files used in the project plus some other information used by Delphi.) The first time you choose this option, a dialog box identical to the one for the Save Project As option opens up. (It will ask for the unit names first and then the project name.)

2

Close   This option closes the current file you are working with.

Close All   The Close All option closes all files for the current project after prompting you to save any changes.

Use Unit   This pops up a dialog box that makes it easier to manage projects with multiple units. (Recall that in Delphi units hold related code. You need to tell Delphi when one unit will use functionality from another unit.)

Add To Project   This option pops up a dialog box that lets you add a form or unit file to the current project. (The difference between this and File|Open is that when you use File|Open, the file is editable but is not part of the project and so, for example, wouldn't be compiled.)

Remove From Project   This option lets you remove a file that was once needed by the project.

Print   The Print option lets you print either the current form or the unit that you are working with. The Print dialog boxes contain options that you can accept or change before you click the OK button.

Exit   Choosing the Exit option is the usual way to leave Delphi. If you've made any changes to the current project, Delphi asks you if you want to save them before ending the session. You'll see the same dialog boxes as for saving the parts of your project option discussed earlier.

Editing

Delphi comes with a full screen editor. Since it is a programming editor, it lacks features like word wrap and print formatting that even a primitive word processor like Microsoft Write has. On the other hand, it does add features like syntax checking that can spot certain common programming typos. The Delphi program editor also color codes the various parts of your code. For example, Delphi commands can be one color, comments another. The colors used are customizable via the Color tab on the Environment Options dialog box (Tools | Options). The Delphi Code Editor defaults to using standard Windows methods for common tasks like insert, overwrite, text selection, copy, cut, paste, and delete.

Tip: You can customize the editor to follow Brief, Epsilon, and IDE Classic (equivalent to Turbo Pascal) conventions in addition to the default setting. See the Editor Options page in the online help system for more on this.

The Edit Menu

The Edit menu contains 17 items that will be available depending on which part of Delphi has the focus. Here are brief descriptions of each of them.

Note: Saying an item "has the focus" is Windows jargon for saying that Windows' attention is focused on that item. It is usually the item that will respond to the user's keypress or mouse click.

Undo/Undelete, Redo   Undo reverses the last edit you made in the Code Editor. Undelete reverses the last deletion you made in a form. Redo reverses the last editing action. The shortcut for Undo and Undelete is CTRL-Z. The shortcut for Redo is SHIFT-CTRL-Z.

Cut, Copy, Paste   You use Cut, Copy, and Paste after you select text or a component. Cut places the text in the Windows Clipboard, Copy places a copy of it there, and Paste takes whatever is in the Clipboard and pastes it into your Delphi application. In particular, you can use this item to exchange information (text or graphics) between another Windows application and Delphi. You can also copy and paste components or groups of components.

2

Delete   The Delete option removes the selected item, but does not place a copy in the Clipboard.

Select All   The Select All option selects all the lines in the Code Editor window or all the components on a form.

Align to Grid   Align to Grid is used to accurately position objects on your forms. See Chapter 4 for more on how to use the grid.

Bring to Front, Send to Back   The Bring to Front option brings the selected object in front of all other objects; the Send to Back option moves the object back when you are developing the project. See Chapter 4 for more on this.

Align   The Align option opens the Alignment dialog box, which allows you to accurately position selected components in relation to each other or to the form. You can also use the Alignment Palette, from the View menu, to position components. The Alignment Palette is a floating toolbar that can stay displayed while you change your form.

Size   The Size option opens a dialog box that lets you resize selected components' height and width (see Chapter 4).

The following commands are available on the Edit menu when a form has focus.

Scale   The Scale option opens a dialog box that allows you to proportionally resize the form and all the components on that form.

Tab Order   The Tab Order option opens a dialog box that allows you to change the tab order of components on a form or within a component that contains other components. (See Chapter 4 for more on tab order and container components.)

Creation Order   The Creation Order option opens a dialog box that allows you to determine the creation order that your application will use when displaying nonvisual components.

Lock Controls   Once you are satisfied with the position of the components on a form, this option prevents you from accidentally moving a component.

Object   This option is used when converting or editing an OLE object that you have inserted on a form. See Chapter 10.

The Search Menu

What follows is a short description of the items on the Search menu. You use the Search menu to locate text, errors, objects, and so on, when you are writing code in the Code Editor.

Find   Opens up a dialog box that lets you search for specific text.

Replace   Opens up a dialog box that lets you search and then replace text.

Search Again   Repeats the previous search.

Incremental Search   This is a nifty way to search without using a dialog box. As you type, the cursor moves to the next occurrence of the text entered to that point.

Go to Line Number   Opens up a dialog box that lets you move the cursor to a specific line number.

Find Error   Moves the cursor to the line of code that caused the last compiler error. Only available after a bad run or bad compile.

Browse Symbol   Opens up a dialog box that searches for a specified symbol. Only available after a project has been compiled. See Chapter 9.

The View Menu

The View menu contains items that deal with displaying and hiding environmental features and the objects and components that make up your application. Here are brief descriptions of each of the menu items. (Which items you see depends on what you are doing in Delphi.)

Project Manager   The Project Manager option displays the Project Manager window. You can use the Project Manager to view what files make up your application as well as add, delete, copy, or save a file to the current project.

Project Source   You use Project Source to view the source code for the Project file in the Code Editor window.

Object Inspector   The Object Inspector option brings the Object Inspector window to the front, allowing you to change object properties and the procedures linked to object events. See Chapter 4 for more on using the Object Inspector.

Alignment Palette   The Alignment Palette option opens the Align window. This allows you to more easily align components with respect to each other or to the form. See Chapter 4 for more on using the Alignment Palette.

Browser   The Browser option displays the Object Browser window. The Object Browser enables you to see the scope, inheritance, and references of classes and methods used in your application. It is available only after you have compiled a program. See Chapter 7.

Breakpoints   Choose Breakpoints to view the Breakpoint List window. You can see details on the breakpoints you have set as well as use the right mouse button to add and edit breakpoints. See Chapter 9 for more on using breakpoints.

2

Call Stack   This option displays the Call Stack window, which shows you the procedure calls that have brought you to your current application location and the arguments passed to each procedure call. This is used as a debugging tool (Chapter 9).

Watches   Choose Watches to display the Watch List window. The Watch List window displays all the currently set watch expressions. This option is also used as a debugging tool (see Chapter 9).

Threads   This option displays the currently running nonprimary thread and its status and location. (Thread programming is not coverered in this book—see the online help for more on this topic.)

Component List   The Component List option allows you to add components to your forms using the keyboard. The Component List window has a Search edit box for entering the name of the desired component, or you can use the component Listbox to make your choice.

Window List   The Window List window displays a list of all open windows in Delphi, allowing you to bring any window to the front. Another way to select this option is to press ALT-0 (zero).

Toggle Form/Unit   The Toggle Form/Unit options allows you to toggle between the form and its Unit window. (F12 is the shortcut.)

Units   Choose Units to display the View Units dialog box. The dialog box allows you to make any unit in the project the active unit in the Code Editor. Another way to select this option is to press CTRL-F12.

Forms Choose Forms to display the View Forms dialog box. The dialog box allows you to make any form in the project the active form. Another way to select this option is to press SHIFT-F12.

New Edit Window The New Edit Window option opens a new Code Editor window whose active unit is the same as the active unit in the previous active Code Editor window. This is a handy way to edit multiple locations in the same unit that otherwise cannot be displayed at the same time in one Code Editor.

Speedbar Choose the Speedbar item to hide or show the SpeedBar (it's a toggle).

Component Palette Choose this item to hide or show the Component palette (it's also a toggle).

The Project Menu

The Project menu contains eight items. Some of the items duplicate functionality found on the File menu—for example, the Add to Project and Remove from Project items. Here are descriptions of the remaining items.

Add to Repository Delphi 32 lets you add forms that you build to its repository that shows up in the various pages of the New Items dialog box. Choosing this item brings up a dialog box that lets you do this. (Click on the Help button of this dialog box for more information.)

Compile The Compile item lets you compile any code that has changed without actually running the project.

Build All This recompiles all the code in the project (as opposed to Compile, which only works with the code that has changed).

Syntax Check This checks your code for correct syntax. This is a lot faster than running the code and waiting for the inevitable error messages that result when working with a larger project.

Information This pops up a dialog box with information that is occasionally useful about the compiled code, such as the total size of the EXE and how much memory was used for various pieces of the program.

Options This brings up an important tabbed dialog box that is used to set various options for the compiler and the resulting code. For example, the Application page on this dialog box lets you set the title, icon, and help filename for the project. You will see how to work with the pieces of this dialog box in the various chapters that follow.

The Run Menu

This menu controls how Delphi runs your project from within the integrated development environment (or IDE as it is usually called). The first item is, naturally enough, the Run item (its shortcut is F9), but the other items are also very useful. They are used mostly for debugging and will be covered in Chapter 9.

2

The Component Menu

Delphi is extendible—that is one of its strongest points. This menu controls the component library. For example, if you choose New, you get a dialog box that lets you start the process of building new components. (See the supplied documentation for Delphi for more on doing this.) Install, on the other hand, pops up a dialog box that lets you install an existing component that is not yet part of the component library. Open library does allows you open an alternative component library. In essense you can have multiple component palettes that you can choose from. The Rebuild library lets you incorporate any changes you have made in an individual component into Delphi itself. Finally, the Configure Palette item lets you customize Delphi's component palette any way you want.

The Tools Menu

This important menu lets you work with Delphi's environment—customizing it the way you want. For example, the Options item opens up the very important Environment Options dialog box, whose tabbed pages let you take control of Delphi. For instance, the Editor page controls how Delphi's Code Editor works, and the Colors page controls what colors Delphi uses to highlight the various parts of your project. Figure 2-2 shows this key dialog box. This dialog box will appear frequently in the chapters that follow.

Tip: I strongly recommend checking off the Editor files option in the Autosave options area of the Preferences page in this dialog box. This option automatically saves your work whenever you compile a project. Developing projects without this is like doing gymnastics without a rubber mat— occasionally very painful.

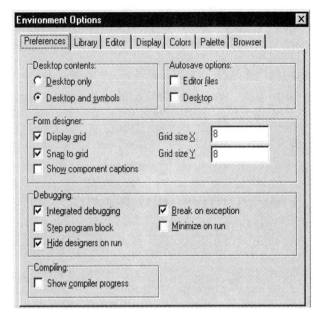

Environment
Options
dialog box
Figure 2-2.

The first two items on this menu are the ones you will use most often. The second one gives you another way to work with the repository that you have already seen.

As an example of how to change an option in this dialog box, let's change the default tab stop settings from 9 and 17 spaces to 4 and 8 spaces. To do this:

1. Click on the Editor options page tab.
2. At the Tab Stops box, type **4**, press the SPACEBAR, then type **8**.
3. Press ENTER.

Other items in this dialog box give you a fixed list of choices. For example, the Editor Speedsetting drop-down list box on the Editor options page lets you choose what key combinations control which editing functions. There are only four possibilities: the default, Classic (Turbo Pascal-WordStar), Brief, or Epsilon.

The Tools Item   This item gives you access to the tools supplied with your version of Delphi. For example, the Database Desktop is supplied with all versions of Delphi and lets you test sophisticated database applications without needing a server. The Add button on this dialog box lets you add other tools that you may make or buy. Like any good Windows application, it comes with its own extensive help system.

Loading and Running Programs

Delphi comes with many interesting sample projects, so let's end this chapter with the procedures needed to run an existing Delphi project. The one described in this section is the Richedit demo. This project demonstrates how easy it is to build a mini–word processor using one of the new Windows 95 components in Delphi 32.

2

If you choose the Open option on the File menu or click on the Open Project tool (the first tool in the SpeedBar), you are presented with the Open dialog box shown here:

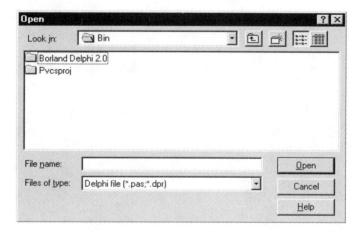

Notice that no files are shown. This is because Delphi keeps track of the files that make up a project in a file with a .DPR extension (for the "Project file"), and there aren't any in the \Program Files\Borland\Delphi 2.0\Bin\ directory that is shown. Of course, you can change the default for the filename extension Delphi will search for, by moving to the File Name list box and typing the new file pattern or shift drives by working with the drive list area of this dialog box.

Move to the drive and directory that holds Delphi (it's below Program Files\Borland\Delphi 2.0\Bin in the default installation), and then move to the Demos directory. Move through the subdirectories of the Demos directory until you get to the one marked "Richedit." Double-click on it and you are placed in the Richedit subdirectory. The Files box now lists the RICHEDIT.DPR file, which contains the names and locations of the files that make up the Richedit project. When you now double-click on this, Delphi loads the Richedit project, which gives you a mini–word processor written completely in Delphi.

After a short delay (possibly interrupted by a dialog box asking you if you want to save your current work), Delphi loads the Richedit project. Since this project, written completely in Delphi, shows off the power that will soon be at your fingertips, you might want to press F9 to run it. (To end this, or any project when it is running, use ALT-F4.) Note that this project is only a couple of hundred lines of code.

Chapter

3

The Delphi 16 Programming Environment

In this chapter, I'll show you how to use the menus and windows that make up the Delphi 16 (Delphi 1.0) environment. (In this chapter, "Delphi" will always mean Delphi 16 and "Windows" will always mean Windows 3.X.) If you are not completely comfortable with the look and feel of Microsoft Windows applications, then this chapter will help. After all, Delphi is itself a well-designed Windows application, and the way its elements respond is typical of Windows programs. Experienced Windows users may want to skim much of this material. Remember, though, that until you are familiar with how a Windows application should look and feel, you can't take full advantage of the power of Delphi. When you're finished with this chapter, you'll be comfortable with the online help, the editing tools, and the file-handling utilities built into Delphi.

If you are developing an application with Delphi for your personal use, then conforming to the Windows standard is not essential. However, if others will be using your application, following the Windows standard essentially eliminates the learning curve for using your application. For example, since Windows users expect a single click with a mouse to select an item and a double-click to activate the item, you must ensure that your application follows this standard.

Note: The most complete guidelines for a Windows application can be found in Microsoft's publication, *The Windows Interface: An Application Design Guide* (part number 28921 or ISBN 1-55615-439-9). Contact Microsoft or your local bookstore for price and availability.

The default settings built into the design process of a Delphi application make it easy to conform to the Microsoft Windows guidelines. As you saw in the last chapter, windows default to the proper shape and can be moved and resized as users expect. Similarly, menus respond the way users are accustomed to. Of course, Delphi doesn't lock you into these defaults, but it is not a good idea to make changes casually.

Note: The Interactive Tutors available on the Help menu are a good complement to some of the material presented in this chapter.

Given the power of Delphi, with its richness of tools and detailed menus, it's easy to be overwhelmed at first. To help reduce any confusion, this chapter gives you a detailed description of what the environment has to offer.

An Overview of the Main Screen

When you start Delphi, you are presented with a splash screen indicating which version of Delphi you have. After a short pause, you are automatically dropped into the Delphi environment, which is shown in Figure 3-1. You can see the four parts of the standard Delphi environment: the menu bar, Object Inspector, Form window, and the Code Editor window (although the Code Editor window is partially obscured). Other windows that provide more specialized features (such as the one for debugging) are also available to you when you need to work with them.

Title bar   Menu bar   Component palette

SpeedBar

Object Inspector

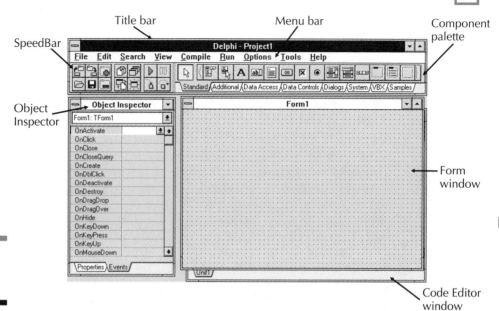

Form window

Code Editor window

3

The Delphi initial screen

Figure 3-1.

Note: Delphi has the ability to remember how you arranged the screens the previous time and reuses that arrangement. For this reason, your screen may look different from Figure 3-1.

The following is a description of the most commonly used parts of the main screen. Subsequent sections of this chapter cover the help system and the most commonly used parts of the menus.

The Caption Bar

The *caption,* or title, *bar* is the horizontal bar located at the top of the screen; it tells you the name of the form and is common to all Microsoft Windows applications. Interactions between the user and the caption bar are handled by Windows, not by the application. Everything below the caption and menu bars (excluding the bottom and side border) in a Windows application is called the *client area.* Your application is completely responsible for the look, feel, and response of the objects you place in the client area.

In Delphi, the caption bar starts out by displaying **Delphi - Project1** when you are using the default name, Project1, for your project. This is typical of Microsoft Windows applications. In sophisticated programs (like Delphi) that have multiple states, the caption bar changes to indicate the different states. For example, when you are running this project within the Delphi environment, the caption bar switches to **Delphi - Project1 [Running]**. And when you are debugging (correcting errors in a project's code) and have temporarily stopped the project, the caption bar reads **Delphi - Project1 [Stopped]**.

The Menu Bar

Selecting items from the pull-down menus listed on a menu bar is one of the most common ways to utilize the power of a Windows application. The same is true of Delphi itself. For Delphi, the menu bar gives you the tools needed to develop, test, and save your application. The File menu contains the commands for working with the files that you compile into your application. The Edit menu contains the editing tools to make it easier to write the code that activates the interface you design for your application. These include the alignment and placement tools. The Search menu contains the search-and-replace editing tools and code positioning tools.

The View menu gives you fast access to the different parts of your project and quick access to the different windows that make up the Delphi environment. The Compile menu contains compile and syntax checking tools. The Run menu lets you test out your application while developing it and it gives you access to the tools used to correct (debug) problems (Chapter 9 offers a detailed discussion of debugging techniques). The Options menu lets you control the Delphi environment. The Tools menu contains external tools like ReportSmith, Database Desktop, and the Image editor. Finally, the Help menu gives you access to the very detailed online help system provided with Delphi.

As with any Windows application, you can open a menu by pressing ALT and the underlined letter, which is called an *accelerator key* (or an access or hot key). If you press ALT alone to activate the menu bar you can move around the bar with the left and right arrow keys and then press ENTER or DOWN ARROW to open a menu. Once a menu is open, all you need to press is an accelerator key to select a menu option. For example, if the Help menu is open, pressing I brings up the Interactive Tutor. Accelerator keys are not case sensitive.

Some menu items have shortcut keys. A *shortcut key* is usually a combination of keys the user can press to perform an action without opening a menu. For example, as is common in Windows applications, pressing ALT-F4 closes the active window or lets you exit Delphi without going through the File menu (when no other window is active).

The SpeedBar

The SpeedBar, shown in the following illustration, is immediately below the menu bar. As is common in Windows applications, Borland added icons to what it calls the SpeedBar to let you activate common tasks without using the menus. Since every item on the SpeedBar has a keyboard equivalent for the same task, which method you choose is a matter of taste. For those times when a picture isn't worth a thousand words and you need help remembering just what each icon represents, Borland has provided "help hints"—move the cursor over an icon and a text description of the icon's function pops up. Table 3-1 shows and describes each SpeedBar icon.

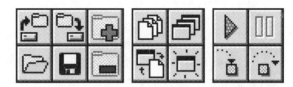

Note: The icons shown in Table 3-1 are the default SpeedBar buttons. You can customize the SpeedBar to suit your needs by clicking on the right mouse button anywhere within the SpeedBar, then selecting Configure from the pop-up menu, and following the onscreen instructions.

3

Icon	Name	Purpose
	Open Project	Opens an existing project (see the section "Loading and Running Programs" in this chapter). Same as Open Project on the File menu.
	Save Project	Lets you save your Delphi project. Same as Save Project As on the File menu. If the project hasn't been saved yet, Delphi will prompt you for a filename.
	Add File to Project	Lets you add an existing form (customizable window) or Unit (source code) file to a project. Same as Add File on the File menu.
	Select Unit from List	Brings up the View Unit dialog box. Same as Units on the View menu.
	Select Form from List	Brings up the View Form dialog box. Same as Forms on the View menu.
	Run	Runs the application. Same as choosing Run from the Run menu (F9 is the shortcut).
	Pause	Pauses a running project. (Programs can usually be continued by choosing Run from the Run menu, or F9.) Same as Program Pause on the Run menu.

The Default
SpeedBar Icons
Table 3-1.

Icon	Name	Purpose
	Open File	Usually used to open an existing Form file or Unit file. Same as Open File on the File menu.
	Save File	Lets you save the selected file. Same as Save File on the File menu.
	Remove File from Project	Removes a form or Unit file from the project. Same as Remove File on the File menu.
	Toggle Form/Unit	Switches focus from a form to its Unit. Same as Toggle Form/Unit on the View menu (F12).
	New Form	Lets you add a new form (customizable window) to a project. Same as New Form on the File menu. See Chapter 5 for more information on using multiple forms in your applications.
	Trace Into	Moves through your project's code one line at a time. It is also a debugging tool and is discussed further in Chapter 9. Same as Trace Into on the Run menu (F7 is the shortcut).
	Step Over	Moves through your project's code one line at a time while executing procedures as a single step. Like Trace Into, it is also a debugging tool and is discussed in Chapter 9. Same as Step Over on the Run menu (F8 is the shortcut).

The Default
SpeedBar Icons
(*continued*)
Table 3-1.

The Component Palette

Located near the top right of the screen in Figure 3-1, just to the right of the SpeedBar, the tabbed Component palette contains over 75 basic tools for developing your application. In the last chapter you saw some of these components at work. Chapter 4 will cover more about the various components that are available.

The Initial Form Window

The initial Form window takes up much of the center of the screen. As you saw in the last chapter, this is where you customize the window that users will see. The code for the forms that make up the visual part of your application is usually stored in a binary format that is not readable by other applications. Form files always have the extension .DFM. See Chapter 4 for more details on forms and the Form window.

Note: Delphi allows you to save your Form files (.DFM) as ASCII text files (see the next chapter).

 Visual **Basic Tip:** It is not too difficult to change the ASCII representation of a Visual Basic form to the ASCII representation of a Delphi form. If you have many forms to create, EarthTrek (617) 273-0308 sells a program that will do (some of) the conversion for you.

3

The Object Inspector Window

The Object Inspector window is where you set the properties that define your application's initial appearance. It also is where you go to set up the code that responds to events such as user actions. The Object Inspector has two pages: Properties and Events. You access these by clicking on the tabs. You use the Properties page to set design time properties of the form and its components. You use the Events page to specify the code to associate with predefined event procedures. For more details about the Object Inspector see Chapters 4, 5, and 6.

 Visual **Basic Tip:** The Properties tab on the Object Inspector is similar to the Visual Basic Property window.

Many people like to have the Object Inspector be the top window at all times. To do this:

1. Move to the Object Inspector and click the right mouse button to open the speedmenu.
2. Choose Stay on Top from this menu.

The Code Editor Window

The Code Editor window is just behind and slightly below the Form window. (You can see the bottom edge of the Code Editor window under the Form window in Figure 3-1.) The Code Editor is the place where you write the code that tells Delphi how to handle events. Event handlers (as mentioned in Chapter 1) are what you use to make Delphi respond to the user's actions. The event handler for a form is kept separate from the visual part of your form. It is kept in a type of file called a *Unit* file. Unit files always have a .PAS extension to indicate that they contain code written in a version of Pascal, called Object Pascal, the language used in Delphi. Unlike Form files, unit files are always stored in ASCII format. (For more on units, see Chapter 6.)

Visual **Basic Tip:** Unit files are similar to Visual Basic Code Modules. One difference from Visual Basic is that a Delphi form does not also contain the code that handles the form's events.

Pascal **Tip:** You can usually reuse units created with earlier versions of Pascal. (Delphi supports the WinCrt unit, for example.) Of course, you may need to rethink the interface, but any code that just processes data should port relatively easily.

The Project Manager Window

Since it is quite common for Delphi applications to share code or previously customized forms, Delphi organizes applications into what it calls *projects*. A project is made up of the visual interface along with the code that activates the interface. Each project can have multiple forms, allowing you to build applications that have multiple windows. The code that is needed for a form in your project (for example, the code to respond to events) is stored in a separate Unit file that Delphi automatically associates to that form. General programming code that you will want shared by all the forms in your application is placed in Unit files as well. Unit files containing general code can be stored separately and added to your project as needed—maximizing reuseability.

What this means is that each project then is made up of one or more Form files (files with a .DFM extension) and one or more Unit files (files with a .PAS extension). To see which files make up your project, you need to use the Project Manager window. You activate the Project Manager window from the View menu. The Project Manager window contains a list of the forms and units that make up your project. Here's what the initial Project Manager window looks like:

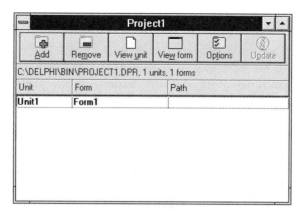

Notice that two items are already listed in the Project Manager window. They are the initial form and its associated unit.

Although Delphi separately stores the files that go into making up your project, it does need to keep track of where they are. To do this it creates a file, called the *Project file*, that tells it (and you, if you look at the file) where the individual files that make up a project are located. Delphi creates the Project file whenever you choose Save Project from the File menu (or use the equivalent Save Project tool from the SpeedBar). Project files always have a .DPR extension in their filename. Moreover, any time you choose Save Project As, Delphi pops up a dialog box that lets you create a different Project file.

T **ip:** If you use a separate directory for the files that make up each project, you will find it much easier to make backups. (Copy the directory using XCOPY.)

The Alignment Palette Window

Sometimes, it can be tricky to line up components on a form. If you select the Alignment Palette option from the View menu you will pop up the Align window. You can use this to align components to each other or to the form. Here's what it looks like:

You'll learn more about the Alignment Palette option in the next chapter.

The Help System

The Setup program that installs Delphi automatically installs the more than 17 MB of help information that comes with it. The online help system contains far more information than the manuals supplied with Delphi. In addition, there are example programs and dozens of useful tables. The Setup program creates icons to launch the various help files.

The online help system contains a very useful feature: it is context sensitive for help. This means that you can press F1 whenever you need help with something and you bypass the help system's Search dialog box in order to go directly to the relevant information. You can get information about any keyword in the Delphi programming language, about an error message, or about the parts of the Delphi environment.

Once you start up the help system, you can move the Help window anywhere you want. You can resize it or minimize it to an icon as necessary.

The following summarizes each item on the Help menu:

♦ **Contents**   Tells you how the Delphi help system is organized.

♦ **Topic Search**   Opens a dialog box that lets you search for help on a specific topic.

♦ **How to Use Help**   Tells you how to use and navigate through help files.

♦ **Interactive Tutors**   A computer-based tutorial. It doesn't go far, but it's worth checking out.

♦ **Windows API**   Gives you access to the Windows 3.1 API Help file. More information on Windows APIs is in Chapter 6.

♦ **Database Form Expert**   The Database Form Expert walks you through the creation of a form that will be linked to a database.

♦ **About**   Gives you the copyright notice and version number of Delphi.

Tip: You can get your version number by holding down the ALT key and typing **version**. Holding down ALT and typing **team** gives you the name of everyone at Borland who is on the Delphi Team.

More on the File Menu

You use the main File menu to work with the files that make up your project. This menu includes commands for saving, loading, and printing files. They are covered briefly here. The File menu also lets you exit Delphi.

(As we've mentioned earlier, another way to exit Delphi when the focus is on the main menu bar is to use ALT-F4 and, like any Windows application, you can also open up the control box (System menu) on the menu bar and choose Close.)

Most of the items on the main File menu are useful only when you've started developing your own applications, and will be discussed in the later chapters of this book. What follows is a brief discussion of each of the items, which should help you to orient yourself.

New Project   The New Project option unloads the current project. If you've made any changes to a project since you've last saved it, a dialog box pops up, asking you if you want to save your work. If you answer Yes, you are led to another dialog box for saving files.

Open Project   The Open Project option lets you work with an existing Delphi application. For more details on how to use this dialog box, see the section "Loading and Running Programs" later in this chapter.

Save Project   The Save Project item saves all the files in the current project and creates the initial Project file. (Recall that a Project file is a list of all the files used in the project plus some other information used by Delphi.) The first time you choose this option, a dialog box identical to the one for the Save Project As option opens up. (Note: It will ask for the unit names first and then the project name.)

Save Project As   The Save Project As option pops up a dialog box that lets you save all the files that make up the current project with a new name. It does this by creating a new Project file and saving the files with their current names. You can also use this option to keep backup copies of the project on a different disk or to save different versions of the project.

Close Project   The Close Project option closes all files for the current project after prompting you to save any changes.

New Form   You use the New Form item to add multiple windows to your application. (See Chapter 5 for more on this option.)

New Unit   You use the New Unit option to add programming code that you'll want to share among all the parts of the application you develop. In Delphi, code is placed in Unit files that may be tied to specific forms.

New Component   You use the New Component option to open the Component Expert that helps you to create a new component. (See the documentation supplied with Delphi for more on creating components.)

Open File   You use the Open File option to view work previously done. Open File does not add the file to your project. You use the Add File option to add already existing forms and Unit files.

Save File   The Save File option saves the active form or unit to disk. The first time you choose this option, Delphi opens a dialog box identical to the one for the Save File As option.

Save File As   The Save File As option pops up a dialog box that lets you save the active form or unit to disk, possibly with a new name. Use this option to keep backup copies of a specific piece of a project on a different disk or to save different versions. You also use this option when part of your current application will be useful in other projects. (In this case, you would use the Add File option to add the file to a different project.)

Close File   The Close File option closes the active form or Unit file and prompts you to save any changes.

Add File   The Add File option opens a dialog box that lets you incorporate work previously done into your application. You can use this to add already existing forms and Unit files to Delphi.

Remove File   Use the Remove File option to remove a file that is currently part of a Delphi application. All this option does is delete the file from your application; it does not delete the file from the disk where it was stored. For that you'll need to use the File Manager built into Windows or ordinary DOS commands.

Print   The Print option lets you print either the current form or the unit that you are working with. The Print dialog boxes contain options that you can accept or change before you click the OK button.

Exit   Choosing the Exit option is the usual way to leave Delphi. If you've made any changes to the current project, Delphi asks you if you want to save them before ending the session. You'll see the same dialog boxes as for the New Project option discussed earlier.

The History List   This keeps track of the three most recently opened Delphi projects. If you click on one of the files listed here, Delphi automatically loads the project. This makes returning to work in progress easy.

Editing

Delphi comes with a complete screen editor. Since it is a programming editor, it lacks features like word wrap and print formatting that even a primitive word processor like Microsoft Write has. On the other hand, it does add features like syntax checking that can spot certain common programming typos. The Delphi program editor also color codes the various parts of your code. For example, Delphi commands can be one color, comments another. The colors used are customizable via the Environment item on the Options menu. The Delphi Code Editor defaults to using standard Windows methods for common tasks like insert, overwrite, text selection, copy, cut, paste, and delete.

T ip: You can customize the editor to follow Brief, Epsilon, and IDE Classic (equivalent to Turbo Pascal) conventions instead of the default setting. See the Editor Options page in the online help system for more on this topic.

3

The Edit Menu

The Edit menu contains 17 items that will be available depending on which part of Delphi has the focus. Here are brief descriptions of each of them.

N ote: Saying an item "has the focus" is Windows jargon for saying that Windows' attention is focused on that item. It is usually the item that will respond to the user's keypress or mouse click.

Undo/Undelete, Redo   Undo reverses the last edit you made in the Code Editor. Undelete reverses the last deletion you made in a form. Redo reverses the last editing action. The shortcut for Undo and Undelete is CTRL-Z. The shortcut for Redo is SHIFT-CTRL-Z.

Cut, Copy, Paste   You use Cut, Copy, and Paste after you select text or a component. Cut places the text in the Windows Clipboard, Copy places a copy of it there, and Paste takes whatever is in the Clipboard and pastes it into your Delphi application. In particular, you can use this item to exchange information (text or graphics) between another Windows application and Delphi. You can also use this to copy components or groups of components (see Chapter 4).

Delete   The Delete command removes the selected item but does not place a copy in the Clipboard.

Select All   The Select All command selects all the lines in the Code Editor window or all the components on a form.

Align to Grid   Align to Grid is used to accurately position objects on your forms. See Chapter 4 for more on how to use the grid.

Bring to Front, Send to Back   The Bring to Front option brings the selected object in front of all other objects; the Send to Back option moves the object back when you are developing the project. See Chapter 4 for more on this.

Align   The Align option opens the Alignment dialog box, which allows you to accurately position selected components in relation to each other or to the form. You can also use the Alignment Palette, from the View menu, to position components. The Alignment Palette is a floating toolbar that can stay displayed while you change your form.

Size   The Size option opens a dialog box that lets you resize selected components' height and width (see Chapter 4).

The following options are available on the Edit menu when a form has focus.

Scale   The Scale option opens a dialog box that allows you to proportionally resize the form and all the components on that form.

Tab Order   The Tab Order option opens a dialog box that allows you to change the tab order of components on a form or within a component that contains other components. (See Chapter 4 for more on tab order and container components.)

Creation Order   The Creation Order option opens a dialog box that allows you to determine the creation order that your application will use when displaying nonvisual components.

Lock Controls   Once you are satisfied with the position of the components on a form, this option prevents you from accidentally moving a component.

Object This option is used when converting or editing an OLE object that you have inserted on a form.

The Search Menu

What follows is a short description of the items on the Search menu. You use the Search menu to locate text, errors, objects, and so on when you are writing code in the Code Editor.

Find Opens up a dialog box that lets you search for specific text.

Replace Opens up a dialog box that lets you search and then replace text.

Search Again Repeats the previous search.

Incremental Search This is a nifty way to search without using a dialog box. As you type, the cursor moves to the next occurrence of the text entered to that point.

Go to Line Number Opens up a dialog box that lets you move the cursor to a specific line number.

Show Last Compile Error Moves the cursor to the line of code that caused the last compiler error. Only available after a bad run or bad compile.

Find Error Opens up a dialog box that searches for the most recent Exception/run-time error.

Browse Symbol Opens up a dialog box that searches for a specified symbol. See Chapter 9.

The View Menu

The View menu contains items that deal with displaying and hiding environmental features and the objects and components that make up your application. Here are brief descriptions of each of the menu items. (Which items you see depends on what you are doing in Delphi.)

Project Manager The Project Manager option displays the Project Manager window. You can use the Project Manager to view what files make up your application as well as add, delete, copy, or save a file to the current project.

3

Project Source   You use Project Source to view the source code for the Project file in the Code Editor window.

Object Inspector   The Object Inspector option brings the Object Inspector window to the front, allowing you to change object properties and the procedures linked to object events. See Chapter 4 for more on using the Object Inspector.

Alignment Palette   The Alignment Palette option opens the Align window. This allows you to more easily align components with respect to each other or to the form. See Chapter 4 for more on using the Alignment Palette.

Browser   The Browser option displays the Object Browser window. The Object Browser enables you to visually see the scope, inheritance, and references of classes and methods used in your application. It is available only when you have compiled a program. See Chapter 7.

Breakpoints   Choose Breakpoints to view the Breakpoint List window. You can see details on the breakpoints you have set as well as use the right mouse button to add and edit breakpoints. See Chapter 9 for more on using breakpoints.

Call Stack   This option displays the Call Stack window, which shows you the procedure calls that have brought you to your current application location and the arguments passed to each procedure call. This is used as a debugging tool (see Chapter 9).

Watches   Choose Watches to display the Watch List window. The Watch List window displays all the currently set watch expressions. This option is also used as a debugging tool (see Chapter 9).

Component List   The Component List option allows you to add components to your forms using the keyboard. The Component List window has a Search edit box for entering the name of the desired component or you can use the Component Listbox to make your choice.

Window List   The Window List window displays a list of all open windows in Delphi allowing you to bring any window to the front. Another way to select this option is to press ALT-0 (zero).

Toggle Form/Unit   The Toggle Form/Unit option allows you to toggle between the form and its Unit window.

Units   Choose Units to display the View Units dialog box. The dialog box allows you to make any unit in the project the active unit in the Code Editor. Another way to select this option is to press CTRL-F12.

Forms   Choose Forms to display the View Forms dialog box. The dialog box allows you to make any form in the project the active form. Another way to select this option is to press SHIFT-F12.

New Edit Window   The New Edit Window option opens a new Code Editor window whose active unit is the same as the active unit in the previously active Code Editor window. This is a handy way to edit multiple locations in the same unit that otherwise cannot be displayed at the same time in one Code Editor window.

Speedbar   Choose the Speedbar item to hide or show the SpeedBar (it's a toggle).

Component Palette   Choose this item to hide or show the Component palette (it's also a toggle).

The Options Menu

The Options menu contains seven items. The first two are the ones you will use most often. The third item, the Tools option, is the same as the Tools menu item. The last three items are used only when you are working with libraries—for example, when you want to add components to Delphi.

The first item, Project, opens up a tabbed dialog box with five pages. The most important parts of this dialog box are covered in Chapter 6. (Consult the online help for the other pages.)

If you choose the Environment option, Delphi opens up a tabbed dialog box that looks like Figure 3-2.

By clicking on the various tabs in this dialog box, you can change the colors, set tab stops, or more generally set certain options that will be useful in programming. For example, you can change the default keymapping for the Code Editor. As an example of how to change an option in this dialog box,

3

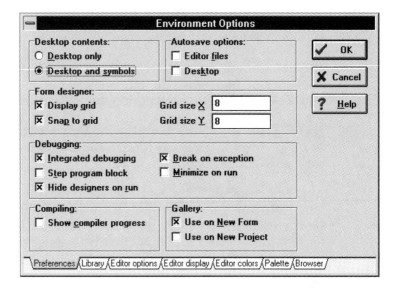

Environment
Options
dialog box
Figure 3-2.

let's change the default tab stop setting from 9 and 17 spaces to 4 and 8 spaces. To do this:

1. Click on the Editor options tab.
2. At the Tab Stops box, type **4**, press the SPACEBAR, then type **8**.
3. Press ENTER.

Items on other pages in this dialog box give you a fixed list of choices to choose from. For example, the Editor SpeedSetting drop-down list box on the Editor options page lets you choose what key combinations control which editing functions. There are only four possibilities: the default (normal Windows editing techniques), IDE Classic (Turbo Pascal), Brief, or Epsilon.

The Tools Menu

The Tools menu gives you access to the tools supplied with your version of Delphi. For example, the Image Editor gives you a fairly complete tool for modifying and building icons and other images that you can use in your program. The initial screen for the Image Editor looks like Figure 3-3. Like any good Windows application, it comes with its own extensive help system.

The other tools include the Database Desktop, used for managing databases, ReportSmith, for doing reports, as well as a tool for configuring the Borland Database.

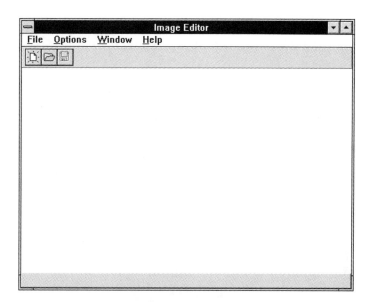

The Image
Editor
Figure 3-3.

3

Loading and Running Programs

Delphi comes with many interesting sample projects, so let's end this chapter with the procedures needed to run an existing Delphi project. The one described in this section is the Filedemo. This project demonstrates how to tie together the various file components. (File programming is covered in Chapter 10.)

If you choose the Open Project option on the File menu or click on the Open Project tool (the first tool in the SpeedBar), you are presented with the Open Project dialog box shown here (possibly after a dialog box asking you if you want to save your work):

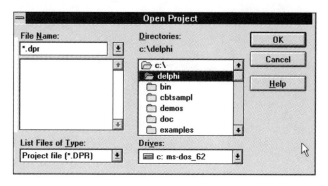

Notice that no files are shown. This is because Delphi keeps track of the files that make up a project in a file with a .DPR extension (for the Project file), and there aren't any in the \DELPHI directory. Of course, you can change the default for the filename extension Delphi will search for, by moving to the File Name list box and typing the new file pattern.

Double-click on the item marked **demos** in the Directories list box. Move through the subdirectories of the demos directory until you get to the one marked **filectrl**. Double-click on it and you are placed in the filectrl subdirectory. The Files box now lists the filedemo.dpr file, which contains the names and locations of the files that make up the Filedemo project.

Double-click on the filedemo.dpr file and Delphi will load the Filedemo project (after a possible interruption of a dialog box asking you if you want to save your current work). Since this project shows off the power that will soon be at your fingertips, you might want to press F9 to run it. (To end this, or any project when it is running, use ALT-F4.)

Chapter

4

Designing a Form: Components, Menus, and Events

This chapter will show you how to customize forms and the components you add to them. Changing a form or component's appearance is most often done by setting properties via the Object Inspector, so this chapter starts by showing you how to work with the Object Inspector. We don't neglect the mouse or the keyboard either. As you saw in Chapter 1, there are techniques that use the mouse for adjusting properties of forms (and components). We cover more of these techniques here and show you the keyboard methods as well. (Note, however, that positioning, resizing, and relocating components are usually done with a mouse except when very precise changes are needed.) We then survey the components, and discuss (some) of their associated properties and events. We also explain the basics of menu design using Delphi's built-in Menu Designer, as well as how to save files in ASCII form so that they can be printed out or viewed in an ordinary word processor.

Note: Depending on which version of Delphi you are using there can be more than a hundred components, which, taken together, have more than a thousand properties. I am in no way attempting to be complete. You must be prepared to consult the online help for more on forms, individual components, and their associated properties and events.

Although not quite precise, a good way to think of properties of visual components is that they affect the appearance of the component. Properties can be changed at design time or at run time. For example, when you drag to change the size and position of a form at design time as you did in Chapter 1, you are indirectly changing the Left, Top, Width, and Height properties as the form moves or changes size.

Note: When properties are changed at run time, the syntax takes the form:

    object.property := new value

(For more on coding techniques with properties, see Chapter 5.)

One way to shorten the learning curve for any version of Delphi is to be aware that regardless of which version of Delphi you have, the various types of components use the same named properties and events. And, in almost all cases, the same name means similar functionality. For example, there is essentially no difference between how one makes a project respond to a mouse click event on a form versus how to make it respond to a mouse click event on a button. Similarly, all components and forms have properties that specify where they are located, or that let you display a little "help hint" when you let the cursor rest on it (just as Delphi itself does).

Working with the Object Inspector

There are several different ways to set properties using the Object Inspector. (The documentation calls these *property editors*.) The following is a picture of the Object Inspector for the 32-bit version of Delphi. Notice that there are two tabbed pages. One is for setting properties and the other is for events.

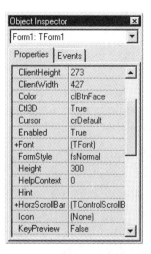

(The 16-bit version of the Object Inspector looks much the same—the only difference is that the tabs are on the bottom rather than the top.)

In the section that follows, we discuss the various methods for setting properties in the Object Inspector—these are the same for both versions.

4

Simple Editor

With this type of editor, you click in the right, or *value,* column and enter the text or the value there. You can use standard Windows editing techniques for cutting and pasting in these boxes. The obvious example is the caption editor for a form as shown here:

Delphi actually checks to make sure that what you entered makes sense. If you enter something that doesn't make sense, Delphi will pop up an "Invalid property value" message box (and reset the value back to its original value). For example, Delphi won't let you enter a string if a number is called for.

Drop-Down List Editor

Delphi uses this type of property editor when you have a finite number of choices for the value of the property. One example of this is the BorderStyle property for a form that controls (as one would expect) what type of border a form has. The following illustration shows this type of editor with the list of possible values dropped down.

There are a couple of ways to choose something from the drop-down list of properties available in these types of editors.

♦ Open the list by clicking the down arrow (or pressing ALT-DOWN ARROW). Then select the item you want.

♦ Keep on double-clicking in the value column until the value you want is shown.

Dialog Box Editor

Delphi follows the standard Windows convention that an ellipsis means a dialog box is available. The ellipsis shows up when you click in the value column. Click on the ellipsis to reveal the dialog box. (You can also double-click in the value column or press CTRL-ENTER to reveal the box directly.) The typical example is the Font property dialog box, as shown here:

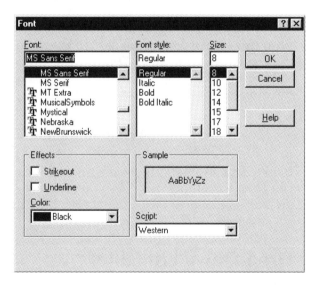

When you are finished adjusting the settings in the dialog box, click OK and they will go into effect.

Nested Properties Editor

This type of editor usually corresponds to properties that come in groups. For example, the BorderIcons property that controls what (standard) icons appear in the title bar of a form has three possibilities: system menu, maximize button, and minimize button (biSystemMenu, biMinimize, and biMaximize). A plus (+) sign to the left of the property name indicates that you have a group of properties that you can set. Double-click on the left column to see the list of properties. Here's a picture of this type of editor with the choices shown.

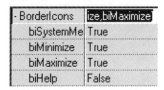

For example, to remove the maximize button from a form, do the following:

1. Double-click on the left column of the BorderIcons property.
2. Set the column for biMaximize to False by clicking on the right (value) column and choosing False from the drop-down list, which appears as shown here:

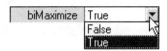

The BorderIcons property is an example of a property that is actually a set of values. This is why the right-hand column shows the values in square brackets, separated by commas. See Chapter 6 for more on sets in Delphi.

T **ip:** Since the Font property for the form also has the + sign indicating a set of properties you can set, you can double-click in the left column to work with individual font properties instead of using the Font dialog box.

4

Setting the Color Property

This is an unusual property in that it can be set two ways. The first is to drop down the list and choose one of the symbolic constants that represent one of any of various colors. (There are also symbolic constants on this list that give the current colors that the Windows control panel is using for standard elements such as the highlight color.) The second way is to double-click on the right-hand column to open up the Color dialog box as shown here.

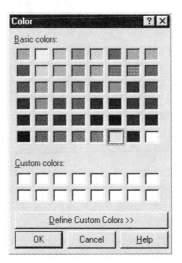

In this dialog box, you can choose one of the colors visually or define a custom color by clicking on one of the blank boxes and then clicking on the Define Custom Colors button and working with blends of the red, green, and blue values (0 is the minimum, 255 the maximum) and the settings for Hue, Saturation (Sat), and Luminosity (Lum) as shown here.

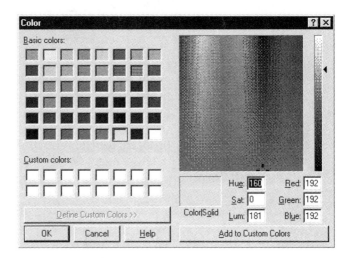

In any case, the color code corresponds to a hexadecimal number that will show up in the Object Inspector.

Tip: If you click inside the color box, Delphi changes the Hue and Saturation values to reflect where you clicked.

Forms

In both versions of Delphi, forms have the same 36 properties you can set at design time with the Object Inspector. Forms in both versions will respond to the same 20 events. The purpose of the next few sections is to introduce you to the most important of these properties and events. We spend somewhat more time on the properties and events associated with forms than we do on the ones for components in the later sections of this chapter. This is because many of these properties and events will recur with similar functionality for the various components.

Form Properties

4

What follows is a short discussion of the most important properties of a form. (See Chapter 12 for more on properties associated with graphics.)

Note: If a property for forms is not covered here and you want to find out more about it, use the online help. The easiest way to do this is to use the context sensitivity built into Delphi: choose the property by clicking or moving the cursor to it, then press F1.

ActiveControl   This property is used when you add components to a form. Use this property to specify which component will have the initial focus when your form is shown. For example, ordinary buttons show they have the focus by an outline that appears around the caption. The ActiveControl property is often used at run time. Using it you can tell which control has the focus and access the properties of that component (with some type casting that you will see how to do in Chapter 7).

AutoScroll   Leave this set at the default value of True to tell Delphi to automatically add scroll bars to a form at run time when there are components that aren't being displayed.

BorderIcons   This property is used to determine if a form shows the standard Windows system menu and maximize and minimize buttons. (See the section "Nested Properties Editor" earlier in the chapter.)

BorderStyle   This property determines the border style, as well as affecting what border icons show up. (See also the section "Nested Property Editors" earlier in the chapter.)

Caption   You saw this property changed in Chapter 1. It determines the text that appears in the title bar of the form.

ClientHeight, ClientWidth   These properties represent the height and width of the usable part of the form—the part excluding the borders. Both are measured in pixels. (*Pixel* stands for "picture element"—it is the smallest unit of resolution for a monitor or printer. This value is maintained by Windows.)

Color   This property determines the background color of the form. The Color property uses a drop-down list editor for the various color codes or a dialog box if you double-click in the right-hand (value) column.

Cursor   This property lets you determine the look of the cursor when the mouse is on the form. There are 15 standard shapes for Delphi 16 and 17 shapes for Delphi 32. They range from the usual arrow to an hourglass to more exotic shapes. The value column in the Object Inspector describes them using constants like crUpArrow that let you guess at the shape—consult the online help for pictures of them.

Note: By use of the Windows API LoadCursor function, it is possible to use a custom cursor. Look up the Cursors property of the TScreen object in the online help for more on how to do this.

Enabled   If this property is changed from the default value of True, the form will no longer respond to any events. Usually this property is manipulated at run time.

Font   This property lets you change the fonts for information displayed on the form via the Canvas property at run time (see Chapter 5). It also controls the default font to display text on components placed on the form. (The default font is the Windows system font in Delphi 16 and MS Sans Serif in Delphi 32.)

FormStyle   There are four possibilities for this property. The default value, fsNormal, says the form becomes a standard window. Change this to fsStayOnTop, and the form will always remain on top of any other forms in your project. The remaining two properties, fsMDIChild and fsMDIForm, are used with MDI forms (see Chapter 13).

Height, Width   These properties determines the height and width of the form in pixels *including the borders* (as opposed to the ClientHeight, ClientWidth properties, which measure the internal space only) or client area of the form.

HelpContext   This property is used when writing a Windows-compatible help system (see Chapter 13) for your application.

Hint, Showhint   The Hint property provides the text for the pop-up help hint, used in conjunction with the OnHint event of the TApplication object. You must have the ShowHint property set to True in order for this event to be activated.

HorzScrollBar, VertScrollBar   These two properties determine if a form has horizontal and vertical scroll bars. These are examples of nested properties, so you double-click in the left column to see a list of the subsidiary properties that you will want to work with. Table 4-1 describes the five nested properties for scroll bars.

To make scroll bars visible, make sure that

♦   The Visible property is True.
♦   The Range property of the scroll bar is bigger than the ClientWidth property (for horizontal scroll bars) or the Height property (for vertical scroll bars).

Property	Description
Increment	Determines how much movement occurs when the user clicks a scroll arrow
Margin	Lets you specify the number of pixels you want components to be from the edge of the scroll bar before a scroll bar actually appears
Position	Determines where the *thumb,* the box in the scroll bar, appears
Range	An integer that determines how far the scroll bars move
Tracking	A rarely used Delphi 32 property only
Visible	Determines if the scroll bars are visible or not

Nested
Properties for
Scroll Bars
Table 4-1.

Icon   This property determines the icon used for the program when the form is minimized. (The icon for your application is set by choosing the Options | Project | Application page in Delphi 16 or the Project | Options | Application page in Delphi 32.)

KeyPreview   The default for this property is False. If you change it to True, then most keystrokes are processed by the form's Key events first—rather than the component that has the focus. (See Chapter 6 for more on the Key events.)

Left, Top   These properties determine where the form is, relative to the left and top edges of the screen. They are measured in pixels.

Menu   This lets you designate which menu will appear on the form. (See "Designing Menus" later in this chapter.)

Name   This property is available for every Delphi object. The Name property lets you give meaningful names to your Delphi objects in order to make programs clearer. Delphi sets up a default name like Form1 for the first form, Form2 for the next, and so forth.

Note: Naming conventions for objects have inspired quite a lot of flaming. Some people prefer to use a prefix that indicates the object followed by the meaningful name. Examples of this might be frmAbout or frmInitial or btnHelp. Others prefer to use something that is close to meaningful English: AboutForm, FormAbout, or HelpButton. Rather than getting involved in the argument, I just want to point out that meaningful names for objects will make debugging easier—following some (documented) convention is always a good idea.

The rules for the name of an object are

♦   You cannot use a reserved word or standard directive (see the online help for a list of them) for an object's name.

♦   Object names can be any length, but only the first 63 characters are significant.

♦   The first character must be a letter or an underscore.

♦   The rest of the name can include any combination of letters, numbers, and underscores.

♦   The case of the letters in the variable name is irrelevant.

(These are actually the rules for Delphi *identifiers*; these rules apply to many Delphi objects. See Chapters 5 and 6 for more on identifiers.)

Tip: If you change the Name property and then click in the right-hand column of the Caption property, the Caption will change to the value of the Name property, if the Caption property has the same string value as the Name property when changing the Name property.

PixelsPerInch, Scaled   Once the Scaled property is set to True, the PixelsPerInch property determines how many pixels are used for each inch of the form. These two properties are mostly used at run time together with the PixelsPerInch property of the Screen object. By combining the two properties you can determine what Windows is using for the numbers of pixels in an inch. Once you know this, you can easily write the code to make your forms independent of the screen's resolution.

PopupMenu   You set this property to the name of the pop-up menu that you want to appear when the user clicks the right mouse button in a blank area of the form. (See "Designing Menus" later in this chapter for how to construct the pop-up menu.)

4

Position   This property gives you an easy way to set the position of the form. There are five possibilities. The two most important are the default value, poDesigned, which leaves the form in the position in which you designed it, and poScreenCenter, which automatically centers the form on the user's screen. The others are poDefault, which lets Delphi determine the location; poDefaultPosOnly, where the size stays as you designed, but Delphi chooses the position; and poDefaultSizeOnly, where the position stays as you designed, but Delphi chooses the size.

PrintScale   This property makes it easier to print the information on a form. The default value of poNone means no scaling will occur, and the form will appear different on paper than it is on the screen. If you set it to poProportional, then Delphi will automatically scale the form so that both the printed and displayed form have the same dimensions. The poPrintToFit value means the proportions remain the same but are rescaled to fit the printed page's size and shape.

Tag   Every form and component has a Tag property that can be used to store an integer that stores information about the form or component that would otherwise not be available.

Visible   This property determines whether the form is visible at run time.

WindowState   There are three values for this property. The default, wsNormal, leaves the form neither maximized nor minimized. You usually use code to change this property to one of the other two values: wsMaximized or wsMinimized—although you can, of course, also do so at design time.

Form Events

Recognizing events is the key to Delphi's power, but unless you write the code in the appropriate event handler, nothing will happen. The first thing you need to do when writing an event handler is to generate the event procedure template. The general method of generating an event procedure template is to double-click in the right column for the event's name.

Note: If you double-click on a component or a form, Delphi pops up the default event procedure template for that object. (For forms, it is the OnCreate event.)

Here are short descriptions of the most important form events.

OnActivate   Delphi uses this event handler when the focus is transferred to the form. In single form projects, as you saw in Chapter 1, this happens automatically when the application runs.

OnClick, OnDblClick   This event is triggered when the user clicks (or double-clicks) in a blank area of the form.

Note: The OnClick event will always be triggered first, even when the user double-clicks.

OnCloseQuery, OnClose   The OnCloseQuery event is triggered when the user *tries to close* the form (for example, by double-clicking on the control box). You can use this event for clean-up code—or even to prevent the form from closing. The OnClose event, on the other hand, is triggered *after* the OnCloseQuery event, but you still have a chance to prevent the form from closing (unlike the Visual Basic counterpart).

The Action variable parameter of the OnClose event can be set to four different values to determine how the form should close (caNone, caHide, caFree, caMinimize).

OnCreate   This event is triggered when the form is first created. You use this to set initial properties for the form and its components.

OnDeactivate   This event is triggered when the user switches (for example, by using the Windows Task Manager or ALT-TAB or the TaskBar in the 32-bit version of Delphi) to another application. Use this event for any code (like file saving warnings) you'll want to process before Windows deactivates your application.

OnDestroy   This event is triggered when the form is destroyed. Windows resources that Delphi allocated will be freed automatically. Nonetheless, this is the place to make sure that any memory you allocated (see Chapter 7) is freed up.

OnDragDrop, OnDragOver, OnMouseDown, OnMouseMove, OnMouseUp These events are used with code to detect mouse movements. (See Chapter 13.)

4

OnHide   You can use code to hide forms (see Chapter 5). If you do, Delphi triggers this event.

OnKeyDown, OnKeyPress, OnKeyUp   These events let you determine what the user is doing with the keyboard. (See Chapter 6.)

OnPaint   This event procedure is where you will most commonly put code to redraw information that may need to be repainted—for example, because information was lost when your window was coverered. (See Chapter 12.)

OnResize   This event is triggered whenever the user resizes a form. You usually place code in this event procedure to resize and reposition components as needed.

OnShow   This event is triggered just before the form is actually shown. It is used mostly with multiple form projects. (See Chapter 5.)

Components

Components are the nuts and bolts of your projects. These are the objects such as the various kinds of buttons or editing areas that make Windows applications easier to use than non-Windows applications.

Note: The documentation distinguishes between components and controls. Controls are those components that the user can see.

Furthermore, Delphi distinguishes between windowed and *non*windowed components. The major distinction is that windowed components can receive the focus and nonwindowed components cannot. (For those who are familiar with the Windows API, nonwindowed controls also do not have a Windows handle.)

Note: We will use the generic term component to refer to both windowed and nonwindowed components.

Just as with a form, components have properties that you can set at design time via the Object Inspector or at run time via code. Many properties, such as Height, Width, ShowHint, and Hint, work essentially the same way for both forms and components.

We first provide short descriptions, in tabular form, of the most common components that occur in both versions of Delphi. (See Chapter 13 for more on the controls specific to the 32-bit version of Delphi.) We then turn to the methods for "painting" them on your forms. Then it's on to short discussions of the most important properties of these components.

Note: We do not cover the components on the VBX page of the Component palette in the 16-bit version of Delphi or the ones on the various Samples or OCX pages here. (The components for data access are summarized in Chapter 14.)

An Overview of the Common Components

The roughly 70 components that are common to both versions of Delphi are displayed on the different pages of the Component palette. The page names are the same in both versions of Delphi.

Note: You can easily add other components to Delphi. For example, since Delphi 16 can add any Visual Basic controls that satisfy the Visual Basic 1.0 specifications, there are hundreds of tools you can add for specialized needs.(But, of course, Microsoft is downplaying VBXs in Windows 95, so I wouldn't recommend using them for applications you intend to port eventually to Windows 95.) Similarly, since Delphi 32 can use any OCX control, you have an ever-growing list of custom components at your disposal in this version as well. To learn how to add components, look at the online help for the page on "Registering Components."

Visual **Basic Tip:** The VBX page in Delphi 16 contains sample Visual Basic controls (the filenames for them end in VBX). However, if you own Visual Basic Professional Edition or a lot of custom controls for Visual Basic, it is possible that the names of the files for the components on the VBX page will be incompatible with your existing controls. For example, the GAUGE.VBX control in Delphi is incompatible with the one supplied with Visual Basic Professional 3.0. You will need to move or rename Visual Basic Professional's 3.0 GAUGE.VBX files in order to avoid crashing your system.

4

The Standard Page

The Standard page of the Component palette contains the components you will probably use most often. They are summarized in Table 4-2. (Remember, the convention in both versions of Delphi is that components have a capitol *T* as the first character in their name.)

The Additional Page

The Additional page of the Component palette contains components that are used in more specialized situations, such as when you need to create tabbed notebooks or graphic-oriented buttons. They are slightly different in the various versions of Delphi. (An * denotes a component that is not available on the Additional page in Delphi 32.) The Additional page is summarized in Table 4-3. (See Chapter 12 for more on graphics.)

The Dialogs Page

The Dialogs page of the Component palette is the same in both versions of Delphi. This page contains what you need to create the dialog boxes Windows users expect to see. It is summarized in Table 4-4 on page 82. (See Chapter 13 for more on dialog boxes.)

The System Page

Most of the components on the System page of the Component palette are the same in both versions of Delphi. The System pages have the components for working with disks and files (see Chapter 11) and for working with DDE

Icon	Name	Purpose
	TMainMenu	Designs ordinary menus
	TPopupMenu	Designs pop-up menus
A	TLabel	Labels other components or displays text that can't change
ab[	TEdit	Displays an area in which a user can enter *one* line of text
	TMemo	Allows users to enter *multiple* lines of text
OK	TButton	Creates command buttons
X	TCheckBox	Creates options when there are only two possibilities
	TRadioButton	Creates group of mutually exclusive options
	TListBox	Displays a list of choices and can also list images (see Chapter 12)
	TComboBox	Usually, combines a list box with an edit area to allow users either to choose an item from the list or to enter their own choice directly
	TScrollBar	Gives an analog method of moving through a range of choices
	TGroupBox	Groups items so they behave as a unit
	TRadioGroup	Special type of group box that makes it easier to work with radio buttons
	TPanel	Container component for other components that you want to treat as a group (see Chapter 13 for examples)

The Standard
Page of the
Component
Palette
Table 4-2.

and OLE (see Chapter 13). It also contains the important TTimer component (see "The TTimer Component" section later in this chapter). This page is summarized in Table 4-5 (see page 83).

4

Icon	Name	Purpose
	TBitBtn	Works like a command button, but allows a graphic to be used for the face of the button.
	TSpeedButton	Used with a panel component to create toolbars (see Chapter 12).
	TTabSet (*)	In the 16-bit version, lets you create the tabbed dialog boxes (like in the Object Inspector) that are becoming more common in applications. Used in conjunction with the TNotebook component when you need more flexibility than the TTabbedNotebook component supplies.
	TNotebook (*)	Used to stack multiple pages in the 16-bit version of Delphi.
	TTabbedNote (*)	Creates multiple pages on a form with a tab on top in the 16-bit version of Delphi.
	TMaskedEdit	Formats the display or hides (masks) the characters the user enters.
	TOutline(*)	Creates outlines in the 16-bit version of Delphi.
	TStringGrid(*)	Used for tabular text data in the 16-bit version of Delphi.
	TDrawGrid	Used to arrange images in a table.
	TImage	Displays a bitmap, icon, or Windows metafile.
	TShape	Used instead of code for displaying circles, ellipses, rectangles, or rounded rectangles.
	TBevel	Used to get a rectangle with a bevel (picture frame) around it.
	THeader(*)	Creates a resizable area in the 16-bit version of Delphi in which to enter text. Commonly used with the grid controls.
	TScrollBox	Creates a scrollable display area inside the form.

The Additional Page of the Component Palette
Table 4-3.

Icon	Name	Description
	TOpenDialog	Creates the Open File common dialog box
	TSaveDialog	Creates the Save File common dialog box
	TFontDialog	Creates the standard dialog box for choosing fonts
	TColorDialog	Creates the standard dialog box for choosing colors
	TPrintDialog	Creates the Print common dialog box
	TPrinterSetupDialog	Bypasses the PrintDialog box to go directly to the Printer Setup dialog box
	TFindDialog	Creates a Find dialog box (i.e., two areas to enter text)
	TReplaceDialog	Creates a Replace dialog box

The Dialogs
Page of the
Component
Palette
Table 4-4.

Adding Components to the Form

Once you decide which component you want to add to a form, there are a
couple of ways to place it there:

♦ If you double-click on the component, Delphi adds the component in
the default size and shape to the middle of the form. (If there are
components already in the center of the form, the new one is placed to
the lower right.)

♦ If you want to add a component at a specific location:

1. Click on the component.

2. Click at the spot on the form where you want the upper-left corner
of the component to appear. The component will appear there in its
default size.

Of course, you may want a component to be smaller or larger than the
default size. To do this, instead of clicking at the spot where you want the
left corner to appear, place the mouse pointer at the spot and drag. As you
drag, Delphi gives you an outline that shows the size and position of the
component. Release the mouse button when you are happy with the
component's size and position.

Icon	Name	Description
	TTimer	Used to activate code at a specified Timer interval
	TPaintBox	Creates an area for graphics
	TFileListBox	Creates a list box that shows files in the current directory
	TDirectoryListBox	Shows the directory structure on the current drive
	TDriveComboBox	Used for navigating among drives
	TFilterComboBox	Used to filter files shown in a TFileListBox
	TMediaPlayer	Used for working with multimedia files
	TOLEContainer	Gives an OLE client
	TDDEClientConv	Used for establishing a DDE client
	TDDEClientItem	Used for specifying what will be sent from the client to the server in a DDE client link
	TDDEServerConv	Used for setting up a DDE server
	TDDEServerItem	Used for specifying what will be sent from the server to the client

4

The System
Page of the
Component
Palette
Table 4-5.

Adding Multiple Components to a Form

You will often want to add multiple components of the same type to a form. (For example, you often need multiple command buttons or edit boxes.)

To add multiple components of the same type:

1. Hold down SHIFT.
2. Click on the component in the palette. (You can actually release SHIFT after you select the component—it will stay selected.)
3. Click at the place on the form where you want the upper-left corner of each copy of the component to appear in the default size and shape or drag the component to size and shape it as you would like.

N **ote:**   If you use this method to add components to a form, be sure to click on the pointer icon to go back to the usual method of working with components. (The pointer icon is always on the far left of each page of the Component palette.)

Container Components

When you use components like radio buttons, they need to be kept in groups. This way, Delphi knows which ones to turn off when one is turned on. There are six components common to both versions of Delphi (besides the form itself) that can serve as *container* components. The idea of a container is that all the components will behave as one at design time (sometimes this is called a *parent-child relationship*). For example, when you move a container component, the child components move with it. These six container components are TGroupBox, TRadioGroupBox, TPanel, TNotebook, TTabbedNotebook, and TScrollBox.

The easiest way to create a container is to add it to the form before you add the child components. Once you have placed the container on the form, make sure that the container component is selected.

Then add components as you normally would, for example, by clicking inside the container. For instance, when you have a container component selected, double-clicking on a component will make it appear (as a child) in the middle of the selected container component.

N **ote:**   You can also add multiple copies of the same component to a container component that is currently active by using the SHIFT-Click method. This is especially useful in making toolbars (see Chapter 13).

Working with Existing Components

Before you can work with a component that is already on a form, you need to select it. This can be done in one of the following ways:

♦   Click inside the component.

♦   Choose the component by dropping down the Object selector, located at the top of the Object Inspector. An example of this is shown in the following illustration:

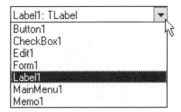

♦ If the focus is in the form, you can also use TAB to move the focus among the components on the form. (What's even better is to select any component and hit ESC until the form has focus.)

When a component is selected on a form, small black squares called *sizing handles* appear on the perimeter. Dragging on them lets you resize the component (see "Resizing and Reshaping Controls" later in the chapter).

Selecting Multiple Components

You will often need to work with many components at once (for example, when you need to align them). The easiest way to select multiple components is

4

1. Hold down SHIFT.
2. Click on each of the components.

There is one other method for selecting multiple components that is occasionally useful.

1. Imagine a rectangle that encloses only those components you want to select. Move to one corner of this imagined rectangle, and click the left mouse button.
2. Hold down the left mouse button, and drag the dotted rectangle until it contains only the components you want to select. Then release the mouse button.

Regardless of which way you select a group of controls, when you finish selecting, you know you were successful when they all show *gray* sizing handles.

Note: If the components are tied to a container object like a TPanel or TGroupBox component, press CTRL before starting to drag.

You can also select all the components on a form by choosing Edit | Select All. Finally, to deselect a group of components, click on a blank part of the form or any component not part of the group.

Moving Components

To move a component to a different location:

1. Select the component.
2. Place the mouse inside the control, and drag the component to its new location. (Be careful not to drag the sizing handles, or you will resize it instead of moving it.)

Notice that as you manipulate the control, it seems to move in fits and starts. As the old computer joke goes, this is not a bug, it's a feature. The positions of components on a form default so that they are located only at grid points. The Environment page available on the Tools menu in the 32-bit version and the Options menu in the 16-bit version let you control this feature. (It's called "Snap to grid.") You can also make the grid more or less fine by changing options in this dialog box.

Note: When you have selected a group of components, they all move in tandem.

Resizing and Reshaping Controls

The sizing handles are the easiest way to change the shape and size of a control. To resize a single component, first select it. You should be able to see the black sizing handles. Now drag the appropriate sizing handle.

You can also select a control and choose Edit | Size to display the Size dialog box, as shown here:

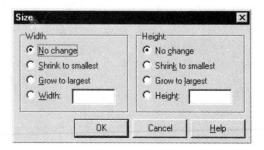

Now fill in this dialog box as you want and choose OK.

Note: If you need to resize multiple components, first select them. Then open the Size dialog box and fill it in as needed.

Deleting Components

If you need to delete components on the form, first select them. Then press DEL, or choose Edit | Delete.

Tip: You can always restore deleted components by choosing Edit | Undelete. You must, however, use the Undelete option before doing anything else!

4

Cutting, Copying, and Pasting Components

Delphi lets you cut, copy, and paste components between forms, or between a form and a container using standard Windows conventions (CTRL-X for cut, CTRL-C for copy, and so on). You can also use the appropriate options on the Edit menu. You need to be aware that whenever you copy a component, Delphi gives it a new name but otherwise uses the same properties. More importantly, Delphi still uses the *old* event handlers that you wrote. (See Chapter 7 for how to work with event handlers shared by multiple components.)

Aligning Components

The trouble with using a mouse to drag components around is that it is hard to get the edges to line up exactly right. To give your applications a more polished look, you'll want to make sure that the components are perfectly aligned. After you have selected a group of controls, there are two ways to align them with respect to each other:

♦   Use the Alignment palette (choose View | Alignment Palette to open the Alignment palette), and click on the button that aligns the components the way you want.

♦   Choose Edit | Align to open the Align dialog box. Then click on the options you like.

Note: Regardless of which method you choose, the first component you select is used as a reference for the alignment. For example, if the first component sticks out a little bit to the left and you choose to align the components by choosing Left sides in the Align dialog box, the others will move to the left.

Some Individual Components

This section discusses some common component properties and events that are important when manipulating the focus for components. We then discuss the more common components. (It is no exaggeration to say that 10 to 15 components make up the bulk of the visual interface in Delphi projects.)

While we discuss some of the most important properties and events that occur time and time again for components, we will not repeat discussions of the many properties and events (such as Color, Cursor, Enabled, Left, Name, Top, Visible, Width, OnClick, OnDblClick, and so on) that work essentially the same for forms and components. Similarly, the procedure for setting up a help hint when the mouse is over a component is the same as for a form. (You should consult Chapter 6 for the keyboard events and Chapter 13 for those dealing with the mouse, such as OnMouseDown or OnDragOver.)

One property worth singling out that many components share is the Align property. This property can be set to values such as alTop, alRight, alBottom, and so on. Setting this property has the effect of securing the component to the specified edge.

Note: Properties that measure where a control is, such as Align, Left, and Top, are always calculated relative to the boundaries of the container component.

Tip: If you select multiple controls, the Object Inspector shows only the properties that all the controls share. This makes it easy to set properties such as Height and Width that you may want groups of controls to share.

Focus Properties and Events

Either the form or a single component on it can be active—that is, have the *focus*—at any given time. You saw one way to determine or set which control has the initial focus: setting the ActiveControl property of the form. If you don't set the ActiveControl property, then Delphi looks at those components whose TabStop property is set to True. It then moves the focus to the visible (and enabled) component with the lowest value for the Tab Order property.

The OnEnter Event   This event is triggered whenever a component becomes active or gains focus. Use this to write any initial code you want for the component.

The OnExit Event   This event is triggered whenever the focus moves away from an active component. Use this to write any code that you want to be processed when the control loses the focus.

Caption Properties and Accelerator Keys   Many Windows applications use accelerator keys to quickly move the focus or to click a button. These keys are indicated by an underline in the caption. Users can then press ALT and the underlined letter to click the button or move the focus.

4

To set up an accelerator key for a Delphi component, add an ampersand (&) right before the accelerator (underlined) letter. For example, if you set the caption property of a Tbutton to &Quit, the user can then use ALT-Q instead of clicking on the button to activate its OnClick event procedure.

The Ctl3D Property   This is a True/False property that determines if a control gives a three-dimensional appearance or not. The default in Delphi is True, so controls appear to have some depth to them.

The TLabel Component

Labels are used for text that identifies the components they are next to (for example, you will want to label edit boxes). They can also be used to display text that users can't edit.

Tip: You can use a label to give an accelerator key to components that do not have a caption property (like edit boxes). The idea is that when the user presses the accelerator key, the control that is the value of the label's FocusControl property receives the focus.

Alignment   There are three ways to align text inside a label. For example, if you set the value of this property to taCenter, Delphi will center the text inside the label. The other two possibilities are taLeftJustify and taRightJustify.

AutoSize   If this property is set to True, then the label resizes automatically to fit the text. You can have the label resize automatically to fit a changing caption if you set the AutoSize property to True.

Transparent   This property is used when you work with graphics (see Chapter 12). If you set this to True, you can see through the label to the underlying picture.

Wordwrap   Set this property to True if you want the text to wrap at the end of lines instead of expanding horizontally.

TEdit Box Component

The TEdit component gives you a place (usually called an edit box) in which the user can type a single line of information. Edit boxes can also be used to display information to a user. For edit boxes, the AutoSize property defaults to True. This lets the box expand to take into account any font changes you may make. It has no effect on the width.

AutoSelect   You can choose to have the text in an edit box automatically selected whenever it receives the focus by setting the AutoSelect property to True. (The default value is, in fact, True.)

CharCase   You can allow the user to enter mixed case text (the default) or restrict entry to upper- or lowercase by changing this property. Delphi automatically changes the case of whatever the user enters to match the setting of this property.

HideSelection   This property controls whether text still shows as selected when the focus leaves the edit component. If you set this to False (the default is True), then Delphi still shows you the currently selected text—regardless of where the focus is.

MaxLength   This integer determines the maximum amount of text the user can enter. The default value of zero means there are no limits except those determined by the system. Any other value will restrict the number of characters.

PasswordChar   If you want to mask the characters a user enters, then change this to a non-null character.

ReadOnly   Set this to True to stop the user from entering text into the box. This is a common alternative to using a label to display unchangeable text.

Text   This determines what text appears initially in the control. The default value is the name of the control.

The OnChange Event   This event is triggered whenever the user changes the data in the edit box.

Caution: Be very careful not to put any code in the OnChange event procedure that changes the contents of the box. This will cause the system to continually trigger the event until the program crashes. (This is usually called an event cascade.)

The TMemo Component

4

The TMemo component gives you a way to work with multiple lines of text. You can even use a TMemo component to quickly read in the data from a file quickly (see Chapter 10). TMemo components can read and store up to 32K of text in the 16-bit version and have essentially no limits in Delphi 32 (it's one gigabyte). Many of the properties of TMemo components, such as MaxLength and ReadOnly, work similarly to those in the TEdit component.

If you want a TMemo component to have scroll bars, set the ScrollBars property accordingly. Although the Align property works much as you would expect, there is a nifty new possibility—if you set Align to alClient, then the Memo component occupies all the space in the form. What follows is a short discussion of the most important properties peculiar to the Memo component.

Lines   This property controls the contents of the component. At design time you can add multiple lines (each up to 255 characters long in Delphi 16 and with no realistic limit in Delphi 32) by double-clicking on the right column. This opens the dialog box (shown in the following illustration) where you can enter the various lines of text.

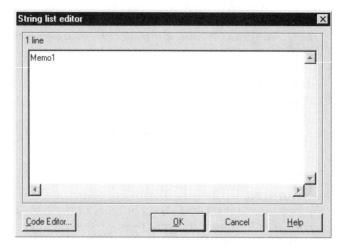

WantTabs, WantReturns   Usually in Windows applications, TAB moves you between controls. If you want users to be able to insert tabs in a Memo component, set this property to True. If you leave this at the default value of False, then users need to press CTRL-TAB. The WantReturns property, on the other hand, defaults to True, so the user can press ENTER to separate lines. Set it to False and ENTER is sent to the form to be processed, and users will need to use the CTRL-ENTER combination to separate lines.

TButton and TBitButton Components

Placing buttons on a form so that the user can click on them in order to do something is very common in Windows applications (although many components can detect the click event and so have an OnClick event procedure associated to them.) The two most common types of push buttons that Delphi supports are examples of TButtons and TBitBtns.

The TButton component may be found on the Standard page of the component palette, and the bit button component (TBitBtn) may be found on the Additional page. Both ordinary and bit buttons give the user an illusion that the buttons are being temporarily pressed in when the user clicks on them or presses the SPACEBAR when the button has the focus. The essential difference of a TBitBtn component from an ordinary button is that you can combine both text and a bitmapped graphic on it. You can use one of Delphi's predefined bitmaps, such as those used for Delphi's OK, Cancel, or Help buttons, or specify your own bitmap for the button.

The two most common properties of both ordinary push buttons and bit buttons are discussed first. Then you'll see short descriptions of the most important properties of bit buttons.

Cancel   Sometimes you want to have the pressing of ESC trigger an event. For this, set the Cancel property of the button to True. Once you have done this, Delphi triggers the OnClick event handler for this button whenever the user presses the ESC key. This is good for a Cancel button of a file delete confirmation.

Default   The OnClick event for a *default* button (one whose Default property is True) is triggered whenever the user presses ENTER. To make a button the default button, set the button's Default property to True.

Note: If the user presses ENTER when a button has the focus, then Delphi triggers the OnClick event for that button. This happens whether or not you have set up a default button. Also, if a TMemo component has the focus whose WantReturns property is True, then Delphi sends the carriage return to the TMemo component (again regardless of whether there is a default button).

4

TBitButton Properties

We now briefly discuss the important properties peculiar to bit buttons.

Glyph, NumGlyphs   The Glyph property lets you specify the bitmap for a bit button. When you set this property in the design environment, Delphi gives you a standard Windows file Open dialog box in order to choose the bitmap. You can use up to four different images for the same button if you want, *but they all must be the same size*. The NumGlyphs property lets you specify multiple images. (See the online help for more on this.)

Kind   The Kind property determines the kind of bitmapped graphic that appears on the bit button. For example, a value of bkOK gives the green check mark "OK" button you see in Delphi. There are 11 possible values. Set it to bkCustom (the default) when you want to use your own bitmap (and then set the Glyph property accordingly).

Layout, Margin, Spacing   The Layout property determines whether the bitmap is on the left, right, top, or bottom of the bit button. The Margin property gives the amount of space between the bit button and its border. The Spacing property gives the space between the caption and the border.

TListBox and TComboBox Components

Both the TListBox and TComboBox components let you display a scrollable list of items that users can select from. The difference is that the user *cannot change the entries in a list box.* (Combo boxes provide an edit area in which the user can enter information.) You need to use the items property editor box or code in order to enter the items in these components, so we will return to these two components in Chapters 6 and 13, where you will also see how to add images to a list box.

The most common event for list boxes is the OnClick event. This is triggered not only when the user clicks on an item, but also when he or she scrolls through the items in the list box with the keyboard. For this reason you will often write the activating code in the OnDblClick event rather than in the OnClick event. (This is pretty much the Windows standard anyway, except for things like the Start bar in Windows 95.)

Here are short discussions of the most important properties of these components that you may want to set at design time.

Tip: Set the IntegralHeight property of a list box to True to make sure that the list box cannot be resized in such a way that an item is only partly visible.

Columns This property only applies to list boxes. It determines the number of columns the user sees in the box.

ExtendedSelect, MultiSelect These properties also apply only to list boxes. If MultiSelect is set to True, then users can select more than one item in the list box using ordinary Windows techniques. The difference is that with both ExtendedSelect and MultiSelect set to True, the user must use SHIFT to select an adjoining group and CTRL to select multiple adjoining groups.

Sorted This property applies to both components. It determines if Delphi keeps the items sorted as you add more items to the list or combo box.

Style This property lets you determine the style of the combo box. There are five possibilities, although only three are very common. The first common value is actually the default value—it's called csDropDown. This gives you the usual drop-down list with an edit area. If you set it to csDropDownList, you get a drop-down list box (that is, no edit area). If you set it to csSimple, you get no associated list of items.

Note: If you set this property to lbOwnerDrawFixed or lbOwnerDrawVariable, then you can mix both text and graphics in the box.

TCheckBox and TRadioButton Components

Use check boxes when you want to provide nonexclusive options to the user. You then use code to determine if the user checks or unchecks a specific check box (using the value of the Checked property). On the other hand, use a group of radio buttons when you need to present mutually exclusive choices to the user. (A good example is the Align dialog box in Delphi.) Whenever a user clicks on one radio button in a group, the other buttons are switched off. In any case, as one would expect, when the user clicks on a box or button, Delphi also triggers the OnClick event for that component.

 Note: Since radio buttons work as a group, the only way two radio buttons on a form can be checked at the same time is if they are in separate container components.

4

The TTimer Component

Use a TTimer component whenever you want something (or "nothing"— such as a pause) to occur periodically. For example, you might want to have a program that wakes up periodically and checks stock prices. On a more prosaic level, if you want to display a "clock" on a form, you might want to update the clock's display every minute or even every second (see "The OnTimer Event" later in the chapter for the one line of code this takes).

Timers are not visible to the user; the icon appears only at design time. For this reason, where you place the timer control at design time is not important. Although timers are an important tool for Delphi programmers, they shouldn't be overused. In fact, Windows restricts all the applications (not just the Delphi ones running at one time) to 16 timers under Windows 3.X. Do not go overboard on the timer control, since too many will use up a large share of precious Windows resources.

The icon for a timer looks like an old-fashioned clock and may be found on the System page of the Component palette. There are two important properties of timer controls: Enabled and Interval.

Enabled

Enabled is a Boolean (True/False) property that determines whether the timer should start ticking. If you set this to True at design time, the clock starts ticking when the form loads. ("Ticking" is meant metaphorically; there's no noise unless you program it.) Also, because timer controls are invisible to the user, he or she may well be unaware that a timer has been enabled. For this reason, you may want to notify the user that a timer is working by means of a message box, an image control, or a picture box with a clock icon inside it.

If you set the Enabled property to False at design time, the timer control starts working only when you switch this property to True in code. Similarly, you can disable a timer inside code by setting its Enabled property to False. (When inside a timer event it is a good idea to turn off the timer while processing the event.)

Interval

The Interval property determines how much time Delphi waits before calling the Timer event procedure (see the next section). The interval is measured in milliseconds, and the theoretical limits are between 1 millisecond and 65,535 milliseconds (a little more than one minute and five seconds). The reason these are only theoretical limits is that the underlying hardware reports the passage of only 18 clock ticks per second. Since there are fewer than 56 milliseconds per clock tick, you can't really use an Interval property any smaller than 56, and intervals that don't differ by at least this amount may give the same results (although you can use API functions, described in Chapter 6, for smaller time intervals.)

The smaller you set the Interval property, the more CPU time is spent waking up the Timer event procedure. If you set the Interval property too small, your system performance may slow to a crawl.

 Note: An Interval property of zero disables the timer.

The OnTimer Event   Delphi tries to trigger the OnTimer event procedure as often as you have set the Interval property. But, since the CPU may be

4

doing something else when the time determined by the interval elapses, you cannot be guaranteed that Delphi will call the OnTimer event procedure exactly when you want it. (Delphi will know when the interval has elapsed; it just may need to finish what it is doing before activating the OnTimer event.) If the time has elapsed, Delphi will call the Timer event procedure as soon as it is free to do so. (You can use code to determine if more time has elapsed than you planned.)

For example, suppose you want to develop a project with a clock that will update itself every second. To design the form, follow these steps:

1. Add a label and a timer to a blank form.
2. Set the AutoSize property of the label to True and the font size to be sufficiently large. Set the Interval property of the timer control to be 1,000 (1,000 milliseconds = 1 second).

Now write the following code in the Timer event procedure for the Timer1 control:

```
Procedure TForm1.Timer1Timer(Sender: TObject);
begin
Label1.Caption = 'The time is ' + DateTimeToString(Now);
end;
```

Delphi will call this event procedure and update the clock's time roughly every second because the Interval property was set to 1,000. (See Chapter 6 for more on the date/time functions we used in this example.)

T ip: If you want to have an OnTimer event procedure do something less frequently than about once a minute (the maximum setting for the Interval property), you need to add a static (typed constant) variable to the OnTimer event procedure. This variable will let you keep track of the number of intervals that has elapsed. See Chapter 5 for more on these kinds of variables.

TStringGrid and TDrawGrid Components

The TStringGrid component lets you build tables of textual data. The TDrawGrid lets you display both text and graphics. The intersection of a row and a column is usually called a *cell*. Most of the properties for the two grid controls work similarly. We only cover the basic properties of grids here. Many of the properties of grids are only useful at run time. For example, the

Cells property both lets you put items in the cells and gives you access to the items in each cell. The key event for grids is the OnDrawCell event. This event is triggered whenever the user selects a cell. (For more on working with grids, please see the online help.)

ColCount, RowCount   These properties determine the number of rows and columns in the grid. The default value for each of these properties is 5, but you can reset them in code or via the Object Inspector.

DefaultColWidth, DefaultRowHeight, Height, Width   DefaultColWidth and DefaultRowHeight specify the width of a column or height of a row. Height and Width, as you probably realize, set the height and width of the whole grid.

FixedCols, FixedRows, FixedColor   Often when you are working with a grid, you will want to use certain cells to display information at all times. For example, regardless of how the user scrolls through a spreadsheet, you may always want to display the column headings. Fixed rows and columns are always displayed in gray and must be at the top and left side of the grid. The FixedColor property gives the color Delphi should use for the fixed cells.

GridLineWidth   This property determines the width of the line between cells. Larger values give you thicker lines, and a value of zero erases the black gridline (although you will still be able to see where the cell boundaries are because of a white border around the cells).

Options   This nested property has 15 Boolean (True/False) settings. These are mostly used for determining how the grid appears to the user, or how he or she can manipulate the grid at run time. For example, if you set the goEditing value of this property to True, then the user can edit text inside a cell. (Consult the online help for more details on this property.)

Designing Menus

Think of menu items as specialized components that you add to your forms. Menu items respond only to a click event. Designing the right kind of menus will make your applications much more user-friendly. Delphi lets you build essentially unlimited levels of menus and add pop-up menus as well.

Menus that contain submenus are usually called *hierarchical* (or *cascading*) menus. Of course, using too many levels of menus can make the application confusing to the user. Four are almost certainly too many; two or three levels are what you usually see. The user knows that a submenu lurks below a given menu item when he or she sees an arrow following the menu item.

Tip: Instead of using lots of submenus, consider designing a custom dialog box for the options.

To add a menu to your form, you first need to add a menu (or pop-up menu) component to a form. Adding a TPopupMenu component lets you create a menu that appears when the user clicks the right mouse button in a component or in the form when it has been assigned to the PopupMenu property of a form or component. To place a TMenu or TPopupMenu component, just double-click on the component, since it doesn't matter where the component appears on a form.

You next need to open the Menu Designer. For this either:

♦ Double-click inside the TMenu or the TPopupMenu component that is on the form, or

♦ Double-click (or click on the ellipsis) in the Items property for the menu component.

4

Delphi then displays the Menu Designer as shown here:

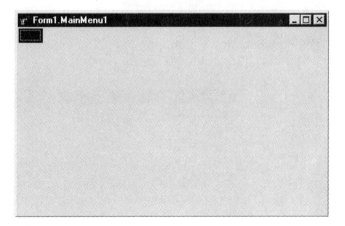

Notice that the first (blank) menu item is highlighted in the Menu Designer. The Menu Designer gives you a sense of what your menus will look like. Look at the illustration on the following page:

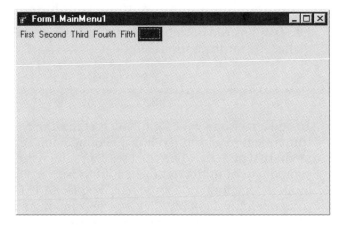

Notice how the items on the main menu bar show up pretty much as they would appear on the form. Of course, you can build menus for the items on the main menu bar as well. Here's an example of a submenu for the first menu item on the main menu bar:

When you design a menu for a pop-up menu component, Delphi only maintains one column as shown here:

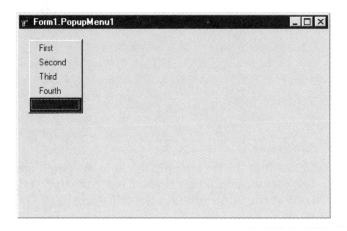

Working with the Menu Designer

Let's suppose you are working with a main menu component. The text you enter in this box becomes the caption for the first menu item—and also, of course, the value of the Caption property. Once you press ENTER, Delphi places dotted boxes to its right and below it, as shown here:

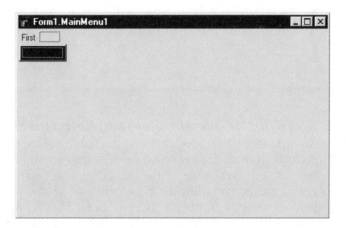

The box below would correspond to the first item in the "First Menu," and the one to the right would be the second main menu item. You can navigate around the Menu Designer with the arrow keys or with the mouse.

Note:　Delphi gives the menu item a Name property based on the caption. To make your code cleaner, you may want to change the Name property in the Object Inspector directly.

Once you add a menu item, you can work with the properties of that item. The most important properties besides the Caption and Name properties are discussed shortly. The Caption property is also where you add the ellipsis a menu item would use to indicate that clicking on the item will pop up a dialog box. You may want to have separator bars for your menus—they have many uses; the simplest is to break long menus into groups. If you have more than five or six items on a menu, see if there is some way to use a separator bar to group them.

4

Tip: If you set the Caption property for a non-main menu to a hyphen (-), a separator bar shows up.

Note: Items on both kinds of menus only respond to the OnClick event.

Specifying Accelerator Keys and Keyboard Shortcuts

As you saw earlier, accelerator keys enable the user to access a menu command from the keyboard by pressing ALT and the appropriate letter, indicated in your code by the preceding ampersand. Just as with components, you indicate the accelerator key by placing the ampersand (&) before the letter in the Caption property for that menu item.

On the other hand, keyboard shortcuts let the user activate the menu item *without having to open the menu.* To give a keyboard shortcut for a menu item:

1. Select the menu item.
2. Enter a value for the ShortCut property of the item. (You can pull down the list box in the value, or right, column in the Object Inspector to see a list of common shortcuts.)

Caution Delphi does not check to see if you have used the shortcut or accelerator before.

Tip: ALT-F4 is not listed as a shortcut because this closes any form as long as you haven't removed the System menu from the form. If you feel you want to indicate that ALT-F4 is the shortcut for an Exit item, add this to the Caption property directly.

The Checked Property

This True/False property controls whether a little check mark shows up in front of the item. It is usually changed at run time via code to reflect what the user did. You can set it at design time as well.

The Break Property

This property is used to set up multicolumn menus. The default is mbNone. If you set it to mbBreak, then Delphi starts a new column with that item. If you set it to mbBarBreak, then Delphi also places a vertical bar between the columns (like the Program item in Windows 95). Obviously you only change the default for this property on submenu items.

The AutoPopup Property (pop-up menus only)

When this is True, a click on the right mouse button pops up the menu. The default value is True.

Adding and Deleting Menu Items

Delphi lets you work within the Menu Designer to insert or delete menu items. Let's start with inserting a new menu item into an existing menu. Menu items are inserted to the left of the selected item on the main menu bar or above the one you selected when you are working with a submenu.

4

To add a menu item:

♦ Move the cursor to a menu item, and then press INS.

To delete a menu item:

♦ Select the item and then press DEL.

Rearranging Menu Items

During design time, you can move menu items in the Menu Designer simply by dragging and dropping them. The only exception is one you would expect: you can't move a menu item into its submenu. While you are dragging menu items, the cursor changes shape.

 Note: When you move a menu item, any menu items beneath it move as well.

For example, to move a menu item along the main menu bar, drag the menu item along the menu bar until the tip of the drag cursor points to the new location. Then release the mouse button. If you move an item into a submenu, then when you start the dragging operation, Delphi opens up the menu the moment the cursor points to the new menu.

Creating Nested Menus

Delphi lets you have a menu item be the gateway into another menu. This is indicated by an arrow to the right of the menu item. To create a nested (cascading) menu, first select the menu item that will have the submenu. Then:

1. Click on the right mouse button in the Menu Designer, and choose Create Submenu from the speedmenu.

2. Enter a name for the first submenu item.

3. Press ENTER (or DOWN ARROW when the focus is in the Menu Designer), to create space for the next submenu item.

Continue this process until you are satisfied. When you are, press ESC to return to the previous menu level, or click inside the Menu Designer to move to a different place. (As always, you can drag an existing menu item to a new location.)

T ip: If you move an existing menu structure to another place in the Menu Designer, its submenus move with it. This gives you a nested menu instantaneously.

Menu Templates

Delphi comes with a few menu templates already built; you can also create your own menu templates for reuse. To add a menu template, you must be in the Menu Designer. Then:

1. Click on the right mouse button to open up the speedmenu.

2. Choose Insert From Template from the speedmenu.

At this point, the Insert Template dialog box pops up, giving you a list of the currently available menu templates, an example of which is shown here:

Choose the one you want to add. (You can then use the techniques you now know to customize it.)

Note: You will have to rewrite the OnClick event handlers for the items on the menu template. You may also have to adjust the Name property of all the menu items if you don't like the ones Delphi creates.

4

After you have designed a menu, do the following to save it for reuse as a template:

1. Click on the right mouse button to open up the speedmenu.
2. Choose Save As Template.

The Save Template dialog box pops up. This dialog box lets you enter a brief description of the menu—you don't have to follow normal DOS/Windows naming conventions.

Making Menu Items Responsive

Menu items only trigger an event when the user clicks on the item. To get to the template for this event handler:

♦ Double-click on the menu item in the Menu Designer.

Or, if you are on the form:

♦ Click the menu item.

The ASCII Representation of a Form

The idea of the ASCII representation of a form is simple: it contains a textual description of the form's properties. This is necessary because Delphi usually stores the form (.DFM) file in a binary format that is unreadable. The ASCII representation of a form is an extremely useful debugging tool. Using it, you can easily check that the properties of the form and its components are exactly what you want. It also is very helpful in version control when you develop a complex project.

Tip: You can modify the properties of a form or its components using an ordinary text editor on the ASCII representation. (Although you should be aware that this is only if you write it out to a text file from Delphi—Delphi knows to read in a DFM and convert it to text and vice versa. Generally speaking, you should use the Delphi editor.)

You have to open a form file to convert it, but you cannot have the same form open simultaneously in both DFM (visual) and TXT (text) formats. In particular, this means that you have to work with an already *saved* .DFM file to convert it. To save a form in ASCII format:

1. Choose File | Open File.
2. Select the form (.DFM) file that you want to convert to ASCII from the dialog box that pops up. Delphi will bring the file into the design environment in ASCII form.
3. Now choose File | Save File As, and use a .TXT file extension for the filename.

To convert a text version of a form file back to the binary (.DFM) format, do the following:

1. Choose File | Open File.
2. Select the text file you want to convert back from text to binary format in the dialog box that pops up. Delphi will bring it into the design environment in ASCII form in the Code Editor window.
3. Choose File | Save File As—only now give the file a .DFM extension.

To see a sample of the ASCII representation for a form:

1. Start up a new project and give the form the caption of ASCII.

2. Add a single TButton in the default size, in the default location, using the default name of Button1.

3. Save the form file.

4. Convert the form file to ASCII using the techniques listed earlier.

The file will look like this:

```
object Form1: TForm1
  Left = 200
  Top = 99
  Width = 435
  Height = 300
  Caption = 'ASCII'
  PixelsPerInch = 96
  object Button1: TButton
    Left = 169
    Top = 120
    Width = 89
    Height = 33
    Caption = 'Button1'
    TabOrder = 0
  end
end
```

As you can see, the ASCII representation contains a textual description of the form and the essential TButtons properties. For example, the form's new caption is reflected by the line of code that looks like this:

```
Caption = 'ASCII'
```

The ASCII format for a component starts out looking something like this:

```
object Button1: TButton
```

This indicates what *class* the object comes from. See Chapter 7 for more on this topic.

4

Chapter

5

Fundamentals of Delphi Programming

By now you have a feel for what a Delphi application looks like. You've seen how to customize forms by adding components, and you've started writing the event handlers that are the backbone of a Delphi application. But, as you've probably realized, the event handlers you've seen didn't do much. To do more, you must become comfortable with the dialect of Object Pascal built into Delphi. This chapter gets you started on mastering this language. In addition to seeing fundamental language constructs like constants, variables, and the loops and decision structures built into Delphi, you'll also start to see how to work with Delphi objects at run time by using the appropriate code in your projects.

You start by learning how to work with the Code Editor window and the basic kinds of Delphi statements. Then it's on to a discussion of setting properties via code and such fundamental programming ideas as variables, numbers, and constants. Then it's on to fundamental programming constructs like types, loops, and if-then statements. Next, we cover the basics of working with Delphi objects at run time. For example, there's a discussion of methods. *Methods* are most commonly operations (functions or procedures) that affect the behavior of Delphi objects at run time. (However, this is not quite precise, as there are methods that work like properties, and properties that work like methods!) Next, we discuss objects that are only available at run time—like Screen, Printer, and Application. This is followed by a short discussion of the various kinds of message and input boxes available in Delphi. The chapter ends with a discussion of the techniques needed to use multiple forms in a single Delphi application.

Before we begin, though, it can't be stressed enough that the key to Delphi programming is recognizing that Delphi generally processes code only in response to events. Think of a Delphi program as a set of independent pieces that "wake up" only in response to events they have been told to recognize. It's also worth stressing that even if you know a more conventional programming language very well, don't force your Delphi programs into its framework. If you impose programming habits learned from older programming languages on your Delphi programs, you're likely to run into problems. For example, don't think of a Delphi program as having a starting line and an ending line, and moving from top to bottom—if you do, you will not be taking advantage of Delphi's power. Delphi is an event-driven programming environment.

You always write code in the Code Editor window. As you have seen, this window opens whenever you double-click a component or form, or click on the Unit tab below (in Delphi 16) or above (in Delphi 32) the form. You can also click on the right-hand (value) field for an event in the Object Inspector. The Code Editor window has a caption that lists the filename for the unit, one or more page tabs, and an area for editing your code. The status bar tells you the line the cursor is currently on, whether you are in insert or typeover mode, and so on.

Depending on what editor option you chose, you have the usual Windows editing techniques, traditional Turbo Pascal, Brief, or Epsilon-style editing techniques available to you. The Options dialog box (on the Tools menu in Delphi 32, the Options | Environment menu in Delphi 16) has an Editor page that allows you to customize the Code Editor window to suit your needs. (It's called Editor options in Delphi 16.) Moreover, a click of the right mouse button when you are in the Code Editor window gives you a speedmenu with quick access to common editing features.

Tip: To quickly get to the code for an event procedure that you have already written, double-click in the right column of the appropriate line in the Events page of the Object Inspector.

Statements in Delphi

A statement in Delphi, as in most programming languages, should be thought of as a complete "sentence." Generally speaking, Delphi statements *do things to Delphi objects*. These objects may be properties of components, numeric expressions, or even more exotic gadgets. When you enter a statement in Delphi, Delphi uses the same technology pioneered in Turbo Pascal to analyze and process it. This happens immediately as you type. Object Pascal keywords are boldfaced, and comments are formatted following the settings on the Editor colors page (in the Environment Options dialog box).

Except within quotation marks, case and spacing and other types of "white space," such as blank lines, are ignored by Delphi. Of course, it's a good idea to stick to a standard method of spacing and formatting in your code.

5

Statements in Delphi do not use line numbers, and each statement generally occurs on its own line. A line can be up to 127 characters long in Delphi 16 and 1,024 characters long in Delphi 32. Provided the statement is syntactically correct, you can break up a statement over several lines by pressing ENTER. A semicolon (;) is always required to separate two statements. Since the semicolon (and not a carriage return or white space) is the statement separator, this lets you, for example, combine statements on one line by placing a semicolon between them and use any indentation pattern you find convenient.

Note: Sometimes in this book you'll see lines that easily fit Delphi's limits but are longer than can fit on one line of a printed book page. Since Delphi doesn't process the next statement until after the semicolon that marks the separation, the key is to look for the semicolon.

The last end statement in your program has a period, just like the period at the end of a sentence. This indicates that your program is over, and no more statements need to be separated.

Note: Delphi, following in the tradition of Pascal, distinguishes between *simple* statements and *compound* statements. A simple statement is one executable line of code. A compound statement is a block of simple statements separated by semicolons and surrounded by **begin**/**end** keywords. (Although you actually don't need the semicolon at the end of the last statement in a compound statement.)

Compound statements are mostly used with constructs like loops and if-thens. See the sections on these constructs later in this chapter for more on them.

Comment Statements

Comment statements are put into programs to explain what code does. Comments are neither executed nor processed by Delphi. As a result, they do not take up any room in the compiled code. There are two ways to indicate a comment. The first is to use a left and right curly brace to delimit the comment:

```
procedure TForm1.FormClick(Sender: TObject);
begin
  {Comments describing the procedure would go here}
end;
```

As usual, the programming lines are indented to improve readability.

The second method to indicate a comment is to use a left parenthesis with an asterisk [(*] to start the comment and an asterisk with a right parenthesis [*)] to close the comment. A comment can extend over several lines:

```
procedure TForm1.FormClick(Sender: TObject);
begin
  (*Comments describing the
   procedure would go here*)
end;
```

You can also add comments to the ends of lines. For example:

```
begin {Comments describing the procedure would go here}
```

Everything within the opening and closing comment marker is treated as a comment by the compiler. If you forget the closing comment indicator, you could accidentally indicate to the compiler that all the following code in the Unit file is a comment. Commenting out executable statements to help debug your programs is a common technique in programming languages.

Ending Programs

When you are developing a program and want to stop it, the easiest (and often best) way to do so is to use the ALT-F4 shortcut when the focus is in the main form, or to choose Close from the system (control) menu box of the (main) form. If you are developing a program, you are returned to the integrated development environment (IDE). If ALT-F4 isn't working, then you usually need to use the Run | Program Reset option (CTRL-F2).

Note: If you choose Run | Program Reset, you may not free up Windows resources that Delphi allocated to your project.

On the other hand, when Delphi processes an Application.Terminate (or the older, but still supported, Halt procedure) statement, the program stops and Delphi frees up any resources that it allocated. In a stand-alone program, after Delphi processes an Application.Terminate (or Halt procedure) statement, all windows opened by the program are closed, and the program is cleared from memory. If you were in the IDE when you developed the program, you are also returned to the development environment.

5

Tip: The Halt procedure takes an optional exit code that you can use if you want your program to have the potential of returning information to another program that started it. Consult the online help for more on this.

You can have as many Halt procedure statements within a Delphi program as you want, but it is obviously good programming practice to restrict the number of events that end a program. Many Delphi programmers restrict the statements that end the program to the OnCloseQuery or OnClose events of the main form.

Note: Delphi will also stop a program when it processes a RunError procedure statement (which is used to generate a run-time error—see Chapter 8) or if it encounters an Exit procedure statement in the main code block.

Setting Properties

Resetting properties via code is one of the most common tasks in Delphi code. Delphi uses a colon and an equal sign (**:=**) for this operation. If you want to change a property setting for a Delphi object, place the object's name followed by a period and then the name of the property on the left side of the colon equal combination, and put the new value on the right side:

object.property := *value*;

For example, suppose you have a TEdit box component named *Edit1* and want to blank it out in code rather than use the Object Inspector. You need only have Delphi execute a line like this:

```
Edit1.Text := '';
```

Since there is nothing between the quotation marks, the text assigned to this property is blank. Similarly, a line like

```
Edit1.Text := 'This is the new text.';
```

changes the setting for the text property to the text in the quotation marks. You can change the setting of a property by using code as often as you need to.

Changing properties with code makes it easy to override design time decisions. For example, if you wanted to make a TButton called Button5 the first button in tab order, you would add a line like this to an event handler:

```
Button5.TabOrder := 0;
```

Now suppose you want a form called Form1 to move around when various buttons are clicked. Suppose one of the buttons is called MoveToLeft. Here is an example of one of the event handlers you would need to activate this button:

```
procedure TForm1.MoveToLeftClick(Sender: TObject);
begin
  Form1.Left := Form1.Left - 75;
end;
```

Look at the key line

Form1.Left := Form1.Left - 75

On the left side of the assignment statement is the property that gets the value, but it seems that the property occurs on the right side as well. What happens is that Delphi first evaluates the right side of any assignment to extract a value from it before performing the assignment. In this case it looks at the current position of the left side of the form (i.e., the current value of the Left property) and calculates the number of pixels it is from the left. It then subtracts 75 from this number. Only after it has done this does it look to the left side. Delphi now changes the old value of the Left property to a new one.

Finally, sometimes Delphi properties are themselves objects. A good example of this is the Font property, which applies to many Delphi objects. Since the Font property is itself an object (the TFont object), to set a value of the Font property, you need a syntax that takes this into account. Here's an example of what you would need to change the font size of an edit box to 24-point type:

Edit1.Font.Size := 24

In general, use periods to navigate down through the object hierarchy. (See Chapter 7 for more on objects and the object hierarchy.)

Boolean Properties

Properties that take only the value True or False are called Boolean properties, after the English logician George Boole. We've discussed many Boolean properties already. Boolean properties specify whether a button is visible, enabled, or whether it is the default or cancel button. When Delphi executes a statement such as

```
Button1.Visible := False;
```

it hides the button. The component stays hidden until Delphi executes a statement like

```
Button1.Visible := True;
```

As another example, if you want TAB to skip over a component while a program is running, change the TabStop property to False, using (for example)

```
Edit1.TabStop := False;
```

The usual way to toggle between Boolean properties is with the Not operator. Suppose you have a statement such as

```
Button1.Visible := Not(Button1.Visible);
```

in an event handler. This statement works as follows: Delphi finds the current value of Button1.Visible, and then the not operator reverses this value. That is, if the value was True, it changes to False, and vice versa.

The with Keyword

When you need to reset a large number of properties at one time, you probably would prefer not to have to retype the name of the object each time. The **with** keyword lets you do this by eliminating the need to type the object's name each time. In addition, using the **with** keyword actually speeds up execution of the statements inside the **with** block.

For example, suppose you want to set the height, width, and color of a TEdit component named DataInput. You could use this:

```
DataInput.Color := clWhite;
DataInput.Enabled := True;
DataInput.Height := 36;
DataInput.Font.Size = 24
```

But it's cleaner and faster (and even often involves less typing) to say

```
with DataInput do
begin {notice the use of the begin/end pair}
   Color := clWhite;
   Enabled := True;
   Height := 36;
   Font.Size := 24;
end;
```

Variable Types

Both versions of Delphi handle around 15 standard types of variables. The 32-bit version of Delphi adds (depending on how you count them) seven more. Usually people break up Delphi's data types into categories: Boolean, Character, Integer, Real, and so on. (It is also possible to define your own variable types, as you will see in the next chapter.) What follows is a short discussion of the different types common to both versions of Delphi. We follow this with a section on the types new to Delphi 32.

Note: In some languages, like Visual Basic, every type of variable has a default value. This is not true in Delphi. You must assign a value to a variable to initialize it—otherwise, unpredictable results will occur. (The only exception is when dealing with objects (see Chapter 7). There, things are initialized but one should not rely on this!)

Boolean

Boolean variables hold the value True or False. A Boolean variable requires 1 byte of memory.

Note: Delphi allows you to use types called ByteBool, WordBool, and LongBool. These use more memory but allow you (as in Visual Basic) to use any nonzero value for True. Most Delphi programmers don't use these types. They exist essentially for compatibility with the Byte, Longint, and Word types discussed next.

5

Integer Number Types

Integer data types are used when you are working with whole numbers (or don't care about the stuff after the decimal point). Arithmetic operations involving variables with integer data are very fast. There are seven integer data types; we discuss the five most important next. (There are also SmallInt and Cardinal types in Delphi 32 but they are used relatively infrequently.).

Integer   Integer variables do not have a fractional part and hold small integer values (between –32,768 and 32,767 in Delphi 16). An Integer variable in Delphi 16 requires 2 bytes of memory. In Delphi 32 on the other hand, this is a 32-bit (4 byte) value that has the range –2,147,483,648 to 2,147,483,647.

Shortint   Shortint variables do not have a fractional part and hold relatively small integer values (between –128 and 127). A Shortint variable requires 1 byte of memory.

Longint Longint variables do not have a fractional part and hold relatively large integer values (between –2,147,483,648 and 2,147,483,647). A Longint variable requires 4 bytes of memory. (So integers in Delphi 32 correspond to long integers in Delphi 16.)

Byte Byte variables also do not have a fractional part and will hold integer values (between 0 and 255). A Byte variable requires 1 byte of memory.

Word Word variables also do not have a fractional part and will hold integer values (between 0 and 65,535). A Word variable requires 2 bytes of memory.

Real (Floating-Point) Number Types

Use variables from one of these types when you don't care about complete accuracy, but do need very large or very small numbers, usually with a decimal point. All operations with these types are approximations. Arithmetic operations involving variables with these types can be much slower than those with integer data.

Note: Most of these data types are available only when the floating-point compiler option (see Chapters 2 and 3) is on. Since any Delphi program that uses the visual component library will not even compile with this option off, you are best off not changing the default!

There are five Real data types (see the section on assignment compatibility later in this chapter for compatibility between these types), as follows.

Real Real variables hold numbers and can have a fractional part of 11-12 significant digits. A Real variable requires 6 bytes of memory.

Note: This type is provided for backward compatibility and should not be used. This is because using a 6-byte data type is non-standard and cannot be used when working with code generated by other languages.

Single Single variables hold numbers and can have a fractional part of 7-8 significant digits. A Single variable requires 4 bytes of memory. The Single data type is only available when the floating-point option (N+) is on. It is on by default and must remain on in most cases for your program to compile properly.

Double   Double variables hold numbers and can have a fractional part of 15-16 significant digits. A Double variable requires 8 bytes of memory. The Double data type is also only available when the floating-point option (N+) is on.

Extended   Extended variables hold numbers and can have a fractional part of 19-20 significant digits. An Extended variable requires 10 bytes of memory. The Extended data type is also only available when the floating-point option (N+) is on.

Comp   Comp variables are unusual in that they hold extremely large integers but throw away the fraction (decimal) part. A Comp variable requires 8 bytes of memory. The Comp data type is also only available when the floating-point option (N+) is on.

Types for Handling Text

The predefined data types for handling text that are common to both versions of Delphi can work with a single character or groups of up to 255 characters.

Char   Char variables use 1 byte to hold one ANSII/ASCII character in the 16-bit version of Delphi and currently do the same thing in Delphi 32. *However, Borland has warned that Char could change in future versions of Delphi 32 to be a Unicode character.* (Unicode is a system that uses 2 bytes to hold character information. This allows more than 65,000 characters. In Unicode, if the high-order byte is 0, the character is then an ordinary ANSI character.)

String   String variables hold up to 255 ASCII characters in Delphi 16. In Delphi 32, however, the default (called Huge strings) is on. *This means that unless you change it, strings in Delphi 32 have essentially no limits on their size. (The actual limit is 1 gigabyte, i.e., 2^{30}.)* In both versions of Delphi you can make strings that can only hold fewer than 255 characters by enclosing the number in square brackets. For example:

```
var
  Name: String[45];
```

Pointer Data Types

Chapter 6 will discuss pointer data types in greater depth. For now, if you haven't programmed with pointers, think of them as the addresses of the places where objects are stored. There are two pointer types common to both versions of Delphi: pointer and PChar.

5

Pointer A pointer type is a value that points to variables of a base type. They can also point to the location of procedures. Most commonly in Delphi a pointer-type variable contains the memory address of a variable. For more on this type see Chapter 6.

PChar This is a pointer to a null-terminated string. Null-terminated strings are used for large strings in Delphi 16, in dealing with the Windows API, and to make some text handling functions easier to write in Delphi 16. See Chapter 6 for more information.

Delphi 32 New Types

Delphi has added a few new types that add quite a bit of power and flexibility to your toolbox. The trade-off is that if you use their power, your programs will no longer be easily ported back to Delphi 16. We discuss these types next.

Delphi 32 Character Types

Windows 95 and Windows NT add support for multiple languages (including ideographic languages like Chinese) through the use of Unicode. Instead of a 1-byte encoding that allows only 256 characters, Unicode uses a 2-byte encoding that allows more than 65,000 characters. The ANSI character set is embedded in those Unicode characters whose first (high-order) byte is 0.

The following table summarizes the new character types:

AnsiChar	This corresponds to the Char type in Delphi 16. It is a standard 1-byte (8-bit) ANSI character.
WideChar	This is a 16-bit Unicode character.

Note: Although the current default is that a Char in Delphi 32 is the same as a Char in Delphi 16, I recommend not using the Char type in Delphi 32. This is because Borland has said that you cannot rely on the current Char type not shifting to WideChar in future versions of Delphi. If you choose to do so, use the built-in SizeOf function to determine the size of a Char.

New Character-Pointer Types

Since you have new character types, you also have new versions of PChar. They are described in the following table:

Pointer Type	Pointer to What Character Type
PAnsiChar	AnsiChar
PWideChar	WideChar
PChar	Char

New String Types

One of the minor disadvantages of Delphi 16 was that strings were usually 255 characters long and in no case could they be longer than 65,536 characters. (And such strings required a fair amount of programming to use effectively—since you had to program the memory allocation and deallocation yourself.) Delphi 32 has completely eliminated the problem by using its long string types.

Note: In Delphi 32, the String type is equal to a large ANSII string type by default. You can change this via a compiler option. (See Chapter 6.)

The following table summarizes the new string types in Delphi 32:

String Type	What It Is
ShortString	The equivalent to Delphi 16's String type. Uses up to 255 ANSII characters.
AnsiString	A long string of ANSII characters—essentially unlimited length (1 gigabyte). The default in Delphi 32 is that String and AnsiString are the same.

5

Note: All Delphi 32 components, where appropriate, support the AnsiString type.

I recommend using the long string types whenever you can. Memory allocation for long strings is done for you (via reference counting); you don't have to worry about garbage collection. Because reference counting is used, string copying is actually faster for long strings than for short strings! Moreover, long strings are completely compatible with the null-terminated C string types that are needed for working with Windows internal functions.

(You will have to do the appropriate typecast to a PChar or a PAnsiChar—see the section on Typecasting in Chapter 6.)

Currency Type

The currency type is designed to avoid any round-off error in the pennies when dealing with currency amounts. (Even when dealing with billion-dollar amounts!) The new floating-point type called Currency is a scaled 64-bit value with four decimal digits, so it will be completely accurate when dealing with currency amounts.

Variant Type

For longtime Pascal users, the new Variant data type will be a hard nut to crack. The variant data type is designed to store all the different Delphi 32 data received in one place. It doesn't matter whether the information is numeric, date/time, or string; the variant type can hold it all. Delphi automatically performs any necessary conversions, so you don't usually have to worry about what type of data is being stored in the variant data type. For example, you can add an integer stored in a variant variable to a real stored in a variant variable without any problem. (Unfortunately for the detection of bugs, you can also add numeric information stored in a variant to a string without causing an error message.)

Using variants rather than a specific type is slower because of the conversions needed and takes up more memory because of additional overhead (16 bytes per variable, to be precise). In addition, many programmers feel that relying on automatic type conversions leads to sloppy programming. One reason is that relying on the machine to do conversions occasionally leads to some weird behavior in your programs (because the conversion you assumed would be made turns out not to be the one that Delphi made).

Note: This book uses the variant data type only when its special properties are needed. It follows the convention that the programmer should be in control at all times and rely on conversions from the variant data type only when he or she is in control of them and thus fully aware of the consequences. If you want to use the variant data type, you will want to study the online help for the VarType function that lets you determine what type of information is stored in a variant variable.

When you do need to use variants (for example, in dealing with OLE automation—see Chapter 13), you will often need to change the type of the data via a *typecast* to one of Delphi's other types. See the section on typecasting in Chapter 6 for more on this.

Variables

Variables in Delphi hold information (values). Unlike Visual Basic, for example, you *must* declare a variable before using it. When declaring a variable, you give the variable a name and a type separated by a colon. You do this after the keyword **var**. For example:

```
var
   Interest: Double;
   Size: Integer;
   BigInteger: LongInt;
   SloppyVariable: Variant;    {Delphi 32 only}
```

Unlike Visual Basic, you can declare more than one variable of the same type by placing a comma between them. For example:

```
var
 Interest, SalesTax: Double;
```

Variable names in Delphi can be any length, but only the first 63 characters are significant. For any variable name over 63 characters, the compiler ignores the extra characters. The first character must be a letter or an underscore. The variable can include any combination of letters, numbers, and underscores. The variable cannot be a keyword or include symbols like $, %, and so on. The case of the letters in the variable name is irrelevant.

5

Note: These are actually the rules for what are called *identifiers* in Delphi. You have seen these rules before: identifiers are used for the Name property of Delphi components.

The following table lists some possible variable names and indicates whether they are acceptable.

Base1_Ball	Acceptable
$Base_Ball	Not acceptable—first character is not a letter, number, or underscore
Base.1	Not acceptable—uses a period
ThisIsLongButOK	Acceptable—fewer than 63 characters long, so all characters count

While the first 63 characters in a variable name are significant, the case is irrelevant. *BASE* is the same variable as *base*. On the other hand, *Base* is a different variable than *Base1,* and both are different from *Base_1.*

As with names of objects, names for variables have inspired much flaming. For example, many people use (some even like) Microsoft's "Hungarian" convention, where you indicate the type of the variable by a lowercase prefix. (For example, iRate for an integer.) Rather then get involved in the flame wars, I'll just reiterate something that is obvious to most programmers: a standard convention which leads to meaningful variable names helps document your program and makes the inevitable debugging process easier.

Note: I will not use the Hungarian convention and will simply use capitals at the beginning of the words that make up the parts of the variable name (for example, *MortgageInterest* instead of *Mortgageinterest*). (This convention is called *mixed-case variable names* and is not, in fact, all that common in older-style Pascal programming.)

You can't use Delphi keywords as variable names. For example, Do is not acceptable as a variable name. However, you can embed keywords within a variable's name. For example, DoIt is a perfectly acceptable variable name. Delphi will present an error message, usually when you compile the program, if you try to use a keyword as a variable name. (See the online help for a list of keywords.)

Assigning Values to Variables

Just as for setting properties, Delphi uses the colon and an equal sign (**:=**) for assigning values to variables. For example:

```
procedure TForm1.FormClick(Sender: TObject);
var
  InterestRate: Double;
  TextEntry: String;
begin
```

```
  InterestRate := 0.05;
  TextEntry := Edit1.Text;
end;
```

The variable name always appears on the left, and the value always appears on the right. Delphi must be able to obtain a value from the right side of an assignment statement. It will do any processing needed to make this happen. For example, the second assignment statement retrieves the value of the edit box text property (a string) and assigns it to the string variable TextEntry. Consider an assignment statement as a way for a Delphi variable to get a (new) value, or as a means of copying information from a source to a destination.

Type and Assignment Compatibility

Delphi is a descendant of Pascal, so it enforces quite strict rules on what kind of assignments you can make between variable types (except, of course, if you are working with Delphi 32 and use the variant data type). For example:

```
var
  IntegerVariable: Integer;
begin
  IntegerVariable = 3.5
```

gives a "Type Mismatch" error message at compile time.

5

Note: Programmers obviously have mixed feelings about this strict type checking. There is little you can do about it in Delphi 16, and I strongly recommend against using variants to get around it in Delphi 32. Besides being a breeding ground for bugs, variants are slower and introduce more overhead.

Two basic types in Delphi are compatible if:

♦   They are both real.
♦   They are both integers.
♦   One is character and the other is string.
♦   They are both string types.

However, to actually make a valid assignment—even between compatible types—the current values must be compatible.

Thus, you can assign a Longint variable holding the value 123 to an Integer variable without raising an exception. (See Chapter 8 for more on this type of exception.)

Constants

A program is easiest to debug when it's readable. Try to prevent the MEGO ("my eyes glaze over") syndrome that is all too common when a program has lots of mysterious numbers sprinkled about. It's a lot easier to maintain (and read) lines of code that use meaningful names for constants. For example, if you set up a constant called TAX_RATE, you can have easier to understand lines of code like:

```
TotalTax := Cost*TAX_RATE;
```

rather than

```
TotalTax = Cost*0.0825;
```

Delphi's named constant feature allows you to use mnemonic names for values that never change during the running of a project. (You can, however, easily make changes for different compiles. This is one of the reasons constants improve maintainability.)

Although Delphi (unlike standard Pascal) doesn't require it, constants are usually declared in a section before the one for variable declarations. You set up the constant by using the name of the constant, an equal sign, and then the value.

```
const
  SALES_TAX = 0.0825;
  LANGUAGE_NAME = 'Delphi';
var
{Variable declarations would go here}
```

Constants, like variables, have types, but a constant derives its type from the value you use in the declaration. For example, the constant SALES_TAX is of type *single* or *double* (depending on the number); LANGUAGE_NAME is of type *string*.

Constant names must be legal Delphi identifiers. Thus, the rules for constant names are the same as for variables: only the first 63 characters matter, and the first character must be a letter or underscore, followed by any combination of letters, underscores, and numerals. As you have seen, I use the convention that user-defined constants are in all caps with an underscore if need be.

You can sometimes define a constant in terms of other constants and/or Delphi's built-in functions. For example:

```
const
  INTEREST = 0.18;
  DAILY_INTEREST = INTEREST/365;
```

(See the online help on "Constant Declarations" for which functions you can use.)

Note: Delphi comes with hundreds of built-in constants for use with its functions and objects.

You have used many of these built-in constants in the last chapter when setting properties at design time. These constants are stored in the units that define the function or object. You do not need to declare these built-in constants. They can be found by looking at the Help topic for the function or object that you are working with. For example, you can use a statement like:

```
Form1.Color = clBlack;
```

which changes the color of the form to black by using the built-in constant clBlack. (Delphi's built-in constants usually—but not always—follow the convention that the initial letters are lowercase, followed by a single capital letter.)

5

The Anatomy of a Delphi Event Handler

At this point you have seen all the elements that can go into writing an event handler (or any Delphi procedure for that matter—see Chapter 6). An event handler starts with a header that gives the things (parameters) for the data it will work with. (For more on this see Chapter 7.) Next comes an (optional) **const** section for the constants, followed by the **var** section, where you declare the variables. After that comes the **begin** keyword that marks the start of the executable code. The executable code ends with an **end** statement that must be followed by a semicolon. (At the end of the program will be the final **end** followed by a period.)

Scope of Variables and Constants

The term *scope* refers to the availability of a variable or constant declared (or used) in one part of a program to other parts of a program. In older programming languages, where all variables and constants were available to all parts of the program, keeping names straight was always a problem. For example, in an older, unstructured language, when you used two variables named Total in different parts of the program, the values could (and would) contaminate each other.

The solution in modern programming languages like Delphi is to isolate variables and constants. Unless you specify otherwise, changing the value of a variable named Total in one procedure will not affect another variable with the same name in another procedure. Thus in Delphi, variables are *local* to procedures unless specified otherwise. In particular, an event handler will not normally have access to the value of a variable in another event handler.

Note: Since Delphi requires you to declare variables, it's a lot harder to fall into the trap caused by side effects accidentally.

Still, it is not a good programming practice to rely on defaults. If you want to be sure a variable is local within an event handler, place it in the **var** section inside the event handler. Of course, since you must declare a variable before you use it, if you *can* use a variable without declaring it locally, you *know* that there is a variable with greater scope with the same name lurking somewhere.

Sharing Values Across Procedures

Of course, occasionally you will want to share the values of variables (and constants) across event handlers or across units. For example, if an application is designed to perform a calculation involving one interest rate at a time, that rate should be available to all the procedures in a unit. Variables that allow such sharing are called *global* variables. Depending on where you declare a variable, the variable can be thought of as a true global variable accessible by any other code in the application, a unit-level variable accessible by any code in the unit, an object-level variable accessible by all the event handlers attached to a form, or a procedure-level variable local to only one procedure or event handler.

You put the declaration statements for unit-level variables in a **var** section in the unit's **implementation** section. You put the declaration statements for unit-level constants in a **const** section in the unit's **implementation** section. To get to this section of the code, open the Code Editor window, go to the top of the form's Unit file, and scan down for the **implementation** section. (See Chapter 6 for more on this section.)

Here's an example of how you could make a variable named InterestRate a unit-level variable and SALES_TAX a unit-level constant:

```
implementation
{$R *.DFM} {Don't worry about what this means yet-but don't
change it either!}
const
  SALES_TAX = 0.0825;
var
  InterestRate: Comp;
```

Now:

♦ The value of the constant named SALES_TAX and the variable named InterestRate will be visible to all the procedures in the unit.

♦ Any changes made to this variable by code in one event handler will persist for other event handlers.

Obviously, the last point means you have to be careful when assigning values to unit-level variables. Any information passed between event handlers is a breeding ground for programming bugs. Moreover, these errors are often hard to pinpoint.

5

Although most programmers don't think it is a good idea, you can use the same variable or constant name as both a local and a unit-level constant or variable. Any **const** or **var** declarations contained in a procedure take precedence over global declarations—they force a variable to be local. Therefore, you lose the ability to use the information contained in the global variable. Duplicating the names makes the global variable invisible to the procedure. Delphi doesn't tell you whether a global variable has been defined with the same name as a local variable. This is one more reason to make sure that variables you want to be local really are local by declaring them inside the procedure. This forces the variable to be local to that procedure.

Tip: Some programmers like to prefix procedure-level variables with the letter *p* (for example, pInterest) and unit-level variables with the letter *u* (for example, uInterest). This makes it easier to tell the scope of variables at a glance.

As you saw earlier, constants work similarly: if you have only one form or want the constants visible to the event handlers for only one form, put them in the **implementation** section of the unit. If you were to define a constant within a procedure, then only that procedure would have access to the constant. (See below for more on multiform programs.)

Note: If you want to create true global constants or variables in a unit (that is, constants and variables that will be visible to any unit which uses that unit), place the declaration in the **interface** section of the unit.

Making Values Persist

When Delphi invokes an event handler, the old values of local variables are wiped out. They go back to the values they are initialized to be. (As mentioned before, you cannot rely on the value of an uninitialized variable, you *must* initialize *all* variables.) Variables that do not retain their values are called *dynamic* variables. However, dynamic variables are not enough for all programming situations. For example, suppose you need to keep track of how many times a button has been clicked. If the counter is always set back to zero, you're in trouble. You could have the values persist by using a unit-level (form-level) variable, but it is generally a good idea to reserve form-level variables only for sharing information. Most programmers would choose this method only if other event handlers needed to work with the counter.

What you need are usually called *static* variables in languages such as Visual Basic. Such a variable is initialized only when the program starts running. After that, the value in the procedure persists; any changes the procedure makes to the variable remain between invocations. In Delphi (which inherits the terminology from the original Pascal) they are called *typed constants*. It is important to remember that they are *not* constants—they are just declared in the constant section. You give the initial value at that time. The syntax looks like this:

```
const
   count: Integer = 1;
```

Visual Basic Tip: Although the terminology is a little peculiar, one advantage of typed constants over static variables in Visual Basic is that you can set the initial value for typed constants to be anything you want.

To see typed constants (static variables) at work, put a push button (a TButton) on a blank form, and try the following OnClick event procedures:

```
procedure TForm1.Button1Click(Sender: TObject);
const
  Count: Integer = 1;
  begin
    ShowMessage(IntToStr(Count));
    Count := Count + 1;  {Inc(Count) is good too}
  end;
```

Now try the following, which uses an uninitialized variable for the counter:

```
procedure TForm1.Button1Click(Sender: TObject);
var
  Count: Integer;
  begin
    ShowMessage(IntToStr(Count));
    Count := Count + 1
  end;
```

Notice the rather weird values for Count. Finally, change the last event handler so as to initialize the Count variable to 1. Notice that every time you run the program and click on the button, you get the same value for the count (1).

5

Tip: Besides being ideal for counters, typed constants (static variables) are ideal for making components alternately visible or invisible (or for switching between any Boolean properties, for that matter) and as a debugging tool. They can also be used inside a TTimer's event procedure to keep track of how many times the event has been triggered. This gives you the ability to handle very large time intervals.

Strings

Since information in Delphi edit boxes is always stored as text, strings are extremely important in Delphi.

Note: String variables in Delphi 16 can hold only 255 characters; therefore you need to use other techniques to handle very large strings. See Chapter 6 for some ways to do this.

To put two strings together (concatenate them), use a plus sign (+). For example, if:

```
strTitle := 'Queen ';
strName := 'Elizabeth ';
strNumeral := 'I';
```

then

```
strTitle + strName + strNumeral = 'Queen Elizabeth I'
strTitle + strName + strNumeral + strNumeral = 'Queen Elizabeth II'
```

Tip: Because of the line limitations in Delphi 16, you need the + to make a string variable hold more than 127 characters. (And you certainly need the + sign if you take advantage of Delphi 32's 1 gigabyte limit on strings!)

The + joins strings in the order in which you present them. Thus, unlike when you add numbers together, order is important when you use the + sign to join two strings. You can use the + sign to join two strings before Delphi will make the assignment statement. Here is an example using the variables defined earlier:

```
strCurrentQueen := strTitle + strName + strNumeral + strNumeral;
```

Tip: It is much faster to build up the string first and then change a string property of an object than to change the string property repeatedly.

If you need to represent an ASCII character, use a # before the ASCII code. For example,

LetterA := #65;

is the same as

LetterA := 'A';

As another example, when you need the NewLine code (combination of ASCII 10 + ASCII 13) use

NewLine := #10 + #13 {you can also use #10#13}

Numbers

Numbers in Delphi cannot use commas to delineate thousands. They can use a decimal point, unless they are integers. If you need to give a numeric value to a variable, place the number on the right side of the assignment statement.

 Note: If you need to work with a real number like .5, you must place a 0 before the decimal point (that is, use Number := 0.5).

If you try to assign a number with a decimal point to an integer variable, it is automatically flagged during the compile.

 Note: You can use hexadecimal representation for the Integer, Shortint, Smallint, Byte, Word, Cardinal, and Longint types by prefixing the hexadecimal (base 16) representation with a **$**.

5

For example, $A and (decimal) 10 are the same to the compiler.

 Note: Your code will behave erratically if you assign a number larger than the limits for the given variable to it, but no error message will be generated unless you tell the compiler to do *range checking*.

If you want Delphi to do range checking so the limits on numeric variables are flagged, set the Range checking compiler option to be on. This may be found on the Compiler page of the Project | Options dialog box in Delphi 32 or Options | Project in Delphi 16. (See Chapter 6 for more on compiler options.) Telling Delphi to do range checking will slow down the performance of your code, so there are definite trade-offs.

Operations on Numbers

The following table gives you the symbols for the four fundamental arithmetic operations. With the exception of the division operator, when you start with two numbers of the same type, you end up with a number of the same type.

Operator	Operation
+	Addition
–	Subtraction (and to denote negative numbers)
/	Division (always gives a real type result—even if you are working with integers)
*	Multiplication

Visual Basic Tip: You must use the built-in Exp function to obtain a counterpart to the ^ operator for raising to a power. (a^b = exp(b*ln(a)))

For integer types, there are two keywords for the arithmetic operations unique to numbers of these types:

Operator	Operation
div	Integer division
mod	The remainder after integer division

Since the ordinary division symbol (/) gives you a value that is a real type, use div if you need to remain within one of the integer types. div throws away the remainder in order to give you an integer. For example, 7 div 3 = 2.

The mod operator is the other half of integer division. This operator gives you the remainder after integer division. For example, 7 mod 3 = 1. When one integer perfectly divides another, there is no remainder, so the mod operator gives zero: 8 mod 4 = 0.

The usual term for a combination of numbers, variables, and operators from which Delphi can extract a value is a *numeric expression*.

Boolean and Binary Operators

Delphi lets you combine Boolean variables or expressions using the operators described in Table 5-1.

Symbol	Function
= (equality)	Tests whether two Boolean expressions are both True or both False
not	Changes a Boolean expression that is True to False and vice versa
and	Returns True only when both expressions are True
or	Returns True if either one of the expressions is True
xor	Returns True if the Boolean expressions are different

Boolean Operators
Table 5-1.

These operators also work on the bit level. If you have an integer and apply one of these operators, it will affect the individual bits in the number or numbers. For example, the and operator returns a 1 only if both binary digits are True (= to 1). Thus:

X and 1 Tells you if the first (rightmost) binary digit is on.
X and 2 Tells you if the second binary digit is on.
X and 3 Tells you if both the first and second binary digits are on.

(This process is usually called *masking* and is occasionally necessary to analyze the return value of Delphi's functions or the Windows API.)

Table 5-2 summarizes how these operators work on the bit level.

5

You can also use the shl (shift left) and shr (shift right) operators on integers or integer expressions. These move the bits over to the left or right, respectively. Thus, they multiply an integer or integer expression by 2 or divide it by 2 very quickly. You can move multiple bit positions by adding an integer to shl or shr. For example, shl 3 shifts the bits three positions to the left, multiplying by 8 very quickly.

Expression Using Bit Operator	What It Does
X and Y	Returns a 1 in a bit position only if both bits were 1 (on); otherwise turns that bit to 0 (off).
X or Y	Returns a 1 in a bit position if either X or Y had that bit on.
X xor Y	Gives a 1 in a bit position if exactly one of the bits was on. (Because of this, xoring with the same number twice does nothing.)
not (X)	Reverses the bits: 1 becomes 0, and 0 becomes 1.

Bitwise Operators
Table 5-2.

Parentheses and Precedence

When you do calculations, you have two ways to indicate the order in which you want operations to occur. The first way is by using parentheses, and most people prefer this method. Parentheses let you easily specify the order in which operations occur. A calculation like 3 + (4 * 5) gives 23, because Delphi does the operation within the parentheses (4 times 5) first and only then adds the 3. On the other hand, (3 + 4) * 5 gives 35, because Delphi adds the 4 and the 3 first to get 7, and only then multiplies by 5.

Here's another example:

((6 * 5) + 4) * 3

The innermost parentheses give 30, the second set of parentheses tells Delphi to add 4 to get 34, and then Delphi multiplies 34 by 3 to get 102.

Delphi allows you to avoid parentheses, provided you follow the rules that determine the precedence of the mathematical operations. For example, multiplication has higher precedence than addition. This means 3 + 4 * 5 is 23 rather than 35 because the multiplication—4 * 5—is done before the addition.

The following list gives the order (hierarchy) of operations:

```
@, not
*, /, div, mod, and, shl, shr, E
+, -, or, xor
=, <, >, <=, >=, <>, in
```

(The last line of operators contains the relational operators. They are described later in this chapter—except *in,* which is used with sets and is described in Chapter 6.)

When you use two operators on the same level, Delphi evaluates the expression from left to right.

More on Numbers in Delphi

If you've tried any calculations involving large numbers in Delphi, you've probably discovered that Delphi often doesn't bother printing large numbers. Instead, it uses a variant on scientific notation. If you are not familiar with this notation, think of the E+ as meaning "move the decimal place to the right, adding zeros if necessary." The number of places is exactly the number following the "E." If a negative number follows the "E," move the decimal point to the left. For example, 2.1E-5 gives you .000021. You can enter a number using the E notation if it's convenient; Delphi doesn't care whether you enter 1000, 1E3, or 1E+3.

Type Conversions

You may often need to convert strings to numbers and vice versa. This is usually called a *type conversion*—since you are changing an object from one type to another. For example, the function IntToStr lets you convert an integer to a string. The FloatToStr or FormatFloat function lets you convert a number from one of the real data types to a string. For example, if Message is a string variable, then you could use a statement like:

```
Message := 'The current count is' + IntToStr(Count);
```

Table 5-3 summarizes the basic type conversion functions.

Note: There are a few other conversion functions available for special situations (Val, Str, FloatToStrF, and FormatStr) and a whole slew of functions for working with date/time strings (for example: DateToStr, StrToDate, TimeToStr, FormatDateTime). The most important are probably the FloatToStrF and FormatStr functions. FloatToStrF is an extended version of FloatToStr that allows you to control the format of the resulting string (see the online help).

5

For more on typecasting please see Chapter 6.

Function	Effect
IntToStr	Converts integers to a string.
IntToHex	Converts an integer to hexadecimal.
StrToInt	Converts an integer (or hexadecimal representation of an integer) to a string. (StringToIntDef allows you to have a default value if the string is not in the format of a number.)
FloatToStr	Converts a floating-point number to a string.
StrToFloat	Converts a string representation of a floating-point number to a number.

Basic Type
Conversion
Functions
Table 5-3.

Repeating Operations—Loops

Suppose you need to repeat an operation. In programming (as in real life), you may want to repeat the operation a fixed number of times, continue until you reach a predetermined specific goal, or continue until certain initial conditions have finally changed. In programming, the first situation is called a *determinate* loop and the other two are called *indeterminate* loops. Delphi allows all three kinds of loops, so there are three different control structures in Delphi for repeating operations.

Determinate (for) Loops

Suppose you want to display ten successive message boxes inside an event handler. The simplest way to do this is to place the following lines of code inside the procedure:

```
var
  I: Integer;
begin
  for I:= 1 to 10 do
    begin
      ShowMessage('This is the' + IntToStr(I) + 'th message box');
    end;
end;
```

In the preceding example, the line with the **for** and **to** keywords is shorthand for "for every value of I from 1 to 10." You can think of a for loop as winding up a wheel inside the computer so that the wheel will spin a fixed number of times. You can tell the computer what you want it to do during each spin of the wheel. This is done in the (block of) statements that are between the **begin** and **end** that mark the compound statement. (If you have only a single statement, as in the above example, you don't, strictly speaking, need the begin/end pair of keywords that marks the compound statement block, but almost all for-next loops use a compound statement in practice.)

The keyword **for** sets up a counter variable. In the preceding example, the counter is an integer variable: I. In this example, the starting value for the counter is set to 1. The ending value is set to 10. Delphi first sets the counter variable to the starting value. Then it checks whether the value for the counter is less than the ending value. If the value is greater than the ending value, nothing is done. If the starting value is less than the ending value, Delphi processes subsequent statements until it comes to the closing semicolon that marks the end of the block. At that point it adds 1 to the counter variable and starts the process again. This process continues until the counter variable is larger than the ending value. At that point, the loop is finished, and Delphi moves past it.

The general syntax for a for loop looks like this:

```
for variable := expression to expression do
   begin {start block}
      statement1;
      statement2;
         .
         .
   end; {end block}
```

More on for Loops

You don't always count forward. Sometimes it's necessary to count backward. You do this by using the **downto** keyword in a for loop. The **downto** keyword tells Delphi to change the counter by minus 1.

For example, a space simulation program would not be complete without the inclusion, somewhere in the program, of the fragment:

```
for I:= 10 downto 1 do
   begin
    ShowMessage(IntToStr(I));
   end;
    ShowMessage('Blast Off!');
```

When you use **downto**, the body of the for loop is bypassed if the starting value for the counter is smaller than the ending value.

Visual Basic Tip: The counter in a for loop cannot be a real number, and there is no equivalent to the **step** keyword. If you need to convert a for-next loop from Visual Basic that uses either one, you'll need to increment the counter inside the loop, or use other variables inside the loop and maintain them by code within the loop.

Nested for-next Loops

Suppose you want to allow not only a range of interest rates in a mortgage table, but also a range of dollar amounts. For each dollar amount, you want to run through an entire range of interest rates. Or, considering the code needed to fill the cells in a grid, you will usually work through the cells row-by-row (or column-by-column). Placing one loop inside another is

5

called *nesting loops.* Let's look at the simple example of a multiplication table. A fragment such as:

```
procedure TForm1.Button1Click(Sender: Tobject);
var I : Byte;
begin
 for I := 1 to 10 do begin
    StringGrid1.Cells[0,I] := '2 x ' + IntToStr(I) + ' =' ;
    StringGrid1.Cells[1,I] := IntToStr(2 * I);
 end;
end;
```

gives you the "twos table." To get an entire multiplication table, you need to enclose this loop with another one that changes the 2 to a 3, the 3 to a 4, and so on. The loop looks like this:

```
procedure TForm1.Button1Click(Sender: TObject);
var I, J : Byte;
begin
  for J := 1 to 10 do begin
    for I := 1 to 10 do begin
       StringGrid1.Cells[J,I] :=
       IntToStr(J) + 'x' + IntToStr(I) +
       ' = ' + IntToStr(J * I);
    end;
  end;
end;
```

Here's what is happening: The value of J starts out at 1, and then Delphi enters the inner loop. The value of I starts out at 1 as well. Now Delphi makes 10 passes through the loop before it finishes. At this point Delphi changes the value of J to 2 and starts the process again.

The rule for nesting for-next loops is simple: The inner loop must be completed before the next statement for the outer loop is encountered. You can have triply nested loops, quadruply nested loops, or even more. You are limited only by how well you understand the logic of the program, not by Delphi.

Indeterminate Loops

Sometimes you won't know exactly how many times a loop should cycle. For these situations Delphi has two kinds of loops that you'll see next. These loops use the relational operators described in Table 5-4.

Operator	Checks For
=	Equality
<	Less than
<=	Less than or equal
>	Greater than
>=	Greater than or equal
<>	Not equal

The Relational
Operators
Table 5-4.

Note: Delphi defaults to using *short circuit evaluation* in its treatment of the relational operators. This means that if you have a condition like A and B and A is false, B is never evaluated. You can change this via the "Complete Boolean evaluation" option on the Compile page of the Project Options dialog box. (I don't know why you would want to, of course, since it just slows down the program!)

The Repeat Loop

Repeat loops repeat a block of code until a condition is met. Such loops are indeterminate—that is, not executed a fixed number of times—by their very nature. For example, suppose you wanted to find out how long at 8 percent interest it would take to get $1,000 up to $1,000,000:

5

```
var
  Money: Double;  {Currency would be better in Delphi 32!}
  Count: Integer;
begin
  Money := 1000;
  repeat {begin the body of the loop}
    Money := Money * 1.08;
    Count := Count + 1;
  until Money > 1000000; {test at end of loop}
ShowMessage('Took' + IntToStr(Count)+ ' years');
end;
```

The general pattern when you write this type of loop in Delphi is as follows:

```
repeat
  begin
    Delphi statements;
  end;
until condition is met;
```

(The begin/end pair is optional in most repeat statements, since the block nature is built into the loop.)

Note: Since the test for whether the condition is True is only done at the bottom of the loop, a Repeat loop is always executed at least once.

The (Boolean) condition in a loop that Delphi is testing need not be simply one for equality or inequality. You can use any combination of the logical operators and, or, not—even xor if you want. The important thing is that the result be Boolean—something that is either True or False.

Visual Basic Tip: A Repeat loop in Delphi is the same as a Do-Until loop in Visual Basic.

The While Loop

Delphi has another kind of loop. This loop moves the test to the top. The syntax looks like this:

```
while condition do
  begin
    Delphi statements;
  end;
```

In this case, since the test is done at the top, it may not be executed at all, and the begin/end pair is needed. Also since the test is being done at the top, you will usually need to make sure that the condition makes sense before the loop is processed. You do not have the luxury of making the changes inside the loop as with a Repeat loop.

Making Decisions

At this point, all your code can do is decide whether to repeat a group of statements. It can't, as yet, change which statements are processed depending on what the program has already done or what it has just encountered. The next few sections take care of this. All the commands in these sections deal with turning into Delphi code the ideas that a programmer would internalize as:

if *condition* then *do something else do something.*

Delphi uses the if-then statement in much the same way that you do in normal English. For example, to warn a user that a number must be positive, use a line like this:

```
if I < 0 then
    ShowMessage ('Number must be positive!');
```

More generally, when Delphi encounters an if-then statement, it checks the first clause (called, naturally enough, the if clause) which is built by use of the relational operators and checks whether it's True. If that clause is True, the computer does whatever follows (called the then clause). If the test fails, processing skips to the next statement.

More often than not, you will want to process multiple statements if a condition is True or False. For this you need the most powerful form of the if-then-else statement, called the block if-then statement. To write this statement in Delphi, you again use that Delphi regards any statements between a begin and an end pair as a single block. The block if-then statement looks like this:

```
if thing to test then
  begin
    lots of statements;
  end
else
  begin
    more statements;
  end;
```

5

Note: When you use the block if-then statement, you do not put a semicolon after the end of the if block, or after the keyword **else** that starts the **else** block statement.

Of course, the else statement block is optional; putting it there means that a statement or another block will follow. This else block will be processed only if the if clause is False.

To create an example of this, let's modify the last sample:

```
if I < 0 then
  begin
    ShowMessage ('Number must be positive!');
  end
else
  begin
    ShowMessage ('Number was positive!');
  end;
```

Again, as usual, the indentation is there to make the program more readable; Delphi doesn't care how you indent.

Using If-Then Statements with Loops

Often when you are working with a loop, you want to force another iteration or leave the loop prematurely in response to a specific condition. The **continue** keyword lets you force an iteration. For example, if you are superstitious:

```
var
 Count: Integer;
begin
  for Count :=1 to 100 do
    begin
     if Count = 13 then
        continue;
     ShowMessage(IntToStr(Count));
    end;
end;
```

This will avoid displaying the number 13, since we force an iteration if the value of count is 13 *before* we display the message box.

On the other hand, the **break** keyword lets you leave any loop prematurely—without finishing the condition. For example, the following modification of the previous program only displays the numbers between 1 and 12.

```
var
  Count: Integer;
  begin
    for Count :=1 to 100 do
      begin
```

```
        if Count = 13 then
          break;
        ShowMessage(IntToStr(Count));
      end;
  end;
```

Tip: Using the appropriate if-then statement with the **break** keyword gives you a loop that tests in the middle.

The Case Statement

Suppose you were designing a program to compute grades based on the average of four exams. If the average was 90 or higher, the person should get an A; 80 to 89, a B; and so on. This is such a common situation that Delphi has another control structure designed exactly for it. It's called the case statement. The case statement makes it clear that a program has reached a point with many branches; multiple if-then statements do not. (And the clearer a program is, the easier it is to debug.)

For example, you could write the following fragment to analyze the value of the AverageGrade variable.

```
case AverageGrade of
    100:      ShowMessage ('A+!');
    90..99:   ShowMessage ('A');
    80..89:   ShowMessage ('B');
end;
```

In general, what follows the keyword **case** is called the *selector*. The selector is a variable or expression taken from either the char type or any integer type. What Delphi is going to do depends on the value of the selector variable or expression. You place the statement to be executed after a colon. (Use a compound statement if you need to do more than one thing.)

The individual case statements use either a single constant, a group of constants (separate them by a comma), or a range of constants (use a double dot). These are usually called *case constants*. You can add an else clause to take care of all the remaining cases at once. As with all Delphi statements, you can replace an individual statement with a begin/end block (compound statement).

5

Note: Only one case statement will be executed. You also cannot have overlapping conditions in the case statements.

For example:

```
case UpCase(chA) of
        'Y':    begin
                    ShowMessage ('Sometimes a vowel.');
                    ShowMessage ('Too tough for me');
                end
        'A', 'E', 'I', 'O', 'U': ShowMessage ('Definitely a
vowel.');
else
        ShowMessage('Consonant!');
end;
```

More on Working with Objects at Run Time

There are both objects and properties of objects that you must use code to work with—neither the properties nor the objects themselves are available via the Object Inspector. For example, if you wanted to find out what Windows is assuming for the height of the screen, you would look at the Height property of the TScreen object—and the TScreen object and its associated properties are available only at run time. Similarly, you can control a printer (through the TPrinter object) only at run time.

Note: It is possible to create instances of almost any Delphi objects at run time. See Chapter 7 for more information on how to do this.

Methods

If you want your Delphi objects to actually do anything, you most often need to work with Delphi's built-in methods. For example, if you want to clear the contents of an TEdit component , you use a statement like:

```
Edit1.Clear;
```

Since there are hundreds of methods (there are 32 for the TEdit component (edit boxes) alone), it would be impossible to cover them all. You must be prepared to work with the online help to see if a component has a method that does what you want. As with properties, your task is made easier by the fact that methods with the same name tend to work in similar ways. For example, the Clear method applies to most controls that handle text—and clears the text from all of them. As another example, the SetFocus method applies to all controls that can receive the focus, and, as you'd expect, moves the focus directly to the component.

 Note: You can modify the behavior of any method for a Delphi component by creating your own version of the component. Consult the documentation supplied with Delphi called "Component Writers Guide" for more on how to do this.

The following is a brief description of some of the more important common methods. Other chapters go into more specialized methods. (For example, the next chapter goes over the most common methods for working with list and combo boxes. Chapter 12 goes over the most common methods for working with graphics.)

BringToFront, SendToBack   This method brings the component (or form if you are using multiple forms) in front of (or sends it behind) all other components or forms (see the section on Z-Order in Chapter 13).

5

Create   This important method is used to create new instances of Delphi objects at run time. It is covered at length in Chapter 8.

Focused   This is an example of a method that works more like a property. It is Boolean (True/False) and is used to determine if a control has the focus. The syntax is most commonly

    If Edit1.Focused Then ...

Hide, Show   Hide makes a form or control invisible. This is the same as setting the Visible property to False. The Show method makes it visible again. Show also invokes the BringToFront method if used on an obscured form (see "Multiple Form Applications" later in this chapter).

Refresh, Repaint   Refresh erases whatever image is on the screen and then repaints the component. Repaint makes the component regenerate the image, but doesn't erase what is already there (see Chapter 12 for more on these methods).

ScaleBy   This lets you rescale any control. For example, if you wanted to make a TButton named Ccommand1 50 percent larger, you would say

```
Command1.ScaleBy(3, 2);
```

In general, the first number is the numerator and the second is the denominator of the scaling factor. In our example this results in a scaling factor of 3/2 (150 percent).

Tip: You may need to reposition and resize controls when the size of the form is changed by the user. Use proportions of the various size properties of the form (or container component) to do this.

The TApplication Object

Whenever you run a Delphi project, Delphi automatically creates the Application object as an instance of the TApplication class. You need to work with properties and methods of this object in order to do things like set the icon for the application or set the name of the project's Help file (see Chapter 12). What follows is a short discussion of the most important properties and methods for the Application object. (See the online help if you need to write event procedures for the Application object. This requires somewhat different techniques than you use for writing event procedures for Delphi objects available at design time.)

Terminate Method   Calling the Terminate method in the form of Application.Terminate is the standard way to end an application. It has the same effect as a Halt procedure statement, but is preferred by most programmers, as there is no guarantee that Halt will be suported in future releases of Delphi.

ExeName Property   This is a read-only property that gives the full pathname you gave the project in compiled form minus the .EXE extension. For example, the name of a compiled Delphi project is C:\DELPHI\PROJECTS\PROJECT1.EXE, so for this we would have

```
Application.ExeName = 'C:\DELPHI\PROJECTS | PROJECT1';
```

HelpFile Property   This is the name of the Help file (see Chapter 13).

Icon Property   When you minimize an application, the value of this property is the icon the user will see. As an example of how you might use this, suppose you have an icon for a butterfly in a directory called ICONS on the C drive. You can then use

```
Application.Icon.LoadFromFile('C:\ICONS\BTFLY.ICO');
```

Minimize, Restore Methods   The Minimize method minimizes the application to an icon. It is especially useful in multiform projects. When the user minimizes the application, the Minimize method is what is actually called. The Restore method returns an iconized application to its previous state.

ProcessMessages Method   This is an extraordinarily important method. It is how you have your application let Windows process events for other applications. Since Windows 3.X can only *cooperatively* multitask, you must use this method if you want Windows 3.X to process its event queue. (It will still be useful in Windows 95 because of legacy programs and also to force Win95 to process its event queue.)

Some common uses of ProcessMessages include

♦   Using it inside code that is making a time-consuming calculation

♦   Using it in a Delphi application that works with other Windows programs (for example, a terminal program that might be receiving data from an online service)

5

Note: Delphi 32 allows you to add multiple threads to the same program. See the online help for more on this.

Title   This is the text that appears below the icon.

The TScreen Object

This essential object tells you what Windows thinks are the properties of the entire screen. For example, the value of Screen.Height is what Windows is using for the height of the screen in pixels. Here are short descriptions of the most common properties and methods for the TScreen object.

ActiveControl, ActiveForm Properties   This tells you what control (or which form) has the focus. ActiveForm is a vital property when you work with multiform applications (see the following) that determines what form the user is working with.

ComponentCount, ComponentIndex, Component, Forms, FormsCounts Properties   These are used when you need to, for example, iterate through the forms in an application or the components on a form. See Chapter 7 for more on Delphi objects.

Cursor Property   Unlike the cursor property for a component, the cursor property for the Screen object has a global effect. It controls the mouse cursor shape for all the forms in the application. (You can override this for an individual component through its Cursor property, however.)

Height, Width Properties   This tells you the height and width of the screen, measured in pixels, as reported by Windows.

PixelsPerInch Property   This tells you how many pixels the current video driver assumes are in an inch.

Fonts Property   This gives you a list of the screen fonts. This is an example of a property that is actually a string list. (See Chapter 6 for more information on string lists.)

Cursors Property   This gives you a list of the cursors available. This is also an example of a property that is a string list.

The TCanvas Object

The TCanvas object is another example of a property of a Delphi object that is an object in its own right. As its name suggests, the TCanvas object is a surface to "paint" on. In Delphi you can use the TCanvas object to display text or graphics. This section explains how to use this object to display text accurately on a form. The section on Printers, which follows, explains how to use it to position text on a printer. (See Chapter 12 for how to use the TCanvas object to do graphics on a form or printer.)

The key method for displaying text is called the TextOut method. Here's an example of how to use TextOut:

```
TepTextWidth := Form1.Canvas.TextOut( 0, 0,
  'This will be at the left corner of the screen');
```

The general syntax is

> *ObjectName*.Canvas.TextOut(*LeftRight, TopBottom, Text*)

where LeftRight gives the horizontal location (X coordinate) as an integer, TopBottom gives the vertical (Y coordinate), and Text is a string or string expression for the text to be displayed.

Often you need to know the height or width of a text string before you decide where to place it. This is done with the TextHeight and TextWidth methods. The syntax for both is essentially the same. For example:

```
TempTextWidth := Form1.Canvas.TextWidth('Text would go here');
```

is the number of pixels the string 'Text would go here' would take up. As you can imagine, this information can be used to resize components or forms as need be.

The Printer (TPrinter) Object

By providing its own interface to the Windows printer driver via the TPrinter object, Delphi does its best to insulate you from having to deal with the confusion of handling multiple printers. This way, when you want to print information, you need only use the properties and methods of the TPrinter object.

There is one fundamental rule for using the TPrinter object: Add a printers clause to the **uses** section of your unit. To do this, move through the Code Editor window until you encounter a section that begins like this in Delphi 16:

```
uses
    SysUtils, WinTypes, WinProcs, Classes,...
```

or

```
uses
    Windows, Messages, SysUtils, Messages,...
```

in Delphi 32.

Now add the **printers** keyword (along with a comma) anywhere in this **uses** clause before the final semicolon. (This tells Delphi to make the Printers unit accessible to this unit in your project.)

5

Tip: To print an image of a form on the printer use the Print method of the form.

If you want to do anything other than print images of forms, you need to initialize the printer. When you finish sending the information to the printer, you need to close the connection. For this:

♦ To start a print job, use the BeginDoc method.

♦ To end a print job, use the EndDoc method.

(Of course, you have to be prepared to deal with printer problems, like running out of paper. The methods for dealing with these exceptions are covered in Chapter 8.)

Generally, use the Canvas property (subobject) of the printer to direct the text or graphics to the printer. The syntax is similar to using the Canvas object for a form. For example:

```
Printer.Canvas.TextOut(0,0, 'Text in top left corner');
```

Note: Most properties of the Printer's Canvas (for example, TextOut, TextHeight, and Fonts) work the same way for printing on forms as they do for working with a printer.

In general, the X and Y coordinate parameters of the Canvas property let you control individual placement of the dots on a printed page.

Note: Printing the contents of a memo box involves techniques similar to working with files.

What follows is a short discussion of the most important printer properties and methods.

Abort Method   This is used to terminate a print job if, for example, a problem occurs.

Printing Property   This Boolean property tells you if the job is still printing. (Of course, if your printer has a large buffer, this will not be relevant, as the buffer in the printer will contain the text, and then the value of this property might be unreliable.)

Printers, PrintIndex Properties   Printers is a string list. (See Chapter 6 for more on string lists.) This list tells you which Windows printer drivers are installed on the user's computer. The value of the PrinterIndex property is the currently selected printer.

NewPage Method   This method sends a form feed to the printer.

Orientation Property   This tells you if the job is printing in landscape or portrait form.

PageHeight, PageWidth Properties   These are the height and width of the current page measured in pixels (that is, dots per inch, for laser printers). For example, on a 300 dpi laser, an 8.5×11 page returns values of 3150 for PageHeight and 2400 for PageWidth properties—reflecting an actual printing surface of about 8×10.5.

PageNumber Property   This gives you the current page number.

5

PrintScale Property   (This is actually not a property of the TPrinter object but rather one of the form itself.) When you print a form by using the Print method, this lets you determine whether the form is left unchanged or scaled. There are three values given by the constants: poNone, poProportional (which keeps the proportions the same as on the screen), and poPrintToFit (which uses the screen proportions, but makes sure the form will fit on a page).

Message Boxes and Input Boxes

Using special-purpose message boxes for displaying information is quite common in a Windows application. You have already seen the most basic mechanism for doing this in Delphi: the ShowMessage procedure whose syntax is ShowMessage(*string*).

Unfortunately, all the ShowMessage procedure does is display a box with the string and an OK button. (The name of your application's executable file is the caption of the message box.)

Note: A variant, ShowMessagePos, does allow you to position the message box anywhere on the screen you want.

Getting more information to the user—for example, giving the user buttons to click on to provide information to the program—is also possible with a message box. This section covers ways of doing this.

Note: All message boxes are *modal*. This means they must be closed before the application will continue.

There are two kinds of message boxes available to you:

♦ The MessageDlg function displays a message box with text, caption, and buttons you specify.

♦ The MessageDlgPos function lets you position the box at the screen location you specify.

The MessageDlg Function

Before we look at the general syntax for dealing with this message box, look at the following code snippet:

```
if MessageDlg('Do you really want to terminate the program?',
mtConfirmation, [mbYes, mbNo], 0) = mrYes then Application.Terminate;
```

As you might expect, this presents the user with a message box that looks something like this:

Notice the Yes and No buttons. When the user clicks a button, Delphi returns a value that depends on the button. In our example, if the user clicks on the Yes button, Delphi would return the value given by the built-in constant mrYes. If he or she clicked on the No button, the function would have the value mrNo. We then test what the value is by checking if it is equal to the constant mrYes. If it is, we terminate the application.

The general syntax for this function in the online help looks like this:

```
MessageDlg(const Msg: string; AType: TMsgDlgType; AButtons: TMsgDlgButtons;
HelpCtx: Longint): Word;
```

Since this is pretty typical of an online help entry, let's spend a little time going over the various pieces. First, the information passed to a function in Delphi is usually called a *parameter*. (You'll see a lot more about parameters in Chapter 6.) The type of the parameter is indicated, just as in declarations, by a colon. Parameters of different types are separated by semicolons. If the keyword **const** precedes the parameter, then the function cannot change it. If you see the keyword **var**, it can.

Notice that this function uses a few types you haven't seen before. For built-in functions, these are most commonly types that are predefined to be certain sets of constants. For example, the TMsgDlgType consists of the predefined constants for the type of message box. They are discussed shortly.

Note: For more on *enumerated types,* which are essentially lists of things, please see Chapter 6.

5

Msg Parameter   This is a string or string expression that Delphi displays as the text in the message box. It is limited to 255 characters.

AType Parameter   This determines the type of message box that appears. Table 5-5 summarizes the possible types. Each message box is given by a different value of TMsgDlgType.

Types of Message Boxes
Table 5-5.

Value for the TMsgDlg Parameter	Type of Message Box
mtWarning	Uses a yellow exclamation point symbol
mtError	Uses a red stop sign
mtInformation	Uses a blue *i*
mtConfirmation	Uses a green question mark
mtCustom	Eliminates any bitmap and forces the caption to be the name of the application's executable file

AButtons Parameter This parameter determines which buttons appear in the message box. To add multiple buttons, surround them with square brackets and separate them by a comma as in the code fragment earlier when we wrote [mbYes, mbNo] to give both Yes and No buttons. (AButtons is actually a set. See Chapter 6 for more on sets.) Table 5-6 summarizes the types of buttons you can use.

As you saw in the code fragment, you can determine which button a user pressed by analyzing the return value of the MessageDlg function. The constants are pretty mnemonic. For example, mrCancel means the Cancel button was clicked, mrNo means the No button was clicked, and so on. (Check the online help for a complete list.)

Note: You can use three predefined constants for commonly occurring sets of buttons. They are mbYesNoCancel (for the Yes, No, and Cancel buttons), mbOkCancel (for the OK and Cancel buttons), and mbAbortRetryIgnore (for the Abort, Retry, and Ignore buttons). Since these are predefined, you don't use a square bracket for them.

HelpCtx Parameter This determines the Help context ID used when you set up a help system. See Chapter 13.

The MessageDlgPos Function

Since the MessageDlg function displays a message dialog box in the center of your screen, you need to use this function if you want to position the

Value	Displays on Button Face
mbYes	A green check mark and the text "Yes"
mbNo	A red circle with a slash mark through it and the text "No"
mbOK	A green check mark and the text "OK"
mbCancel	A red X and the text "Cancel"
mbHelp	The text "Help"
mbAbort	A red check mark and the text "Abort"
mbRetry	Two green circular arrows and the text "Retry"
mbIgnore	A green man walking away and the text "Ignore"
mbAll	Green double check marks and the text "All"

Types of Buttons Available in a Message Box

Table 5-6.

message box anyplace else on the screen. The syntax for each is similar, except for the addition of two parameters for the coordinates (in pixels) where you want the dialog box to appear.

```
function MessageDlgPos(const Msg: string; AType: TMsgDlgType;  AButtons:
TMsgDlgButtons; HelpCtx: Longint; X, Y: Integer): Word;
```

The X and Y parameters are integers that indicate the screen coordinates (in pixels) where you want the top-left corner of the message box to appear.

InputBox Function

Although the TEdit and TMemo components are the most common way of receiving user input, there are times when you want to stop the application by using a modal dialog box to get some essential (and usually brief) piece of information. For example, you might want to get the user's password before running the core of the application. The InputBox function displays an input dialog box that looks like this:

Here's an example of a code fragment that generated the input box shown earlier:

```
UserName := InputBox('Need your name', 'Please enter your name', '');
```

The general syntax for the input box function is

   StringVariable := InputBox(const: *ACaption, APrompt, ADefault*: string);

(Input boxes are functions, so they return values. See Chapter 6 for more on functions.)

The ACaption parameter is the caption of the input box, the APrompt parameter is the text you want to appear in the box in order to prompt the user. Finally, the ADefault parameter is set to a string that you want to appear in the edit box when the dialog box first appears. You can set this to be nothing by using empty single quotes (' '). If the user chooses the Cancel button (which is the same as pressing ESC), then the value of the InputBox

5

function is the default string. If the user chooses the OK button, then whatever was entered in the edit area is the value of the function.

InputQuery Function

This extension of a simple input box lets you determine whether the user pressed the OK button or pressed Cancel (or ESC). The syntax is very similar to that of an InputBox function.

> function InputQuery(const *ACaption*, *APrompt*: string; var *Value*: string);

The ACaption and APrompt parameters work as before. In this case, though, the Value parameter is the string that appears in the edit box when the dialog box first appears. *However,* because of the keyword **var**, when the user enters a string in the edit box and chooses OK, Delphi changes the Value parameter to be a string that reflects what the user entered. In addition, the function itself returns True or False depending on whether the user chose OK or Cancel (or ESC). Notice that since this function needs to give back two pieces of information, there has to be a parameter that can be changed—otherwise a function can return only one value.

For an example of how to use this function, start up a new project and add the following OnClick event procedure to it.

```
procedure TForm1.OnClick(Sender: TObject);
var
  UserData: String;
  OKClicked: Boolean;
begin
  UserData := '';
  OKClicked := InputQuery('Input Query Box', 'Press OK to enter data',
UserData);
  if OKClicked then
    ShowMessage('You entered ' + UserData);
end;
```

Multiple Form Applications

Until now all our projects used a single form. This section covers some of the techniques you'll need to create multiform projects. The ideas are the same in both versions of Delphi, but the mechanics are a bit different.

Note: For multiform projects that follow the MDI (multiple document interface) model, please see Chapter 13.

Adding Extra Forms to a Delphi 16 Project

Let's start by assuming that you have a new project and want to add a second form to it. Open the File menu and choose New Form (or use the New Form SpeedBar button). The Form gallery that looks like Figure 5-1 will open. (If it doesn't, look at the Gallery section on the Environment Options dialog box, and make sure the Use on New Form option is checked.) Notice in Figure 5-1 that you have various templates for commonly occurring forms or an option for a blank form. Regardless of which option you choose, when you create a new form, Delphi adds another form (.DFM) file and its associated unit (the code file with a .PAS extension) module. It also modifies the project file to indicate the presence of a new form and unit.

5

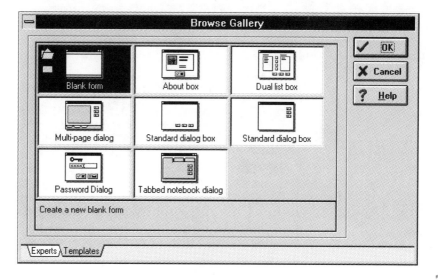

The Forms gallery

Figure 5-1.

Note: You can also add an existing form to a project. Choose File | Add File (or use the Add SpeedBar button) to open a dialog box that lets you choose the form (.DFM) file to add.

When you add an existing form to a project, Delphi requires you to add the name of the form to the uses clause of all units that access the code or the form. However, Delphi automatically adds the necessary references to the uses clause in the Project (.DPR) file.

Adding Extra Forms to a Delphi 32 Project

Let's start by assuming that you have a new application in Delphi 32 and want to add a second form to it. Open the File menu and choose New (or use the New Form SpeedBar button). The New Items dialog box that shows the current contents of the Object Repository pops up (see Figure 5-2). Notice in Figure 5-2 that you have various templates or an option for a Blank form. Regardless of which option you choose, when you create a new form, Delphi adds another form (.DFM) file and its associated unit (the code file with a .PAS extension) module. It also modifies the project file to indicate the presence of a new form and unit.

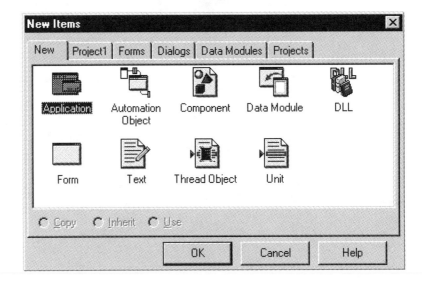

The New Items dialog box for the repository

Figure 5-2.

Note: You can also add an existing form to a project. Choose File | Add to Project (or use the Add SpeedBar button) to open a dialog box that lets you choose the form (.DFM) file to add.

As in the 16-bit version of Delphi, when you add an existing form to a project, Delphi requires you to add the name of the form to the uses clause of all units that access the code or the form. However, Delphi automatically adds the necessary references to the uses clause in the Project (.DPR) file.

Working with Multiple Form Projects

To switch among forms or between forms and units in a project, regardless of which version of Delphi you are using:

1. Choose View | Forms (press SHIFT-F12 or use the Select Form from list SpeedBar button).
2. When the View Form dialog box pops up, select the form that you want to work with, and then choose OK.

You will also need to switch among the code units associated with the various forms:

5

1. Choose View | Units (press CTRL-F12 or choose the Select Unit from list SpeedBar button).
2. When the View Unit dialog box pops up, select the unit you want to work with, and then choose OK.

Saving Forms

Consider saving a copy of a form under a different name. Although this wastes space, it makes it easier to ensure that you have an archival copy of the form. As you might expect, you use File | Save File As to save a form under a different name or location. However, only its unit (.PAS) file is displayed when you save the file. This is not a problem since Delphi saves both the form and its associated unit file at the same time.

Working with Form Templates

If you have designed a complicated form that you know you will want to use again, you will probably want to save it for reuse. In Delphi they are called *form templates*. Once you do this, Delphi adds your custom form to the

Delphi forms gallery that pops up when you choose to add a new form in Delphi 16 or the Object Repository in Delphi 32.

To save the current form as a template, it is best to have saved the form first (and it is *necessary* that you do so in Delphi 32). After doing this, make sure you have selected the form. Then:

1. Open the form's speedmenu and:

    ◆ In Delphi 16 choose the Save As Template.
    ◆ In Delphi 32 choose the Add to Repository item in Delphi. (This opens up the Save Form Template dialog box.)

2. A dialog box will pop up. In the Title edit box, enter a name for the template (you also should consider adding a brief description of this template in the Description area).

You can also add a bitmap for your new template by clicking on the Browse button and finding a bitmap you like.

Note: It is possible to turn a form file into a DLL. See the online help page on "Building a DLL."

Removing a Form (and Its Associated Unit) from a Project

Because the form (.DFM) file is always tied to its associated unit file containing the code file (the .PAS file), you can't remove one without removing the other. When you remove a form from a project, Delphi also deletes the reference to the Unit file in the uses clause of the Project (.DPR) file.

You have a choice of two ways to remove a form and its associated Unit file:

◆ Select the unit or units you want to remove, and then choose the Remove file from project button on the SpeedBar.

Or:

◆ Select the unit or units you want to remove, and then choose the Remove File SpeedBar button.

(You can also select the tab for the unit you want to remove, and then choose File | Remove File from the File menu in Delphi 16 or File | Remove from the Project menu in Delphi 32.)

Specifying the Main Form for the Project

When you deal with multiform projects, you have the option of choosing which form will be displayed automatically when a user runs the application. This called the *main* form. All other forms will need code to be displayed (see the following).

Note: When the user closes (for example, by using ALT-F4) or the program closes the main form, the application terminates. (It is also the best way to end a project you are running within the development environment.) In other words, closing the main form is the same as using code to call Application.Terminate.

The first form you create becomes the main form by default. If you want to change this at design time:

1. Go to the Project Options dialog box (available off the Options menu in Delphi 16 and the Project menu in Delphi 32). See Figure 5-3 for the Delphi 16 version which is similar in Delphi 32.)
2. In the Forms page, select the form you want to be the main form in the Main Form drop-down list box and click on OK.

Form Behavior at Run Time

If you look at Figure 5-3, you'll notice there are two boxes: one is labeled "Auto-create forms," and the other, "Available forms." Any form listed in the Auto-create box will be created (*instantiated* is the technical term) automatically at run time. (See Chapter 9 for how to deal with forms that you do *not* want Delphi to create automatically at run time.) The default is that all forms are auto-created.

Note: It is also possible to create a form at run time without having added it at design time. See Chapter 9 for how to do this.

5

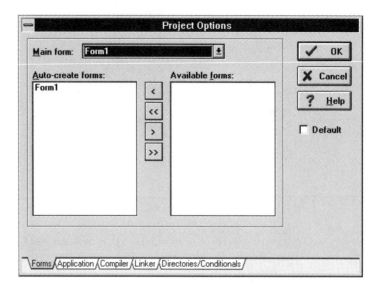

If you want to have one form work with another form and its components, add the name of its Unit file to the **uses** clause of the calling form. You must do this yourself, as Delphi does not do this automatically. (In Delphi 32 you can use the File | Use Unit option to make this process simpler.) Once you have done this, you can work with the objects and properties of one form in the code associated with another. For example, suppose you have two forms. Let's say the forms are named Form1 and Form2, and the Unit (.PAS) files are named Unit1 and Unit2. Let's also suppose that each one has an edit box (say, Form1EditBox and Form2EditBox).

Here's the code you need in the Form2 unit to make the contents of the Form1EditBox appear in the Form2EditBox:

```
Form2EditBox.Text := Form1.Form1EditBox.Text;
```

(Remember, though, unless you have added Unit1 to the **uses** clause of Unit2, this code can't work.)

In general, once forms have been told to recognize each other by placing the appropriate unit name in a **uses** clause, you refer to the properties of the objects on one form by using the form's name together with periods as needed. (As in the preceding example, you do not need to give a form name if you are writing code about it in its Unit file.)

 Note: When two forms need to work with each other's objects, then you can cause the compiler to generate a circular reference error by adding both of the unit names to the respective uses clause. To avoid this, add the name of the other form to a uses clauses in the **implementation** section of their respective Unit files.

(If the code unit doesn't have a **uses** clause in the **implementation** section, you will need to add this as well. Just add the keyword **uses** below the keyword **implementation**.)

Note that even if a secondary form is auto-created at run time, it will *not* be visible to the user until you write the code that makes it so. Here are short descriptions of the methods you need in order to work with a form at run time.

Show Once Delphi has created a form, use the Show method to make it visible *and to also make it the active form.*

For example, to make Form2 (unit name Unit2) available from Form1:

1. Add Unit2 to the **uses** clause of Form1.
2. Have Delphi process a line of code like this: Form2.Show.

 Tip: Remember to also set the FormStyle property to fsStayOnTop if you want a form to always be on top.

Hide, Close The Hide method simply hides a form. It doesn't remove the form from memory. For this, use the Close method (which has the same effect as choosing Close from the control box menu) or the ALT-F4 shortcut.

5

Modal Forms

Sometimes you want to make a form *modal*—so the user won't be able to switch to another form in your application without working with the modal form (for example, you may be designing a custom dialog box).

Note: The Windows convention is that dialog boxes lack any icons in the title bar and are not resizable.

(Recall that to do this to a form, you must change the values of the various BorderIcons properties to False and change the BorderStyle property to bsDialog.)

To make a form modal, use the ShowModal method rather than the Show method. The usual syntax is

FormName.ShowModal;

or

if *FormName*.ShowModal = mrOK then...

(Note: ShowModal stops code execution, Show doesn't.)

Once you have made a form visible with this method, the user *must* interact with the form. If he or she doesn't do what it takes to trigger the code that hides the form, the modal form will remain on the screen.

To actually close a modal form, you must have Delphi change the value of its ModalResult property to a nonzero value. You can do this with code in any event procedure for the form or component on the form. However, except for an occasional use of the Timer event, the standard way to change the ModalResult property and close the form is to add buttons to the form. Then set their ModalResult property to the appropriate value. For example, with an OK button, you would want to set the ModalResult property of the button to mrOK. When the user clicks on any button on a modal form whose ModalResult button is set to be nonzero (mrOK, mrCancel, mrAbort, and so on), then Delphi assigns this value to the ModalResult property of the form—closing the form.

T **ip:** The TBitBtn has a Kind property that makes this kind of code easier.

Programming with Forms

Especially when dealing with multiple form applications, be aware of the possibility that all the forms may be hidden—but the application is still running! (Of course, you can use the OnHide event to prevent a form from being hidden, but what I am referring to is when the main form gets hidden early on and all the other forms are closed via Windows shortcuts like ALT-F4.)

The trick is to use the OnCloseQuery and OnClose events to monitor why your forms are closed. We cover these important events next.

OnCloseQuery Event

The OnCloseQuery event occurs when the user takes an action that *tries to close* the form. Thus, the OnCloseQuery event handler is the place to intercept a form's closing and prevent it. For example, use the OnCloseQuery event handler to ask users if they are sure they really want the form to close. The first line of an OnCloseEventHandler looks something like this:

```
procedure TForm1.FormCloseQuery(Sender: TObject; var CanClose:
Boolean);
```

If you change the CanClose parameter to False in the body of the event procedure, the form will not be allowed to close down! For example:

```
procedure TForm1.FormCloseQuery(Sender: TObject; var CanClose;
Boolean)
  begin
    if MessageDlg('Are you sure you want to close the form?',
mtConfirmation, [mbOK, mbCancel], 0) = mbCancel then
CanClose := False;
  end;
```

5

The OnClose Event

Unlike in Visual Basic, the OnClose event gives you one last chance to prevent the form from closing. However, most of the time Delphi programmers use this event for cleanup code. The Action parameter in the OnClose event handler has four possible values. They are given in the following table.

Action Value	Meaning
caNone	The form is not allowed to close; corresponds to setting CanClose parameter to be False in the OnClose Query event.
caHide	Instead of closing the form, you hide it.
caFree	The form is closed, so all its allocated memory is freed by Delphi.
caMinimize	The form is minimized, rather than closed. (This is the default action for MDI child forms—see Chapter 13.)

Chapter

6

Advanced Programming Techniques

The last chapter showed you the basics of Delphi's built-in programming language. This chapter takes you further along the road to mastering it. We start by showing you how to extend Delphi's built-in types by constructing your own types. Then it's on to lists, arrays, and records. These are used when you need to work with groups of data at one time. Then there is a short treatment of pointers and memory management. Next, there is a short discussion of Delphi's built-in functions and procedures and, following that, a section on writing your own functions and procedures. We end the chapter by spending a bit of time on the anatomy of a project and a unit, what you need to know to more efficiently use Delphi's compiler when you generate stand-alone programs, and the infamous goto.

Types Revisited

Delphi's programming language is an example of a *strongly typed* language. This means that all variables must have types. In Delphi 16 type boundaries were pretty strict; in Delphi 32, using the new variant data type, they can be much less so. Nonetheless, some barriers remain: for example, regardless of which Delphi version you are using, if a variable is declared to be a Double, then you cannot assign it to an Integer. On the other hand, as was mentioned in the last chapter, you can assign values of type Char to a variable of type string, or assign a value of type Integer to a Floating Point type, or make assignments between two Floating Point type variables or two Integer type variables when the values are compatible. And (some people would add, "unfortunately"), if you are using the variant data type, you can assign variant variables that hold strings to variants that hold numbers without causing any error messages.

Note: See the online help topics on "Assignment Compatibility" and "Type Compatibility" for exactly what intratype assignments you can make when not using the variant data type.

Using Delphi 32, I am convinced that in the long run, my programs will be easier to debug (and run faster) if I rely on variants only when I need their special properties (usually in OLE applications—see Chapter 13). Of course, some programmers regard the strongly typed features in Delphi as a straitjacket and welcome the variant data type that was added to Delphi 32, so the choice is yours!

Ordinal Data Types

Many of Delphi's built-in data types, such as String or Integer, can be refined or combined to create new data types. While you can create many different kinds of types in Delphi, we start with the techniques needed for creating new examples of *ordinal data types*. Although we haven't used the term "ordinal data type" yet, you have already seen the most common examples of them: all the integer types as well as Char are ordinal data types. The defining characteristics of ordinal data types are

♦   They consist of a finite number of elements.

♦   They must be ordered in some way.

In particular, in any ordinal types, it must make sense to move forward and backward to the next element. Real types are not ordinal because moving backward or forward doesn't make sense: the question "What is the next real after 1.0?" is meaningless. The basic ordinal types in both versions of Delphi are the Boolean types, Char, and all Integer types.

Working with an Ordinal Type

Both versions of Delphi come with the same built-in functions for working with ordinal types. They are listed in Table 6-1.

Note: If you try to wrap around the elements (say, by using Succ when you are at the last element), then as long as range checking is on, Delphi will generate a run-time exception. (See Chapter 8 for how to handle exceptions.)

Enumerated Data Types

The easiest way to create a new example of an ordinal type is simply to list a bunch of elements in some order. Each element is defined by a Delphi identifier. (Recall that this means they must satisfy the same rules as for variable or component names.) Doing this gives you what is called an *enumerated data type*. Here are some examples of how to create enumerated data types:

```
type
   Clone = (Compaq, Dell, Gateway, Packard, Micron, Zeos, Other);
   WorkDays = (Monday, Tuesday, Wednesday, Thursday, Friday);
```

Once you define an enumerated data type, you can declare variables to be of that type using the standard syntax, an example of which is shown here:

```
var
   YourComputer: Clone;
```

6

Function	Effect
Pred(X)	Goes to the element listed before X in the type.
Succ(X)	Goes to the element listed after X in the type.
Dec(X; n)	Moves n elements back. (If you leave off the n, moves back 1.)
Inc(X; n)	Moves n elements forward. (If you leave off the n, moves forward 1.)
Ord(X)	Gives you the index of the element.

Functions for Working with Ordinal Data Types
Table 6-1.

The primary purpose of an enumerated data type is to make clear what data your program will manipulate. In general, an enumerated data type:

♦ Consists of no more than 256 elements

♦ Has a unique *identifier* for each element in the type

Delphi allows you to work with the elements in an enumerated data type using an *index* that comes from the order that they were listed in. Delphi indexes the elements in an enumerated data type starting at 0 (*not* 1). For example, in our Clone type example earlier, Compaq has index 0, Other has index 6. The functions for ordinals that were listed in Table 6-1 let you move through the elements in an enumerated data type.

Subrange Types

You have already seen subrange types at work in the case statement (as discussed in Chapter 5). When we had a statement like

```
case AverageGrade of
  90..99: {do something};
```

we were using a subrange of the integers that consisted of the numbers 90 through 99. In general, you can define any subrange by starting with any ordinal type (including a previously defined enumerated type) and using a double dot. For example:

```
type
  ControlChar = #0..#31;  {using # for an ASCII Character}
  UpperCase = #65..#90;
```

Again, the point of a subrange type is to clarify what data your code is manipulating.

Sets

Sets work much like enumerated data types, but they are not ordinal data types, because the order of the elements is no longer important. You use a set when you are more concerned with *what* elements are in the set rather than the *order* of them. Like enumerated types, sets can hold up to 256 elements, but *all the elements must be taken from the same ordinal type* and, *if the elements are numeric, they must be between 0 and 255.* In particular, you cannot make up a set that consists of both characters and integers, or one containing elements like 20,000. Here's an example of a set declaration:

```
type
  Characters = set of Char;
  Primes = set of Byte;
```

To actually create the set, use square brackets and separate the items by commas:

```
var
  SmallPrimes: Primes;
  LCaseVowels, UCaseVowels, Vowels: Characters;
begin
  SmallPrimes := [2, 3, 5, 7, 11, 13, 17];
  LCaseVowels := ['a', 'e', 'i', 'o', 'u'];
```

The operators for handling sets are described in Table 6-2. Here are some examples of how the operators used with sets work:

```
Vowels := ['A', 'a', 'E', 'e', 'I', 'i', 'O', 'o', 'U', 'u']
```

and

```
LCaseVowels := ['a', 'e', 'i', 'o', 'u'];
UCaseVowels := ['A', 'E', 'I', 'O', 'U'];
```

then as a set

Vowels = LCaseVowels + UCaseVowels
LCaseVowels = Vowels – UCaseVowels

Sets can make code much clearer—and even shorten it—by avoiding cumbersome case statements. For example, a line of code like

```
if YourCharacter in Vowels then ...
```

is both clearer and shorter than the corresponding **case** statement would be.

6

Arrays

You use a variable array (or simply, "an array") when you need to set aside space in the computer's memory for a group of related values that are all the same data type. You can use arrays to store large strings as well as lists and tables. Arrays are the first examples you have seen of what are called *structured types* in Object Pascal. The defining characteristic of a structured

Operator	Function
= (equality)	Determines if two sets are equal. Returns a Boolean (True/False) result.
<> (not equal)	Determines if two sets are not equal. Returns a Boolean (True/False) result.
< = (inclusion)	Checks if all the elements of one set are in (*included*) in another. Also returns a Boolean (True/False) result. (This condition is commonly called *being a subset.*)
> = (containment)	Checks to see if one set contains all the elements of another. (This is often called *being a superset.*)
+ (union)	Returns a set consisting of *all* the elements from both sets.
* (intersection)	Returns a set consisting of the elements *common* to both sets.
– (set difference)	Returns a set obtained by removing the elements of one set from another.
in	Tests to see whether the value of an expression or constant is in a set. Returns a Boolean (True/False) value.

Operators
Used with Sets
Table 6-2.

type is that you can both manipulate the object as a whole and work with the individual elements in it. A structured type can use up to 65,520 bytes of memory in Delphi 16 and 2 gigabytes (!) in Delphi 32.

One-Dimensional Arrays

To Delphi, a one-dimensional array (or simply, a "list") is just a collection of values, each of which is identified by two things:

♦ The name of the list

♦ The position of the item on the list

For example, suppose you are writing a program that lets a user enter an "errand list" at the beginning of each day. You would probably choose to store the information on a list. You could call this list Errand, and each errand might be stored as Errand[1], Errand[2], and so on.

The number in the brackets is usually called the subscript or index. The term "subscript" comes from mathematics, where the item M[5] is more likely to be written M₅. To Delphi, M5 is the name of a single variable, but M[5] is the name (position) of an element on a list called M.

Visual Basic Tip: Remember, array indexes in Delphi use *square brackets,* not parentheses.

To use a list, you must first declare it. Here are some examples of how the declarations would look for two arrays—one for strings and the other for integers:

```
var
   StateNames: array[1..50] of String;
   RangeOfInteger: array[-100..100] of Integer;
```

This is actually not the best way to create arrays for sophisticated programs. Normally you should create a type for each array, rather than implicitly declaring the type as part of the variable declaration. This makes it possible to pass these arrays as parameters to a subprogram (see next). For example:

```
type
   ElectionResults = array[1..51] of Longint;
var
   ResultsIn1996: ElectionResults;
```

The general form of the syntax for declaring an array is

   ArrayName: array[*Index Type*] of *Type*;

where *Index Type* is any ordinal (or subrange of an ordinal) data type except Longint in Delphi 16. (You can use Longint in Delphi 32.)

You can also have typed constant arrays when you want to specify the initial values (and have the values persist—to be *static* variables, as with ordinary typed constants). An example of this would be

```
Const
   CutOffForGrades: array[1..4] of Integer = (90, 80, 70, 60);
```

(Note the parentheses for the initial values and that the array was created in the Const section.)

6

The string types in Delphi 16 are actually arrays of characters starting at one and continuing to the length of the string. (The "zeroth" position is used for the number of characters.) For example, if

```
var
   S: String[80];
```

then s is actually stored as an array of characters of the following type:

```
S: array [0..80] of Char;
```

In Delphi 16 (or if you choose to have Delphi 32's string type be the same as in Delphi 16), the 0th position is used to store the length of the string. The actual string would be stored in s[1] for the first character, s[2] for the second, and so on. Because Delphi doesn't distinguish between the array of characters and the string, you can isolate individual characters in a string the same way you isolate an element of an array. For example, a line of code like:

```
S[37] := '!';
```

would change the 37th character in the string to an exclamation point.

 Note: Remember in Delphi 32, Integers have the same range as the Longint type in Delphi 16.

You can partially get around Delphi 16's limitation on 255 characters in a string by making an array of characters larger than 255. However, as you will see in the section on "Null-Terminated Strings and PChar" later in this chapter, you are best off using an array of character variables that also starts with an index of zero (you will use the extra space for bookkeeping). For example, if you need a string that would hold 20,000 characters in Delphi 16, use

```
var
   TextInMemo: array[0..20000] of Char;
```

which sets aside 20,001 spaces (one space for bookkeeping) instead of using an index of 1 to 20,000. (Although the disadvantage of this type of array is that you are using up memory in the local heap—see later in this chapter for more on the heap.)

Caution: When you use large strings (that is, greater than 255 characters long) in Delphi 16, memory management becomes more important. See the "Pointers" section in this chapter for more about this.

Delphi 32 automatically reclaims the memory used for its large strings, so you don't have to worry about memory management for strings when you are using Delphi 32.

String Lists

Both versions of Delphi maintain a lot of information about certain components, such as the items in a list or combo box, the available fonts, or the lines of text in a memo box, in what are called *string lists*. Essentially, a string list is a array of strings *maintained* by Delphi, so that they are easy to manipulate.

Tip: You can tell if a property is stored in a string list by looking to see if there is a TStrings in the value column of the Object Inspector. (TStrings is the name of the string list object. There will be more on the TStrings object in Chapter 7. You'll see, for instance, how to create your own string lists at run time.)

6

For example, you can copy one string list to another just by a simple assignment statement. If you want to have the lines in a memo box appear in a combo box, the one line of code shown here would suffice to make the item's property point to the same place in memory!

```
ComboBox1.Items := Memo1.Lines;
```

To make a true copy use:

```
ComboBox1.Items.Assign(Memo1.Lines);
```

(Both the Items property of a combo box and the Lines property of a memo field are of type TStrings.)

Tip: Delphi has the ability to maintain a list of objects in parallel to a string list. One common use of this, for example, is to associate a picture to each item in a string list. For more on this, look at the online help entries on "Adding Objects To A String List" and "Adding Graphical Objects To A String Lists," which are subtopics of the String List Topic.

What follows is a short discussion of the most common properties and methods of string lists.

Strings Any string list has a Strings property that is best thought of as an array of the strings being stored. The list starts at zero. For example, a memo box maintains the lines in it in a string list called (naturally enough) Lines. So

```
Memo1.Lines.Strings[1]
```

is the *second* line in the memo box. (Memo1.Lines.Strings[0] is the first.)

Note: Since Strings is the default property of a string list, you don't actually have to use it. The compiler also understands a line like *Memo1.Lines[1]* to be the second line in the Memo component.

Count The Count property gives you the number of items in the list. This means that the last item in a string list has index Count-1. For example:

```
Memo1.Lines.Strings[Count-1] := 'Hello' {assign to last line in
box};
```

or

```
NumberOfFonts := Screeen.Fonts.Count; {number of screen fonts
available};
```

In general, since string lists are zero-based, to iterate over all the items, use the following syntax:

For *Index* := 0 to *StringList*.Count - 1 do

IndexOf   This function takes a string and returns the index where the string is located. If the string isn't found, Delphi returns -1. For example:

```
If Memo1.Lines.IndexOf('Test string') = -1 Then
   ShowMessage('String not found')
else
  ShowMessage('String found');
```

Add   The Add method puts a string at the end of a string list if the Sorted property is False and in the appropriate sorted position if the Sorted property is True. For example, the Items property on a list box is a string list that holds the items. If you wanted to add the names of the presidents to a list box, the code might look like this:

```
President.ListBox.Items.Add('George Washington');
President.ListBox.Items.Add('John Adams');
```

You can also use Add as a function. In this case, it will tell you the index in which the string was entered. For example:

```
IndexOfLastEntry: = ListBox1.Items.Add("This is the last entry');
```

Insert   The Insert method lets you add an entry at a specific place to a nonsorted string list. For example, if you left out the ninth president, William Henry Harrison (a common mistake since he was president for only one month), you would use the following code. (Remember that string lists are zero-based, so the ninth entry is at index 8.)

```
President.ListBox.Insert(8, 'William Henry Harrison');
```

6

In general, the first entry is an integer for the index, and the second is the string to insert.

Move   The Move method lets you rearrange items in a string list. For example, to make the tenth item in a list box first, use

```
President.Items.Move(9, 0);
```

In general, the first entry is the index of the item to be moved; the last entry is the place to move it.

Clear, Delete   The Clear method erases all strings in the list. The Delete method takes a specific index and deletes that entry. For example:

```
PresidentListBox.Items.Delete(0);
```

would delete George Washington's name.

Multidimensional Arrays

You can also have arrays with more than one dimension; they're usually called *multidimensional arrays*. Just as lists of data lead to a single subscript (one-dimensional arrays), tables of data lead to double subscripts (two-dimensional arrays). For example, suppose you want to store a multiplication table in memory—as a table. You could do this as:

```
var
  I, J: Integer;
  MultiTable: array[1..12,1..12] of Integer;
begin
  for I := 1 to 12 do
    for J := 1 to 12 do
      MultiTable[I, J] := I*J;
end;
```

To compute the number of items in a multidimensional array, multiply the number of indexes. The variable declaration above sets aside 144 (12 * 12) entries, and there are 12 rows and 12 columns. In general, the number of entries in an array is the product of the numbers specified in the declaration.

When you use a two-dimensional array to represent a matrix, the mathematical convention is to refer to the first entry as giving the number of rows and the second, the number of columns. Following this convention, we would say this code fragment fills an entire row, column by column, before moving to the next row. (Notice that this is the opposite of the convention Delphi uses for a grid's Cell property.)

Records

Suppose you want to have three one-dimensional arrays for 100 employees in a company. The first array is for names, the second for salaries, and the third for Social Security numbers. Each list would have matching indexes, and plenty of extra code would be required to maintain all these lists in parallel.

The way around this extra work is to use a new structure called a *record*. Essentially, a record is a new type that can mix any of Delphi's types, including any types you may create.

The code in the example shown here defines the record type for our hypothetical employee:

```
type
  TVitalInfo = record
    Name: String;
    Salary: longint;
    SocialSec: String[11];
end;
```

Usually people say that this record has three *fields* (the Name, Salary, and SocialSec parts of this record). Once you have set up the record type, then from that point on in the program, you can declare a variable to be of type TVitalInfo. TVitalInfo is now just as good a variable type for variables as any of Delphi's built-in types like Integer or String. Of course, to actually create a variable of TVitalInfo type, you need to declare it:

```
var
 YourName: TVitalInfo;
```

Once you have a record, you use a dot (period) to isolate the fields of this record:

```
YourName.Name := 'Howard';
YourName.Salary := 100000;
YourName.SocialSec := '036-78-9987';
```

The **with** keyword that you learned about for working with deeply nested properties also works for records, as you can see in the following code:

```
with YourName do
  begin
    Name := 'Howard';
    Salary := 100000;
    SocialSec := '036-78-9987';
  end;
```

6

You can also set up an array of record variables:

```
Employees: array [1..100] of TVitalInfo;
```

As with arrays or other variables, you can have typed constant records in which you initialize the record by separating the entries, as in the following example:

```
const
  BossRecord: TVitalInfo =  (Name: 'Big Cheese'; Salary: 1000000;
SocialSec: '001-01-0011');
```

Since a record type is as legitimate as any other Delphi type, you can have a field of a record be a record itself. For example, you could make up a RecordOfSalary type to keep track of monthly earnings along with the previous year's salary:

```
type
  TRecordOfSalary = record
    SalInJan: Integer;
    SalInFeb: Integer;
    SalInMar: Integer;
    SalInApr: Integer;
    SalInMay: Integer;
    SalInJun: Integer;
    SalInJul: Integer;
    SalInAug: Integer;
    SalInSep: Integer;
    SalInOct: Integer;
    SalInNov: Integer;
    SalInDec: Integer;
    SalInPrevYear: LongInt;
  end;
```

Now you can set up a record of records:

```
type
  TExpandedVitalInfo = record
  Name: String;
  Salary: TRecordOfSalary;
  SocSecNumber: String[11];
end;
```

Of course, filling out all the information needed for a single record is now that much harder, and you will appreciate the **with** keyword even more. It also gets a little messy to refer to the information in records such as TExpandedVitalInfo. You work your way down by using more periods. After using

```
var
  GaryStats: TExpandedVitalInfo;
```

to set up a variable of this new type, use a statement like

```
ShowMessage(IntToStr(GaryStats.Salary.SalInPrevYear));
```

to display information in one of the nested fields.

Pascal Tip: Delphi does support variant records, but you are usually better off using an inherited object. (See Chapter 7.)

Pointers

Although pointers are considered a subtle concept, you can make them a lot more concrete if you always keep in mind:

♦ Everything used in a program is stored somewhere in the computer's memory.

♦ A pointer to that item simply gives (points to!) the application to that memory location.

As with all Object Pascal types, you must declare a pointer before you can use it in your program. The syntax uses a caret (^). Most of the time, pointers in Delphi point to a specific type. For example:

```
IntegerPointer: ^Integer;
RealPointer: ^Double;
```

Since a pointer is an address in memory, you must tell the compiler the location of that address. This is done with the @ operator (or equivalently, the Addr function).

6

```
var
  Foo: Integer;
  PointerToFoo: ^Integer;
begin
  Foo := 2;
  PointerToFoo := @Foo {or addr(Foo)};
```

Since Foo is a variable, its value must be stored somewhere. After these lines of code, PointerToFoo would contain that address. In particular, this means PointerToFoo's value isn't 2; it is the memory address where Foo's value is currently stored.

Note: The Convention is to use a prefix 'P' for pointers, so that most code would actually denote what I called PointerToFoo simply by PFoo.

Unassigned pointers are dangerous. Using them can lead to spectacular program crashes. This is because pointers let you work directly with memory locations, and if you inadvertently write to a crucial protected location in memory, you will get a general protection fault (affectionately called a GPF) in Delphi 16, or an access violation in Delphi 32, at best, or lock up your machine, at worst. For this reason, you should always initialize a pointer to the special value of **Nil**. (Using **Nil** means that the pointer is not currently referring to a specific memory location.) Then when you use a pointer, first check whether the pointer is **Nil**. (Using a nil pointer doesn't prevent a memory violation, checking for it does!)

```
if PInteger = Nil then
  {don't do anything}
else
  {do what you want}
```

Pascal Tip: Although Delphi supports the Ptr function that lets you work with an absolute memory location, using absolute memory locations is a very bad idea in Windows programming!

Once you have a pointer, you use the caret *after* the pointer to get the data at that location. (This is called *dereferencing the pointer.*) For example:

```
PFoo^ := Foo + 4;
```

but

```
Foo := PFoo + Foo;
```

makes no sense—you can't add a pointer to an integer in Delphi (unlike C or C++).

You can also point to arrays or records. If you set

```
type
  IntegerArray: array: [1.. 100] of Integer;
  PIntegerArray = ^IntegerArray;
```

then

```
var
  ExampleOfArray: IntegerArray;
  ArrayPointer: PIntegerArray;
```

gives you an integer array and a pointer to an integer array. To actually dereference the pointer ("point the pointer"), you again use the @ operator:

```
ArrayPointer := @ExampleOfArray;
ArrayPointer^[99] := 37;   {make the 99th entry = to 37};
```

The ability to have pointers to arrays and records makes it much easier to set up such complicated data structures as linked lists and trees as well as parameter passing of large data structures. (If you don't know what these are, please consult any book on data structures.) Here's an example of the type declaration for a simple linked list:

```
type
  PNextListItem = ^ListItem; {forward declaration}
  ListItem  = record
    FirstItem: String;
    SecondItem: String;
    NextRecord: PNextListItem;
  end;
```

The idea, of course, is that you can use the pointer contained in the NextRecord field to give you the address of the next linked item.

6

Note: This is the only case in which you can reference an identifier before you declare it.

Pascal **Tip:**   Delphi, like later versions of Turbo Pascal, supports pointers to functions and procedures. These are rarely used, so we refer you to the online help if you are in the unusual situation of needing a pointer to a function. (Although you should be aware that every event handler such as OnClick is actually a pointer to a procedure.)

Pointers and Memory Management

Until now we have only used pointers to refer to the location of objects that already exist. The real power of pointers comes from the ability to set aside memory while the program is executing. The easiest way to do this is with the New procedure. Here's an example of how to use this procedure:

```
var
  PIntegerPointer: ^Integer;
begin
  New(PIntegerPointer);
  PIntegerPointer^ := 37;
end;
```

Once you tell Delphi to set aside memory for the pointer's data using the New procedure, use a line such as

PIntegerPointer^ := 37;

to fill the memory location with the correct value. If you allocate memory using New, you must be sure to reclaim the memory using the Dispose procedure. (Usually you do this in a try/finally block as described in Chapter 8.) The syntax for the Dispose procedure is simply:

Dispose(pointer); {sets pointer to Nil}

Note: It is extremely important that you synchronize the use of New and Dispose. For example, if you allocate the memory for the same variable twice without disposing of it first, you will never be able to reclaim the memory set aside the first time.

Pascal Tip: Delphi also supports the Mark/Release pair of procedures for memory allocation.

In all cases, memory that you allocate for a pointer is taken from a special part of memory that Windows manages called the *global heap*. The maximum memory you can allocate for a single object in Delphi 16 is 64K and is essentially unlimited in Delphi 32 (2 gigabytes), but the global heap (and thus the amount of memory that you can allocate for what is pointed to by your pointers) is *in both versions of Delphi* generally limited only by Windows itself. Unfortunately, there is another limit set by Delphi 16: the memory used for the static data area (global variables and typed constants), the stack (used for local variables and parameters), and the local heap (used for temporary storage of things like edit control buffers) are limited to one single 64K data segment. (These limits explain why programmers use pointers in Delphi 16 whenever possible—they don't use up precious space in the data segment—only a few bytes for bookkeeping.)

In any case, it is possible to make the stack or Delphi 16 local heap larger as long as the total remains less than 64K. You do this using the Linker page of the Project Options dialog box. If you need to override Delphi 16 defaults for these objects, consult the online help for more on how Delphi manages the heap.

Tip: Since the global heap does have *some* limits, to avoid a run-time error, check that sufficient contiguous memory exists on the global heap before actually allocating the memory. You do this using the MaxAvail function.

Allocating and Deallocating Blocks of Memory

The New and Dispose procedures are used when you want to allocate space for a single object. If you want to allocate (and then deallocate) a block of memory for an object, like an array that may vary in size during the project, use the GetMem and FreeMem pair of procedures. (And as with Dispose, you will usually deallocate the memory in the finally block, as described in Chapter 8.) Here's a very simplified example of how to use GetMem. (See also the following note for the correct way to use GetMem, which uses concepts that won't be introduced until Chapter 8.)

6

```
type
  BigString = array [0..20000] of Char;
var
  BigStringPointer: ^BigString; {could have used PChars of course}
begin
  Getmem(BigStringPointer, 20001); {space from the global heap}
end;
```

Note: Although it uses the try/finally structure that won't be introduced until Chapter 8, you should be aware that the correct way to code the memory allocation part of the previous example looks like this:

```
try
  BigStringPointer^[0] := 'A';
  ...
finally
  Freemem(BigStringPointer, 20001);
```

Visual Basic Tip: If you need an analog to RedimPreserve, you can use GetMem to build up an arraylike structure that can change dynamically. (Another possibility is to use the TList object.)

Null-Terminated Strings and PChar

Note: This section is mainly of interest to Delphi 16 programmers. Delphi 32 programmers would most likely use the large string type (and its built-in "garbage collection," which reclaims memory automatically.)

An ordinary string in Delphi 16 is simply a sequence of bytes. However, Delphi uses the first byte in this sequence to tell it how many characters are stored. Since a byte can only hold integers between 0 and 255, this limits the number of characters in an ordinary string to 255.

Both versions of Delphi (following the lead of C) have a type called *null-terminated strings* that gets around this limitation; you can use it to handle up to 65,535 characters at once in Delphi 16. (And there are essentially no limits in Delphi 32—but the default behavior, or declaring a wide string, gives you this for free!)

In Delphi 16 a null-terminated string is simply a sequence of up to 65,535 characters that ends with an ASCII 0 (#0). Delphi uses the ASCII 0 character to mark the boundary of the string. This means there is essentially no difference between a null-terminated string and an array[0..NumberOfCharacters] of type Char, where the end of the string is marked by an ASCII 0.

Delphi lets you avoid messing around with pointers to zero-based arrays when handling null-terminated strings by using the predefined type PChar. Think of a PChar as being a pointer to a null-terminated string or to the array that represents one. What it actually does is point to the first character in the null-terminated string. Delphi then uses the ASCII 0 to find the end of the string.

Since PChars are pointers, you will usually want to allocate (and deallocate, of course!) memory on the global heap for them. Although this can be done with the GetMem/FreeMem pair of procedures, it is most common to use the StrNew and StrDispose pair. StrNew has the advantage that you will actually assign the string at the same time you allocate the memory for it—see the online help for more on these important procedures. These functions are especially convenient when passing Object Pascal strings to a Windows API function that requires a null-terminated string or a PChar.

If you turn on the extended syntax option, which is available on the Compiler page of the Project Options dialog box, then Delphi lets you manipulate strings using PChar in much the same way you manipulate arrays or ordinary strings.

```
var
PointerChar: PChar;
ArrayOfChar: array[0..1000] of Char; {this is in the
data segment!}
begin
   PointerChar := ArrayOfChar; {both point to the same place in
memory};
   StrPCopy(PointerChar, 'Am assigning a String to a PChar');
   ShowMessage('The eighth character is' + PointerChar[7]);
end;
```

6

Besides the StrNew function, there are lots of other functions you will find useful for working with PChars. For example, StrPCopy lets you convert an ordinary (255-character limit) string to a null-terminated string. The function StrPas converts a (small enough) null-terminated string back to an ordinary string. For more on the functions that work with PChar, please consult the "String Handling Routines (Null-terminated)" topic in the online help.

 **N**ote: Although you can assign an ordinary string to a PChar when the extended syntax option is on, this tends to mess up the data segment; you are much better off using StrNew.

Functions and Procedures

The usual difference between a function and a procedure is that a function can return a value, and a procedure generally will not do so.

 Pascal Tip: In Delphi, the differences between procedures and functions have become a bit more subtle than they were in "standard" Pascal. A *procedure* is always called as a stand-alone statement. A *function* is normally called as part of an expression, so it can return a value, but it can also be called like a procedure (where the return value is ignored when you have the extended syntax option on).

As you saw in the last chapter, the information that a function or procedure works with is the *parameter* or *argument*. For example, let's look more closely at the InputQuery function you saw in the last chapter. Its syntax in the online help looks like this:

    function InputQuery(const *ACaption*, *APrompt*: String;
    var *Value*: String): Boolean;

As this example indicates, the type of a parameter follows its name and a colon. It also shows that you can use multiple parameters of the same type by separating them with a comma. Parameter declarations are separated from each other by semicolons. This example uses three parameters (ACaption, APrompt, and Value) all of which are of String type.

ACaption and APrompt are what are called *constant* parameters (indicated by the keyword **const**). Constant parameters are passed by reference but cannot be changed by the function or procedure. The Value parameter, on the other hand, is passed as a **var** (or *variable*) parameter.

With a **var** parameter, because it is passed by reference and the compiler does not prevent you from changing it (as with Const parameters), you can make changes to it persist simply by having it on the left side of an assignment statement.

Note: The names of parameters in a function or procedure are placeholders. Although they have to follow the conventions for Delphi variable names, they have no independent existence.

Event procedures can use **const** or **var** parameters as well. For example, consider the OnKeyPress event procedure whose header for an TEdit box might look like this:

```
procedure TForm1.Edit1KeyPress(Sender: TObject; var Key: Char)
```

When the user presses a key, the ASCII code for the character is sent as the value of the Key parameter. Since it is a variable (**var**) parameter, you can make changes to it inside the event procedure and have them reflected in the original TEdit box. For example, if you have a line of code like this:

```
If Key = '!' Then Key = #0;
```

users will have any exclamation points they type blanked out.

 Note: There are two other key event procedures available. They let you deal with keys like control keys or combinations of keys that do not have standard ASCII codes. Check out the online help concerning OnKeyDown and OnKeyUp for more information.

6

 Pascal Tip: For compatibility reasons, Delphi still supports the older **value** parameters that indicate a parameter that is passed by value (that is, the compiler makes a copy of the variable, so memory and speed are an issue). However, **const** parameters have all the speed advantages of **var** parameters and none of the memory disadvantages. The built-in functions and procedures use them in place of the older **value** parameters.

Variable (**var**) parameters are *passed by reference* (that is, the compiler passes the memory location of the variable). This is what happens for **const** parameters as well, but with an extra step added. The compiler checks to see that you haven't made any assignments to the **const** parameter. If you have, the compiler generates a compile-time error. This avoids the overhead involved in making a copy as would be done if you used a **value** parameter.

Note: As event procedures themselves show, you can have parameters that are Delphi objects. You can also call an event procedure directly rather than having it triggered by an event (for example in a self-running demo). Please see Chapter 7 for more on both of these tasks.

The Built-in Runtime Library (RTL)

Table 6-3 provides short descriptions of the most common functions and procedures that you haven't already seen. (For file handling routines, please see Chapter 10.) Since there are hundreds of built-in functions and procedures, we suggest you work with the online help for more details. (Try starting at the "Procedures and Functions Categorical List" topic.)

RTL Routines	Description
Abs	Gives the absolute value of the argument
AnsiCompareStr	Case-sensitive string comparison
AnsiCompareText	Case-insensitive string comparison
AnsiLowerCase	Converts string to lowercase
AnsiUpperCase	Converts string to uppercase
AppendStr	Adds one string to another string
ArcTan	Gives the arc tangent of the argument in radians
Chr	Returns a character with a specific ASCII/ANSII code
CompareStr	Does a case-sensitive comparison of two strings
CompareText	Does a non-case-sensitive comparison of two strings
Concat	Joins together a sequence of strings
Copy	Makes a copy of part (a *substring*) of a string
Cos	Gives the cosine of the argument (the argument is assumed to be in radians)
Date	Gives the current date as stored in the system clock
DateTimeToStr	Converts a value from time format to a string
DateToStr	Converts a value from date format to a string
DayOfWeek	Returns the current day of the week
Delete	Removes a substring from a string
Exp	Raises e (the base of natural logs, e is about 2.718...) to a power specified by the argument

The Most Common Built-in RTL Routines

Table 6-3.

RTL Routines	Description
Frac	Gives the fractional part of the argument
Insert	Inserts a string into another string
Int	Gives the integer part of the argument, returns something of Real type
IntToHex	Converts an integer to its hexadecimal representation
IsValidIdent	Checks if the string is a valid Delphi identifier
Length	Gives the length of a string
Ln	Gives the natural logarithm of the argument
LowerCase	Changes the string to lowercase
Now	Gives the current date and time as stored in the system clock
Pi	Gives you the value of π to 14 places (3.14159...)
Pos	Lets you search for the position of a substring inside a string
Random	Returns a (pseudo-) random number
Randomize	Reseeds the built-in random number generator using the system clock
Round	Rounds a Floating Point-type value to return an Integer-type value
Sin	Gives the sine of the argument (the argument is assumed to be in radians)
Sqr	Provides a quick way to square an argument
Sqrt	Provides the quickest way to take the square root of the argument
StrPas	Converts a null-terminated string to a Pascal-style string; can only be used if the null-terminated string has fewer than 256 characters in Delphi 16
StrPCopy	Copies a Pascal-style string to a null-terminated string
StrToDate	Converts a string to a date format
StrToDateTime	Converts a string to a date/time format
StrToTime	Converts a string to a time format
Time	Gives the current time as shown in the system clock
Trunc	Truncates a Floating Point value and returns an Integer-type value
UpCase	Converts a character to uppercase
UpperCase	Converts the given string to uppercase

6

The Most Common Built-in RTL Routines (*continued*)

Table 6-3.

Note: In Delphi 32 the string RTL routines (subprograms) all work with long strings. In Delphi 16, they work only with the 255-character-limit strings. There is an entirely different set of functions for working with null-terminated (PChar type) strings. See the online help for more on these—you may need to use pointer arithmetic for these functions.

Note: As Table 6-3 indicates, there are many built-in RTL functions (like Round) that take arguments of one type and return values of another. You will find these type conversion functions very useful in a strongly typed language like Delphi.

Using the Windows API

Although they are not, strictly speaking, functions built into Delphi, you also have complete access to the many hundreds of specialized functions that make up Windows. These functions are usually called Windows Application Programming Interface (API) functions.

Caution: If you use API functions at all carelessly, your system will lock up, and you will have to reboot. We strongly suggest that you enable the Autosave options in the Preferences page of the Environment Options dialog box before experimenting with Windows API calls.

Most of the time, Delphi is rich enough in functionality that you don't need to bother with API functions. But some tasks, like learning which chip (such as an 80386 or a 486 or a Pentium class CPU) a computer is using, if a computer has a numeric coprocessor (such as an 80387 or a 486DX or a Pentium), or if the user has swapped the left for the right mouse button, must be done with an API function. You can even use an API function, ExitWindows, to end Windows. (However, if you need to use the Windows API extensively, be prepared for a lengthy study—the standard references for the API run around 2,000 pages, and there are both subtle and not-so-subtle differences between the 16-bit and the 32-bit API.)

Tip: Both versions of Delphi come with the appropriate version of the Windows API reference that is adapted to Delphi's syntax (rather than C syntax). You can copy and paste the function headers for the API functions inside your program freely.

One of the simplest useful Delphi 16 API functions is the GetWinFlags function that returns a long integer. (The closest Win 32 counterpart is called GetSystemInfo.) You can use this integer to determine what kind of processor the computer is using. Here's an example of the code you need in Delphi 16 (it will not run under Delphi 32):

```
var
 NeedToAnalyze: Longint;
begin
  NeedToAnalyze := GetWinFlags;
  if (NeedToAnalyze and WF_80x87) = WF_80x87 then
     ShowMessage('You have a math coprocessor');
  if (NeedToAnalyze and WF_CPU286) = WF_CPU286 then
     ShowMessage('You still have a 286 chip?');
```

As another example of using a Windows API function, consider the GetSystemMetrics function. The syntax for this function looks like this:

function GetSystemMetrics(*Index*: Integer): Integer;

In this case, you send this function an integer value that tells the function what information you want reported back. (Most of the constants you need are available as built-in constants in Delphi—check the API online help for them.) The GetSystemMetrics function gives you very detailed information about the system used by your application. For example, you can use this API function to find out if Windows is reporting that a mouse is in use or if the mouse buttons have been swapped. Here's a fragment that checks whether there is a mouse:

6

```
If GetSystemMetrics(SM_MOUSEPRESENT)<> 0 Then
  ShowMessage('You have a mouse.');
```

Note: Windows API calls often require that you send them the object's *handle*. In Delphi this is the value of the (run-time) property called, naturally enough, Handle. The Handle property is available for all windowed components.

User-Defined Functions and Procedures

As with any sophisticated programming language, Delphi allows you to break up the code for your program into manageable pieces. Like Visual Basic (but unlike C), Delphi distinguishes between functions, which generally return values, and procedures, which do not. In Delphi, the term "subprograms" refers to both functions and procedures. The term is useful if it helps you keep in mind that, for all practical purposes, functions and procedures act like miniprograms. In particular, they can have their own type, constants, typed constants, and variable declarations defined inside them. They can even have subprograms of their own embedded inside them. (The reason to embed one subprogram inside another is because of the scope rules for subprograms. An embedded subprogram is local to the container subprogram and cannot be used by other parts of the program. Similarly, variables declared in an embedded subprogram are local to that subprogram.)

Note: How much to modularize a program is a matter of taste. I like to keep both event procedure and subprograms to one screen length or so.

For example, here's a function that counts the number of times a character appears in a string and returns this (integer) value:

```
function CountOccurrences(const Foo: String; const WhichChar:
Char): Integer;
var
  i, count, LengthOfString: Integer;
begin
  LengthOfString := Length(Foo);
  count := 0;
  for i := 1 to LengthOfString do
    begin
      if foo[i] = WhichChar then Count := Count + 1;
    end;
  CountOccurrences := Count;
end;
```

The idea of this function illustrates many standard concepts. First off, notice the *function header:*

```
function CountOccurrences(const Foo: String; const WhichChar:
Char): Integer;
```

A subprogram must begin with a header. The header begins by specifying whether it is a function or a procedure. The header must also name the subprogram and list the parameters. The name of a subprogram must follow the standard rules for an identifier in Delphi (see Chapter 4). Parameters must have their type declared using the colon, and they are separated from one another by semicolons. In fact, the general syntax for parameters in user-defined functions and procedures is the same as for built-in subprograms. For example, you can have **var** parameters, **const** parameters, or **value** parameters. (For the CountOccurrences function given earlier, the parameters are all **const** parameters—because we do not want the original values of the parameters to change.)

Functions, since they return values, must have a return type declared at the end of the header. (In our example, the return type is Integer.) Finally, the return value of a function is given by the (final) assignment to its name. In our example, this is the line

```
CountOccurrences := Count;
```

You can also use the implicitly defined local variable Result to capture the final value of a function. For example, adding this line in the preceding function:

```
Result := Count;
```

6

would be another way to capture the final value for the function. Here's a somewhat shorter version of the previous program that uses Result.

```
function CountOccurrences(const SearchStr: String;
const WhichChar: Char): Integer;
var
  Index : Integer;
begin
  Result := 0;  {Use Result instead of the procedure name}
  for Index := 1 to Length(SearchStr) do
     if SearchStr[Index] = WhichChar then Inc(Result);;
end;
```

As an example of a procedure, let's write one that takes a string and two different characters and changes all occurrences of the first character to the second. It might look like this:

```
procedure ChangeOldCharToNew(var Foo: String;
const OldChar, NewChar: Char);
var
  i, LengthOfString: Integer;
begin
  LengthOfString := Length(Foo);
  for i := 1 to LengthOfString do
    begin
      if Foo[i] = OldChar then Foo[i] := NewChar;
    end;
end;
```

Notice that in this case, we do want to change the original string, so we make it a **var** parameter. But we do not want to change the other two parameters, so we leave them as **const** parameters.

Positioning Subprograms

You always place a subprogram in the **implementation** section of the unit. These subprograms can be used (the jargon is "called") by any event procedure or subprogram in the same unit that is defined *after* it. (You can get around this limitation. See the section "Recursion" later in this chapter.)

Recall that the uses clause of a unit tells you which units it can call. However, if you want a specific subprogram in a unit (say a unit named Unit1) to be usable by the subprograms in another unit (say Unit2), you must not only add the appropriate identifier to the uses clause of Unit2 (add a Unit1 to the uses clause of Unit2), but you also need to place a copy of the header for the subprogram in the **interface** section of the original unit (Unit1, in our case).

Subprograms whose headers are given in the **interface** section are *global* in scope. For example, event procedures headers are always given in the **interface** section, so they can be used by other units after the appropriate modification to the calling unit's uses clause.

Using Subprograms

When you can call a procedure from inside its own unit, you use its name and enclose whatever parameters are needed inside parentheses. For example, suppose we want to have a TButton component that changes all the occurrences of "U" in the Edit1 box to "W." Add the procedure

ChangeOldCharToNew defined earlier to the **implementation** section of the form, and use code like this:

```
procedure TForm1.Button1Click(Sender: TObject);
var
  TempStr : String;
begin
  TempStr := Edit1.Text;
  ChangeOldCharToNew(TempStr, 'I', 'W');
  Edit1.Text := TempStr;
end;
```

If you call a function, however, you normally either assign it to a value or use it in an expression. For example:

```
procedure TForm1.Button1Click(Sender: TObject);
var
  TempStr : String;
begin
  If CountOccurrences(Edit1.Text, 'U') = 0 Then
    ShowMessage('No ''U'' to change')
  else begin
    TempStr := Edit1.Text;
    ChangeOldCharToNew(TempStr, 'U', 'W');
    Edit1.Text := TempStr;
  end;
```

N ote: If you have the extended syntax compile option on, you can use a function like a procedure and disregard the return value.

6

Finally, if you need to call a global subprogram (one declared in the **interface** section) from another unit, use the name of the unit followed by a period. For example, once you add Unit2 to the uses clause of Unit1, you can call a procedure in Unit2 from Unit1 with code that looks like this:

```
Unit2.NameOfProcedure(parameters);
```

Passing Arrays to Subprograms

Delphi, following Turbo Pascal 7, allows you to use *open* parameters for passing arrays to subprograms. Open parameters give you the flexibility of passing any array to a subprogram without needing to declare the array's limits beforehand. To use an open parameter in a subprogram, first declare an array type. Then declare a variable in the parameter list to be of that type, as shown in the following syntax:

ArrayName: array[StartIndex..EndIndex] of Type

Once you have done this, you can use the built-in functions Low and High to determine the first and last indexes in the array. For example, if you wanted to write a general function to calculate the average of an integer array, you could use

```
function AverageValue(IntegerArray: Array Of Integer): Double;
var
  NumberOfEntries, i: Integer;
  Total: Longint;
begin
  Total := 0;
  NumberOfEntries := High(IntegerArray) - Low(IntegerArray) + 1;
  For i :=  Low(IntegerArray) to High(IntegerArray) do
    Total := Total + IntegerArray[i];
  AverageValue := Total/NumberOfEntries;
end;
```

Using External DLLs

You can write almost anything in Delphi, so there is rarely a need to call functions written with other languages. The most common exceptions are

♦ The occasional use of the Windows API that you have seen earlier in this chapter

♦ Library functions written in C or C++

The first point to remember is that C/C++ functions are case sensitive and Delphi's are not. The second problem is that the stack is popped in opposite order in the default C/C++ convention. It is therefore *much* easier if the C/C++ code was compiled with the PASCAL keyword in the function header. Trust me: you do not want to deal with the problems of trying to use a DLL whose exported functions were not compiled with this keyword.

However, if the exported functions in the DLL were compiled with the PASCAL keyword in their headers (and, in fact, most DLLs are), using a DLL from Delphi is not difficult. The trick is that you need to know the names of the exported functions in the DLL. This is simple, *providing you know and have access to the compiler that created the DLL or a tool like BoundsChecker.* For example, all compilers have a tool for analyzing the contents of a DLL to find the names of the exported functions. In Borland C++ the tool is called TDUMP.EXE.

Suppose you have a procedure called @InfiniteMultiply that you want to call that is in a library called BigArithmetic. Since you can't use an @ in the name of a Delphi procedure, you need to give it an alias. Put the following code in the **implementation** section of the unit for Delphi 16:

```
procedure InfiniteMultiply; {Delphi 16}
  far; external 'BigArithmetic' name @InfiniteMultiply;
```

and, in Dephi 32:

```
procedure InfiniteMultiply; {Delphi 32}
   external 'BigArithmetic.dll' PASCAL name '@InfiniteMultiply';
```

Now you can use the InfiniteMultiply function just like any other Delphi function.

Note: In Delphi 32 there is no concept of far calls. Thus, the far keyword is removed, and you must specify the calling convention of a C DLL because Delphi 32's default calling convention is FastCall. This passes parameters different than the usual Pascal calling convention.

Recursion

Recursion is a general method of solving problems by reducing them to simpler problems of a similar type. The general framework for a recursive solution to a problem looks like this:

> Solve recursively (problem)
>   If the problem is trivial, do the obvious
>   Simplify the problem
> Solve recursively (simpler problem)
>   (Possibly) combine the solution to the simpler problem(s)
>   into a solution of the original problem

A recursive subprogram constantly calls itself, each time in a simpler situation, until it gets to the trivial case, at which point it stops. For the experienced programmer, thinking recursively presents a unique perspective on certain problems, often leading to particularly elegant solutions and,

6

therefore, equally elegant programs. For example, most of the very fast sorts such as QuickSort are recursive.

For Delphi programmers, beside sorting routines, one common use of recursion is when you need to deal with the subdirectory structure of a disk. For example, if you wanted to delete a file but didn't know where it was, you would need to search on deeper and deeper subdirectories until you had exhausted all the subdirectories on that disk.

There are actually two types of recursion possible. In the first, the subprogram only calls itself. This is called *direct recursion*. Using direct recursion in Delphi is simple—just call the subprogram the way you would call any subprogram. The second type is called *indirect recursion*. This occurs, for example, when a subprogram calls another subprogram, which in turn calls the first subprogram.

Let's look at the standard example of the greatest common divisor (GCD) of two integers. (For those who have forgotten their high school mathematics, this is defined as the largest number that divides both of them. It's used when you need to add fractions.) Therefore

GCD(4,6) = 2 (because 2 is the largest number that divides both 4 and 6)
GCD(12,7) = 1 (because no integer greater than 1 divides both 12 and 7)

Around 2,000 years ago, Euclid gave the following method of computing the GCD of two integers, *a* and *b*:

If *b* divides *a*, then the GCD is *b*. Otherwise,
GCD(*a*,*b*) = GCD(*b*, *a* mod *b*)

(Recall that the mod function gives the remainder after integer division.) For example:

GCD(126, 12) = GCD(12, 126 mod 12) = GCD(12, 6) = 6

Here's the code for a recursive GCD function:

```
function GCD (Const P, Q: Integer): Integer;
begin
  If Q mod P = 0 Then
    GCD := P
  else
    GCD := GCD(Q, P mod Q);
end;
```

Here the pattern is to first take care of the trivial case. If you are not in the trivial case, then the code reduces it to a simpler case—because the mod function leads to smaller numbers. (In this example, there is no need to combine results as there would be in, say, a sorting routine.)

The second type of recursion, indirect recursion, is where a function or procedure calls itself via an intermediary. For example, function A calls function B, but B also calls A. The problem with using this type of recursion in Delphi is that Delphi doesn't ordinarily let one subprogram call a subprogram that is defined after it.

The way around this is with a special type of declaration called a *forward declaration*. To make a forward declaration, add the keyword **forward** and a semicolon at the end of the header of the subprogram. Then place the header with the extra forward declaration before the code for the subprogram that will call it.

Here's an example of using a **forward** declaration:

```
procedure TheSecondOne(foo: Integer); forward;
procedure TheFirstOne(bar: Integer);
begin
  TheSecondOne(1);
end;
procedure TheSecondOne(foo: Integer);
var
  I: Integer;
begin
  for I = 1 to foo do
    ShowMessage('This is now OK');
end;
```

Note: If you use very complicated recursive procedures, you may need to enlarge Delphi 16's default stack size (16,384 bytes). This can be done via the Linker page of the Project Options dialog box. The maximum size of the stack in Delphi 16 is 65,536 bytes. (In Delphi 32 it defaults to 1 megabyte and can be increased.)

6

Managing Projects and Units

Projects store all the information for your application while it is being developed. The dialog box that pops up when you choose View | Project Manager lets you get easy access to the forms and units in your project. From this dialog box, you can add or remove forms and units as well.

Most of the options for a project are set from the various pages of the Project Options dialog box. For example, as you saw in the last chapter, you use the

Forms page to determine which forms Delphi will automatically create. As another example, you can choose the icon that Delphi will use for the stand-alone executable from the Application page of this dialog box. (We cover the Compiler page in the "Compiler Essentials" section. For the parts of this Project Options dialog box that we do not cover, please consult the online help.)

A project is made up of a single Project file (.DPR) that lists all the forms and units in the project. Although you can look at and even edit the Project file by choosing View | Project Source, generally speaking, let Delphi maintain the DPR file. You only have to work with the DPR file when you are creating a DLL rather than a stand-alone application or need some start-up code, such as a splash screen before the main form is created by Delphi.

Tip: It is a good idea to use a separate directory for each project— you will usually store all the files in each project there. Otherwise, Delphi defaults to storing them all in its own \BIN directory, which will get awfully unwieldy.

Whether you run a project from the development environment or make it into a stand-alone file, Delphi uses the name of the Project file for the name of the EXE file that it creates. You can control where Delphi places the resulting EXE file by using the Directories | Conditionals page on the Project Options dialog box (the default is Delphi's \BIN directory).

Tip: Since Delphi actually creates an EXE file every time you run a program from the development environment, you may need to periodically clean out Delphi's \BIN directory of unneeded EXE files—if you do not change this option.

More on Units

Since units store the code for your project, units are the basis of Delphi programming. When you start building libraries of useful routines, you will probably store them in a unit. The possibility of building up a project out of units makes it easier to add a library of tested routines to your project. For example, when you buy a third-party tool, it will probably come as a unit. Many programs make it a habit to put all their programming code in units and just have the event handlers call the appropriate procedure or function.

♦ To add a new unit in Delphi 32, choose File I New from the File menu and then click on the New Unit icon and click on the OK button in the dialog box..

♦ To add a new unit in Delphi 16, simply choose File I New Unit.

Tip: If you often need to share units between projects, consider putting the units you will share into a special directory and setting the Search Path box on the Directories/Conditionals page of the Project Options dialog box accordingly.

Every time you create a new form (that is, a DFM file), Delphi automatically creates its associated unit (.PAS file). All units can have user-defined types, global and local variables, subprogram declarations, and the like. Whenever you create a unit, Delphi adds the following automatically to its definition:

♦ Unit heading

♦ **interface** section

♦ **implementation** section

Note: A unit must end with the keyword **end** followed by a period.

6

A fourth part, called the **initialization** section, is optional in both versions of Delphi. Delphi 32 allows a new **finalization** section that you can use for code you want to be processed when the application shuts down.

Note: The **finalization** section in Delphi 32 corresponds to the ExitProc in Delphi 16.

The following sections briefly describe these parts of a unit.

Unit Heading

The unit heading begins with the keyword **unit** and then gives the unit's name. The default unit names are Unit1, Unit2, and so on. You need to use the unit's name when you refer to the unit in the uses clause of another unit.

Note: You should never change the name of a unit except via the File | Save As option. Otherwise your project files will get messed up.

Whatever name you use to save the unit becomes the unit's name. Of course, the name must be unique, and Delphi will not let you use two units with the same name at the same time, nor a project with the same name as a unit. The rules for a name of a unit must follow the standard eight-character naming convention for DOS files in Delphi 16 and the 255-character limit in Delphi 32, and must have a .PAS extension. If you save the unit with a name like MyFirstUnit.PAS, then the unit will be called MyFirstUnit in any **uses** clause.

interface Section

The **interface** section contains the **uses** clause that lists the other units that will be used by your project. Delphi automatically adds the standard units such as SysUtils, Controls to the uses clause of a form's unit. As you add new components to a form, Delphi adds the appropriate names to the **uses** clause of the form automatically as well. Once units are added, though, Delphi doesn't remove them even if the components that required them are removed from the project.

Note: Delphi does not add a **uses** clause to the **interface** section of the code units you create—you need to do that manually.

As you saw earlier, the **interface** section is where you declare *global* constants, types, variables, procedures, and functions (that is, things that you want to be visible to all the units that use the unit). As you also saw earlier, only the headings for these global procedures and functions are given in the **interface** section.

Pascal Tip: If you want to reuse a unit created with an earlier version of Borland Pascal for Windows that uses WinCrt, be sure to add the WinCrt unit to the **uses** clause of that unit. WinCrt is not added automatically to the **uses** clause of a form's unit, although some early versions of the documentation in Delphi 16 say it is.

You should also be aware that Delphi automatically adds the necessary declarations for the visual parts of your form to the **interface** section of the unit associated to the form—see Chapter 7 for more on this. You will almost never want to change information that Delphi adds to the **interface** section of a form's unit.

implementation Section

This is where you place the code for the procedures and functions, whether or not they are declared in the **interface** section. Any Delphi objects declared here will be available only to code within the unit. The **implementation** section of a form's unit starts with a compiler directive that looks like this:

```
{$R *.DFM}
```

Do not accidentally erase this, as this is the line of code that tells Delphi to link in the form's visual (DFM) part and is where external references are resolved like DLL prototypes..

initialization Section

This section is optional. It is not automatically generated when you create a unit. You must insert the keyword **initialization**, followed by any statements you want executed in order to initialize the unit. Delphi initializes units in the order that the units appear in the uses clause of the main form.

6

Pascal Tip: Delphi recognizes the older **begin** keyword as well as the newer **initialization** keyword but this confuses the IDE and should be avoided.

Compiler Essentials

When you compile your project into a stand-alone application, you can change the kind of code Delphi generates by using compiler options. The most commonly used compiler options are available on the Compiler page of the Project Options dialog box (Options | Project in Delphi 16). Some of the options, like Pentium Safe FDIV (division), have their fans, while others, like Extended syntax, are useful when you know your program will work with PChar and null-terminated (large) strings. Many options—for example, the ones listed in the Debugging section of this dialog box—are usually turned on when developing a project but turned off for the final compile, because they bloat and slow down your code.

 Note: You can also insert compiler options directly into code by using the appropriate switch. To use one of these directives in code, place the switch (as given previously or in the online help) inside comment braces and precede it with a $. Compiler directives usually need to be placed before the declaration part of the unit you are compiling. Use a + sign to turn it on and a – sign to turn it off. For example, {$X+} turns on extended syntax, while {$X–} turns it off.

You can also have Delphi compile your code into a dynamic link library (DLL) so that it can be used by other Windows programs. To do this, you need to manually edit the Delphi DPR (project) file in the following way:

1. Change the keyword **program** to the keyword **library**.
2. Remove the reference to the Forms unit from the uses clause in the DPR file.
3. Remove *all* the code between the begin/end pair.
4. Add the **exports** keyword as the line above the begin/end block.
5. Add any units to the **uses** clause that have functions or procedures to be exported.
6. List all the function headers you want to export after the **exports** keyword.

For more details on how to do this, consult the online help topic "Compiling a Project into a DLL" or the "Component Writers Guide" supplied with Delphi.

Common Compiler Options
We now briefly discuss the most important options available on the Compiler page that are common to both versions of Delphi.

Default Check Box   If you check this box, Delphi will save the current project options to be used in every new project.

Pentium-Safe FDIV   This generates code that detects the infamous floating-point Pentium bug! This corresponds to {$U}.

Range Checking   This checks that array and string subscripts are within bounds. Having this option on will slow your code down, so it is most often used only during the development cycle. This corresponds to {$R}.

Stack Checking   This checks that space is available for local variables when you call a procedure or use recursion. It slows code down, so it, too, often is used only in development. This corresponds to {$S}.

I/O Checking   This checks for input /output (I/O) errors after every I/O call. It is better to use exceptions (see Chapter 8). This corresponds to {$I}.

Overflow Checking   This checks overflow for integer operations. Again, this is a very useful option to have on during testing. This corresponds to {$Q}.

Strict Var-Strings   When this option is on, Delphi lets you, for example, pass a string of size 20 to a procedure expecting a string of size 255. This corresponds to {$V}. When you have Open parameters selected, this option doesn't apply.

Complete Boolean Eval   Usually you want this option off. When it is on, Delphi checks all the expressions in a Boolean expression rather than stopping when it knows enough. For example, if you use the and operator on two expressions and the first expression is False, there's no need to evaluate the next one. This corresponds to {$B}.

6

Extended Syntax   This is needed for PChar support (see the section "Null-Terminated Strings and PChar" earlier in this chapter). This also lets you call a function just like a procedure by ignoring the function result. This corresponds to {$X}.

Typed @ Operator   This controls whether Delphi checks if pointer assignments make sense. It controls the type of pointer returned by the @ operator. This corresponds to {$T}.

Open Parameters   This is a good one to have on. This lets you use open string parameters in procedure and function declarations. This corresponds to {$P}.

Debugging Information Options   These options are covered in more detail in Chapter 9. Generally, however, these options should be on during development and off for the final compile.

Unique Delphi 32 Compiler Options

We now briefly discuss the most important options available on the Compiler page for Delphi 32 that are not available in Delphi 16.

Optimization   This is a good one to have checked, and it is checked by default. If you let it, Delphi 32 uses some extremely good optimizations for its code. You can turn this off to speed compilation during the development cycle.

Aligned Record Fields   This aligns the elements in a data structure to correspond to 32-bit boundaries. Equivalent to {$A}.

Assignable Typed Constants   Enable this for backward compatibility with Delphi 16. When enabled, the compiler allows assignments to typed constants. Corresponds to {$S}.

Huge Strings   This sets the default for the String type to be long strings.

Show Hints   Determines whether Hint messages are shown.

Show Warnings   Determines whether warning messages are shown.

Unique Delphi 16 Compiler Options

Here are the most important options available on the Compiler page for Delphi 16 that are not available in Delphi 32.

Force Far Calls   This is a fairly esoteric switch that is only necessary because of the segmented architecture of the Intel chip. There are essentially no circumstances under which you want this option to be on. The Delphi compiler is usually sufficiently intelligent to know when to use Far Calls. This corresponds to {$F}.

Word Align Data   This enlarges your program by making the data more easily accessible. It adds filler to make sure that your data is stored on even-numbered addresses. Because of certain peculiarities in the Intel chip architecture, putting this filler in by having this option on *may* speed up your program. You might want to experiment with both possibilities before doing the final compile. This corresponds to {$A}.

Smart Callbacks   *Always leave this on!* Otherwise you have to start really messing around with Windows messages. This corresponds to {$K}.

Windows Stack Frame   Leave this off unless you absolutely need to generate code that may run under Windows 3.0. (We say "may" because we don't think a lot of time was spent checking Delphi's ability to generate Windows 3.0 compatible code.) This corresponds to {$W}.

Pascal **Note:**   This switch may be needed when compiling older OWL-based programs.

Conditional Compilation

Often you want to produce two versions of the same project without maintaining two versions of the source code. This is especially common when dealing with language issues involved in internationalizing products. It would obviously be nice if you could maintain only one file with the source code and have Delphi do the bookkeeping in the various cases. The key to this is what is usually called *conditional compilation*.

Here's an example:

```
{$DEFINE FRENCH}
{$IFDEF FRENCH}
ShowMessage ('Bon-jour.');
{$ELSE}
ShowMessage ('Good day.');
{$ENDIF}
```

Similarly, you can leave debug code in your source code and either compile the source code or not by commenting out a statement like:

   {$DEFINE DEBUG}

or under Windows 95 you can use:

   {IFDEF WIN32}

6

The following table summarizes the condition compilation switches:

Conditional Switch	What It Does
$DEFINE	Defines the conditional compilation symbol and sets it to True
$ELSE	Used when the conditional compilation symbol is not in effect
$ENDIF	Ends the conditional compilation
$IFNDEF	Compiles when the symbol is not currently in effect
$UNDEF	Sets a previously true conditional compilation symbol to False

 Note: Unfortunately, it is very difficult to take advantage of the different features of Delphi 32 simply via conditional compilation. Generally, features like large strings require too much conditionally compiled code to be practical.

The goto

Like most programming languages, Delphi retains the unconditional jump or goto. To paraphrase the old joke about split infinitives—modern programmers may be divided into three groups: those who neither know nor care about when they should use the goto, those who do not know but seem to care very much, and those who know *when* to use it.

Obviously, routine use of the goto leads to spaghetti code: code that is hard to read and harder to debug. On the other hand, there are times when using the goto actually makes your code cleaner and easier to understand. (In Delphi this situation typically comes up when you are deep inside a nested loop and some condition forces you to leave all the loops simultaneously. You can't use **break** because all that does is get you out of the loop you are currently in.)

To use a goto in Delphi, you must first declare a label by using the keyword label followed by the identifier for the label—separate the identifiers by commas if there is more than one. Like any declaration, label declarations end with a semicolon. Here's an example:

```
label
  BadInput, BadOutput;
```

Labels must be defined before the code block and must follow the rules for Delphi variables, although you can use numerals between 1 and 9999. Use as descriptive a label as possible.

You can use a previously declared label at any point in the code block after its declaration (you cannot jump out of a unit). To do this, place the label identifier on its own line followed by a colon:

```
BadInput:
  {Code we want to process can goto here}:
```

For example, suppose we are using a nested For loop to input data and want to leave the loop if the user enters a 'ZZZ':

```
var
  i, j: Integer;
  GetData: String;
  cells : array[1..10,1..100] of string[20];
label
  BadInput;
begin
  for i := 1 to 10 do
    for j := 1 to 100 do
    begin
      GetData := InputBox('Data Input', 'Enter data, ZZZ to end', '')
      if GetData = 'ZZZ' then
        goto BadInput
      else
        cells[i,j] := GetData;
    end;
BadInput:
  ShowMessage('Data entry ended at user request');
```

6

Notice how using the **break** keyword would be cumbersome here. For example, it would require extra code in order to break completely out of the nested loop.

Chapter 7

Objects

At this point, you are probably pretty comfortable with the basic techniques for manipulating Delphi's built-in objects. To go further with Delphi, however, you need to know something about Delphi's implementation of object-oriented programming. Object-oriented programming (OOP) seems to be the dominant programming paradigm these days, having replaced the "structured" programming techniques that were developed in the early '70s. If you haven't worked with objects before, you are probably wondering what all the hoopla is about. This chapter is designed to show you (well, at least to give you a glimpse). Since there's a fair amount of terminology needed to make sense of OOP, we'll start with some concepts and definitions. After this, we'll show you the basics of how Delphi implements OOP.

I should note, however, that it is possible to write endlessly about object-oriented programming. A quick survey of *Books In Print* shows there are more than 150 books about object-oriented programming, and more seem to appear each week. Fully describing OOP as implemented in Delphi would take a book at least as long as this one—and probably much longer. I intend only to introduce you to OOP in this chapter. In particular, I do not discuss how to build your own visual components in Delphi. For this, please refer to the *Component Writer's Guide* supplied with Delphi (which, I cannot help pointing out, is roughly one half the length of this book and is, unfortunately, quite sketchy nonetheless).

Getting Started

Let's start with a question that, on the surface, seems to have nothing to do with programming: How did Gateway 2000 become a billion-dollar company faster than any other company in American history? Most people would probably say they made good computers and sold them at rock-bottom prices. But go further—how did they do *that*? Well, a big part of the answer is that they farmed out a lot of the work. They bought components from reputable vendors and then assembled them. They didn't invest any money in designing and building power supplies, disk drives, motherboards, and so on. This made it possible for them to have a good product at a low price.

Ask yourself for a second how this could work. The obvious (and to a large extent, correct) answer is that what they were buying was "prepackaged functionality." For example, when they bought a power supply, they were buying something with certain properties (size, shape, and so on) and a certain functionality (smooth power output, amount of power available, and so on). Object-oriented programming springs from the same idea. Your program is made up of objects with certain properties and functions. You depend on the objects to not interact in undocumented ways with other objects or the code in your project. Whether you build the object or buy it might depend on the state of your wallet or how much time you have free. In either case, as long as the objects satisfy your specifications, you don't much care how the functionality was implemented. In OOP, the way people put it is that what you care about is what the objects *expose*.

So, just as Gateway doesn't care about the internals of a power supply as long as it does what they want, most programmers don't need to care how the TButton component is implemented in Delphi as long as it does what *they* want. And, as you certainly know by now, on the whole, Delphi's objects do what you would expect them to!

The key to being most productive in object-oriented programming is to make your objects as complete as possible and, *as much as possible,* have the other objects and parts of your program tell the objects what to do. OOP jargon describes this by saying that what you do in object-oriented programming is *have clients send messages to objects*. By designing your objects to handle all appropriate messages and manipulate their data internally, you maximize reusability and minimize debugging time.

By this point you have seen pretty clear evidence that Delphi's built-in objects fit this paradigm well. They are extremely rich in functionality. Of course, occasionally you may need to add your own objects to Delphi by either buying them from third-party vendors or writing them yourself. Generally speaking, it is rarely worth reinventing the wheel. If it takes you 40 hours to build a component and you can buy it for $200, one should really ask: is it worth it? Commercial vendors such as MicroHelp produce quality products that are worth the (usually) small cost. I have always used commercial products in our applications and have been generally happy with the results (especially if the source code was supplied so that I can further customize the component if needed).

However, if you do have to write your own objects, another tenet of OOP makes this easier as well: objects can be built on other objects. When you do this, the new object starts out by inheriting all the properties and functions of its parent—you can pick and choose whether you want to keep or modify any property or function of the parent. Given the functionality built into Delphi and the third-party tools available, I suspect that you will almost never need to build a new visual component. What I find in my programming is that most of the objects I create are nonvisual and that I almost never create components. For example, if you are using Delphi 16, creating a BigString object that adds string functions for manipulating larger strings to Delphi 16 is an obvious thing to do. I used it a lot and it was worth the time needed to build it.

The Vocabulary of OOP

7

Traditional structured programming consists of designing the data structures and then manipulating them with functions in specific ways that are theoretically sure to terminate. (These are usually called algorithms.) This is why the designer of the original Pascal, Niklaus Wirth, called his famous book on programming *Algorithms + Data Structures = Programs* (Prentice Hall, 1976). Notice that in Wirth's title the algorithms came first and the data structures came after. This mimicked the way programmers worked at that time. First, you decided how to manipulate the data, then you decided what structure to impose on the data in order to make the manipulations easier. OOP puts both algorithms and data structures on the same level.

The rest of this section explains the basic terminology of OOP. There's a fair amount of it but it is worth learning for two reasons. The first is that you will need some of this terminology to understand the discussions in this chapter, the second is that knowing this terminology in absolutely necessary in order to read the *Component Writer's Guide*, or to go further with OOP.

Classes

A *class* is usually described as the template or blueprint from which the object is actually made. The standard way of thinking about classes is to think of them as the cookie cutter and the actual object as the cookie. The "dough" in the form of memory will sometimes need to be allocated as well. Delphi is pretty good about hiding this "dough preparation" step from you. When you create an object from a class, you are said to have *created an instance* of the class.

Encapsulation

This is the key concept in working with objects. Formally, *encapsulation* was nothing more than combining the data and behavior in one package. Some people like to think of an object as a special type (see Chapter 7) that not only has data but also functions and procedures built into it. This new type corresponds to the object's class and this is, in fact, the syntax used by Delphi for creating objects (see "Creating an Object in Delphi" later in this chapter). (In fact, in Delphi, objects really are simply a special type!)

 Note: The data in an object is usually called its *instance variables* or *fields*, and the functions and procedures are its *methods*.

A key rule in making encapsulation work is that programs should *never* (well, *almost* never) access the instance variables (fields) in an object directly. Programs should interact with this data only through the object's methods. (Properties in Delphi are designed to give you a way to interact with the instance variables without violating encapsulation.) Encapsulation is the way to give the object its "black box"-like behavior, which is the key to reuse and debugging efficiency.

Inheritance

Inheritance is the ability to make classes that descend from other classes. The purpose of inheritance is to make it easier to build code for specialized tasks. The instance variables and methods of the descendent (sometimes called the *subclasses*) start out being the same. This is efficient for the designers of the language: they always have a foundation on which to build the new class. For example, the designers of Delphi started out with a quite general edit box from which they built both masked edit boxes and ordinary edit boxes. Even more generally, all objects in Delphi descend from a single class called, naturally enough, TObject. Classes that other objects are built from are sometimes called *parent classes* or *base classes*.

Inheritance is efficient for the end programmer as well. For example, learning Delphi would be much more difficult if properties like Left and Top worked differently for the different components. Since all visible components descend from the same parent, they inherit the Left and Top properties from it. Since there was no need for the designers of Delphi to redefine how Left and Top work in other components, they behave the same for all components.

Another reason for the efficiency becomes apparent when you start to build your own components. If you need to build a custom edit box of your own, you can start out with the quite general parent of all the edit boxes (TCustomEdit) or with one of its children. By starting with the appropriate parent or base class, you know that much of the work has already been done for you. The collection of base classes and subclasses is called the *class hierarchy*. Class hierarchies are a bit like the species classifications you learned about in Biology: vertebrates are one of the subsets of chordates, and birds, mammals, reptiles, amphibians, and fishes are subsets of vertebrates. Delphi has its own hierarchy of objects, as shown in Figure 7-1. It is occasionally useful to know this. For more on the class hierarchy in Delphi see the section on the ObjectBrowser below.

Usually subclasses will use (inherit) the same methods as the parent class. OOP (and Delphi) allows you to define a new method in a subclass but give it the same name. This is called *overriding*. A true object-oriented language like Delphi allows you to go beyond simply overriding a method into what is usually called *polymorphism*. The idea behind polymorphism is that while the message may be the same, the *object* determines how to respond. Polymorphism can apply to any method that is inherited from a base class.

7

Polymorphism is vital because it makes a programmer's job simpler. For example, when you define a new object based on an existing object, you would not want to rebuild the parent's code in order to take into account that a new object exists. (Imagine some giant case statement in the parent class that just grows and grows!)

The key to making polymorphism work is called *late binding*. This means the compiler doesn't generate the code to call a method at compile time. Instead, every time you use a method with an object, the compiler generates

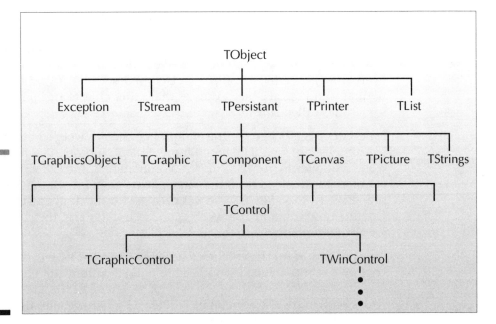

A simplified version of Delphi's Visual Component Library (VCL) object hierarchy

Figure 7-1.

code that lets it calculate which method to call using pointer information built into the object that called it.

Methods that allow late binding are called *virtual methods* because they do not exist in the .EXE file but are only potentially there.

Note: If it is a virtual method then a lookup is performed against the Virtual Method Table (VMT) (which contains the pointer to the routine) and if it is a dynamic or message method then a lookup is performed against the Dynamic Method Table (DMT).

Creating an Object in Delphi

Let's start by imagining that I want you to provide a toolkit for the designers of computer-generated card games. You obviously need an object that takes the place of a deck of cards. So that I don't get bogged down in a lot of details, let's make this a nonvisual object. As a first approximation (building objects also benefits from the stepwise refinement you have probably used in program development before), I decided that this object will have data (an instance variable) consisting of a 52-entry string array for the cards, and two procedures and one function for its methods. One procedure would initialize the cards, a second would shuffle them, and the function would deal a card.

The code for creating this nonvisual object might look like this: (Note this has some flaws that are discussed in the next section—I am giving the code only for the basic structure.)

```
type
  TDeckOfCards = class(TObject)   {Types usually start with a 'T'}}
  FCards: array [1..52] of Byte;  {Note: Fields in a class
usually start with an 'F'--FCards}
  procedure Initialize;  {This should actually be handled in a
Create constructor--see below}
  procedure Shuffle;
  function Deal(CardNumber: Integer): String;
end;
```

Note: When you define a new Delphi object, the definition usually goes below the type statement where the form itself was declared in the Interface section of a unit. You can also define a class in the Implementation section of a unit; however, it can only be used in that unit.

Let's go over this object declaration more closely. As mentioned before, syntactically speaking, an object declaration is a type declaration and usually occurs after the form declaration. Notice, however, that the first line must have the statement that derives the object from Delphi's basic class (TObject) using the syntax:

ObjectName = class(TObject)

Pascal Tip: Although for backward compatibility Delphi supports the Object keyword for creating objects, you are best off using the above syntax in order to descend from TObject. Among the other advantages of this descent is that the new object model allocates the memory for the class object on the global heap rather than the local heap automatically and also because the need for pointer dereferencing is eliminated.

7

Next come the declarations for the data (the instance variables or fields) and then come the declarations for the methods (functions and procedures) for this object. If I actually wanted to implement this object, I would then need to write the code for the various methods.

You actually write the functions and procedures that give the methods in the **implementation** part of the unit where the object is defined.

Constructors

The way I have written this object, we have a special procedure to initialize the object. Presumably, this would occur after the object was created. Although there is nothing wrong with this in theory. it is *much* safer to initialize the data fields (instance fields) at the same time the object is created. This avoids dealing with the case where the user of your class creates the object but forgets to initialize it. (Since Objects in Delphi are actually pointers, the result is a badly initialized pointer—and a likely GPF in Delphi 16 or an 'access violation' in Delphi 32.)

The way you initialize the data fields when an object is created is via a special procedure called a *constructor* that is declared inside the object. Constructors are special in the object model because they are automatically invoked when an object is created.

Like all object methods, the constructor method is declared in the object but the actual code is written after it. One way to write a constructor method is to use, naturally enough, the **constructor** keyword. Here's an example of this in the following rewritten version of the previous example.

```
type
  TDeckOfCards = class(TObject)
  FCards: array [1..52] of Byte;  {Note: Fields in a class
usually start with an 'F'-- hence FCards}
    Constructor Create; Virtual;  //makes this a virtual method
    procedure Shuffle;
    function Deal(CardNumber: Integer): String;
  end;
```

The actually code for the constructor must begin with the keyword **constructor** rather than the keyword **procedure**. For example:

```
constructor TDeckOfCards.Create;
var
  I: Integer;
begin
  for I :=1 To 52 do
     FCards[I] := I;
end;
```

Note: Constructors can take parameters.

One commonly confusing area when dealing with objects is deciding what parameters to use for its methods. For example, you might have expected the initialize constructor to take an FCards parameter. This is not the case and would give an error at compile time. The reason is each call to an object's methods (including the constructor method) implicitly includes a parameter for the object itself. Therefore, when you implement the method you can access the instance variables directly.

Note: There are also **destructors** that will be called when the object is about to be destroyed—you use these methods to free up any memory that was allocated for the object.

Further Refining the Deck of Cards Object

I thought about the DeckOfCards object some more and decided that it would be better to have the individual cards themselves be objects. That way I can further refine their definition (possibly including a visual component later on). I would then use an array of them as an instance field in a new Deck object. (Objects can have other objects as instance fields but the parent object needs to dynamically create and free the instance of the class object that it has as a field.) I further refine the model by allowing a create constructor, one procedure, and one function for its methods. The constructor would initialize the cards, a procedure would shuffle them, and the function would deal a card.

The type declarations for this nonvisual object might look like this:

```
type
  TCard = class(TObject)
  public {used for methods that should be accessible outside the
unit}
    FValue: Byte;
    FSuit: String[8];
    constructor Create(V : String; S: String); virtual;
  end;
type
  TDeckOfCards = class(TObject)
  private
      FCards : array [0..51] of TCard;
  public
      constructor Create; virtual;
      destructor Destroy; override;
{     procedure Shuffle; not yet written}
```

7

```
      procedure Deal(const I: Integer);
   end;
```

Notice that this more sophisticated object includes the optional **public** keyword. Things declared in the **public** section will be available to other units. (There can also be a **private** section for procedures that will not be visible to other units.) This means that as long as you are trying to access an object from the same unit, there is no difference between public and private. The syntax for using publicly declared data or methods just involves giving the name of the object or form. The general syntax for accessing a public method from another unit uses a period to identify the unit. An example of this looks like:

NameOfUnit.NameOfObject.NameOfPublicMethod

Note: There are two other possible keywords for the methods in an object in both versions of Delphi: **protected** and **published**. Protected methods can be used by the class itself and any new classes that are derived (descend) from it. The **published** keyword is essentially only used when you create components—so I refer you to the "Components Writers guide" for more details on this keyword. (There is also an Automated keyword for objects in Delphi 32—I refer you to the online help for this as well.)

The syntax for defining a method mimics Delphi's own: you use a period between the object's name and the name of the method. Defining the object type and its methods is not enough. To use the object, you must tell Delphi to create it (in OOP, this is usually called *instantiating an object by a constructor call*). The following code creates an instance of a deck and then uses a push button to check that the object was correctly instantiated.

```
type
  TCard = class(TObject)
  public
   FValue: String;
   FSuit: String[8];
   constructor Create(V : String; S: String);
  end;
type
  TDeckOfCards = class(TObject)
   public
      Cards : array [0..51] of TCard;
      constructor Create; Override;
      destructor Destroy; Override;
```

```
{      procedure Shuffle; not yet written}
       procedure Deal(const I: Integer);
   end;

type
  TForm1 = class(TForm)
    Button1: TButton;
    procedure Button1Click(Sender: TObject);
  private
  public
      MyDeckOfCards: TDeckOfCards;
  end;

var
  Form1: TForm1;

implementation

{$R *.DFM}

constructor TCard.Create(V: String; S: String);
begin
  inherited Create;
  FValue := V;
  FSuit:= S;
end;

constructor TDeckOfCards.Create;
var
  I: Integer;
  Value: String;
  Suit: String;
  SuitInteger: Integer;
  C: TCard;
begin
  inherited Create;
  for I := 0 to 51 do
    begin
      Value := IntToStr(I mod 13);
      SuitInteger := I div 13;
      case SuitInteger of
        0: Suit := 'Clubs';
        1: Suit := 'Diamonds';
        2: Suit := 'Hearts';
        3: Suit := 'Spades';
      end;
      C := TCard.Create(Value, Suit);
      FCards[I] := C;
```

7

```
    end;
  end;

destructor TDeckOFCards.Destroy;
var
  I: Integer;
begin
  for I := 0 to 51 do
    FCards[I].Free;
end;

procedure TDeckOfCards.Deal(const I: Integer);
var
  TestString: String;
begin
    TestString := FCards[I].FValue + ' of ' + FCards[I].FSuit;
    ShowMessage(TestString);
end;
{quick test procedure}

procedure TForm1.Button1Click(Sender: TObject);
var
  I: Integer;

begin
  I := 5;
  MyDeckOfCards := TDeckOfCards.Create;
  MyDeckOfCards.Deal(I);
  {Usually objects such as this one would created in the Form's
   OnCreate event and destroyed in the form's 'OnDestroy event.}
end;

end.
```

Notice, as always, you must first declare the type of any variable. By declaring it in the public section of TForm1, we are sure that the lifetime will be as long as the form is around.

```
public
      MyDeckOfCards: TDeckOfCards;
```

The syntax to create our example is

```
MyDeckOfCards := TDeckOfCards.Create;
```

Delphi's Create method is what tells Delphi to set aside memory for your object. (Objects in Delphi are actually pointers.) For this reason, you must be sure to release the memory when you are done with your object. You do this with the Free method (which I placed in the Destructor methods).

Note: In actual practice, you must be sure that Delphi processes the Free method. You do this by placing the Create/Free methods in a **try/finally** block as described in Chapter 8.

Visual Component Library Objects

If you have looked at a unit both before and after you added new components, you have probably observed the dramatic changes that Delphi made in the code. Most of these changes occur when you create new Delphi objects from the Visual Component Library, or VCL as it is usually called.

It's worth going over a little bit more closely the code added to a unit when you add components. So, start up a new project and bring up the unit for it. Notice that the lines right below the **uses** clause in the Interface section for a form look like this:

```
type
  TForm1 = class(TForm)
```

Here's what's going on under the hood:

♦ By using the **class** keyword I know Delphi is creating a new object derived from the TForm object type.

♦ Since the object declaration is in the **interface** section, other units can have access to this object.

Next, you see the lines that looks like this:

```
var
  Form1: TForm1;
```

This indicates that Delphi is declaring a new variable of type TForm1.

Next, add a component, say, a TButton, to this form. The type declaration below the **uses** clause now changes to:

```
type
  TForm1 = class(TForm)
    Button1: TButton;
```

7

Notice that Delphi has automatically added a Button1 instance variable (field) to the TForm1 object. Finally, add a button and its OnClick event procedure to your form. The type clause changes to:

```
type
  TForm1 = class(TForm)
    Button1: TButton;
    procedure Button1Click(Sender: TObject);
```

If all of this is starting to look like the definition of the DeckOfCards object, you are not seeing things. A key point in working with Delphi is to realize that what Delphi is really doing is making it easier for you to create visual objects that have certain methods associated with them. As this example shows, your form is itself a Delphi object. More precisely, this code shows that Delphi has written the code for you that is needed to create a new visual object (in our case, a window with a button on it). And, of course, Delphi objects inherit from the VCL an incredible amount of functionality! (One nice extra benefit of having Delphi create the declarations is that it makes any necessary changes as you add or remove components. Delphi also takes care of allocating memory for components from the VCL. You don't have to worry about freeing up the memory for objects created from the Visual Component Library.)

 Note: Be sure that you don't put your own object definitions in the type statement that Delphi maintains for the form. (Declarations of object variables are fine though.) This information is saved in the form file (.DFM) and any changes will make it difficult (sometimes impossible) for Delphi to create the form.

The Private and Public Regions of a Form Declaration

If you look further at the type statement that defines a form when you first use it, you see that there are seven lines that look like this:

```
type
  TForm1 = class(TForm}
  private
    {Private declarations}
  public
    {Public declarations}
  end;
```

As with objects you create, the main difference is that any data or methods declared in the **private** section will not be visible to other units, and anything declared in the **public** section will be available to other units. (This means that as long as you are trying to access a component from the same unit, there is no difference between **public** and **private**.) The syntax for using publicly declared data or methods also just involves giving the name of the form. The general syntax for accessing a public method from another form uses a period. It looks like this:

NameOfForm.NameOfPublicMethod

The Sender Parameter

By now you have seen that all event procedures use a Sender parameter of type TObject. Since TObject is the starting place for all the objects in the Visual Component Library, the Sender parameter, when used properly, can give an incredible amount of flexibility in your code. What the Sender parameter does is let you know which component triggered the event. This makes it easy to use the same event procedure for two different components. For example, suppose you want to have a button and a menu item do the same thing. It would be silly to have to write the same event procedure twice. To share an event procedure in Delphi, do the following:

1. Write the event procedure for the first object.
2. Select the new object or objects.
3. Go to the Event page on the Object Inspector.
4. Click the down arrow that appears in right column of the event you want to share. (Delphi will give you a list of all the compatible event procedures that exist on the form.)
5. Select the event from the drop-down list.

That's all you need to do. Delphi will now call the shared event procedure whenever the event happens in any of the shared components. (You can also select the components first and write the shared event procedure later.)

Of course, you have to have a way to distinguish which component called the shared event procedure. You do this by analyzing the Sender parameter via code. For example, you might have code like this:

```
begin
if Sender = Button1 then
   {code for button 1 goes here}
else
```

7

```
    if Sender = Button2 then
        {code for button 2 goes here};
end;
```

In general, you check if the Sender parameter is equal to the name of the component or simply check its type with the 'as' operator. (See the online help for more details on using the **as** operator.)

Object Variables

An object variable is simply a variable in Delphi that is declared to be of a certain type. For example:

```
var
    Form: TForms;
    AnEditBox: TEdit;
    ArrayOfEditBox: array[1..10] of TEdit;
```

Notice that you can create arrays of Delphi objects (you can even use them in records).

Object variables are used constantly in more sophisticated Delphi projects. For example, when you start sharing event procedures you will need to check what type of object the Sender parameter is. Is it a TEdit, which doesn't have a caption property, or a TLabel, which does? You do this by using the **is** operator with an object variable.

For example, add a TEdit, named Edit1, and a TLabel, named Label1, and share the OnClick event procedure for the Edit1 component with the TLabel component. Then try the following code:

```
procedure TForm1.Edit1Click(Sender: TObject);
  if Sender is TEdit then
TEdit(Sender).Text := 'Clicked in edit box'
  else
 TLabel(Sender).Caption := 'Clicked in the label';
end;
```

In general, you check whether the Sender is a TEdit, TButton, TLabel, or some other component, using, naturally enough, the **is** operator.

However, since the Sender parameter is of type TObject, you cannot test for things like the component's Name property directly. A statement like Sender.Name makes no sense because the TObject class doesn't have a Name property— a TObject can be any Delphi object. What you need to do is usually called *casting* an object of one type to another type. Of course, you cannot cast an object to an incompatible object. You can't make an Edit box into a Memo component, for example.

Suppose you have a bunch of Edit boxes that share an event procedure. You want to find out the name of one that is nonempty inside the shared event procedure.

```
procedure TForm1.Edit1Click(Sender: TObject);
var
  EditBox: TEdit;
begin
  EditBox := (Sender as TEdit);{use the 'as' operator for object
casting}
  if EditBox.Text <> '' then ShowMessage(EditBox.Name);
end;
```

Note: In addition to using the **as** keyword to do a temporary cast, you can also cast an object in Delphi more permanently. To do this use the class name as a function and the object variable (usually of type TObject) as the parameter. It is usually preferable to do a temporary cast with **as**.

Just as event procedures take objects for parameters, you can write your own subprograms that use object variables as one or more of the parameters. For example, if you wanted to write a procedure that would turn the text in any edit box to uppercase, you could use code that looks like this:

```
procedure UppercaseTextInEditBox(EditBox: TEdit);
begin
  EditBox.Text = UpperCase(EditBox.Text);
end;
```

As another example of using object variables: suppose you need to write code that iterates through all the components on a form, finds the Edit boxes, and then blanks out the information in each Edit box. To do this you need to use the Components and ComponentCount properties of the form. These properties give you access to the components on a form. Here's an example of the code you might use

```
procedure BlankEditBoxes(FormName: TForm);
var
  i: Integer;
begin
```

7

```
for i := 1 to FormName.ComponentCount - 1 do
  if FormName.Components[i] is TEdit then
    (FormName.Components[i] as TEdit).Text = '';
end;
```

Note: Delphi also has a Controls property. The difference is that the Components property of an object gives you a list of all the components owned by the object whereas the Controls property gives you a list of all the components that are child windows of the object. This becomes important when you use a container component like a group box. Components in a group box are still owned by the form and so are listed in the form's Components property. They are, however, child windows of the group box and so are not listed in the Forms Controls property but rather in the group box's Controls property.

Creating Delphi Objects at Run Time

It is quite common to need to create new Delphi objects at run time. You may need a new string list, for example, to store data, or you may find you need to plop a new edit box on a form in response to a special situation. You may even need to create a new form. (You could, of course, create the edit box or form at design time and then hide it until it is needed. However, this not only wastes memory but if you do this too often, your project will slow down and become rather demanding on Windows' limited resources.)

Suppose, for example, you want to create a new string list at run time. Any string list must be derived from Delphi's TStrings object. Here's an example of the code you need:

```
var
  MyStringList : TStringsList;
begin
  MyStringList :=  TStringList.Create;
  try
    {code for the string list}
  finally
    MyStringList.Free;
  end;
end;
```

(TStringList is a descendent of TStrings that is used when you need to maintain the list.)

Note: As with any object you create, you need to release the memory by using a **try/finally** block as indicated in the preceding listing. See Chapter 8 for more on these techniques.

You occasionally will need a string list that is available for the entire time the application is running. For this:

1. Declare a field of type TStringsList in the form declaration.
2. Create the string list in the form's OnCreate event handler.

Note: Be sure to free the memory you allocated for any string list. The OnDestroy event procedure is the most common place to do this.

Creating New Visual Objects at Run Time

Suppose you wanted to create an edit box at run time. An example of the code needed looks something like this:

```
var
   NewEditBox: TEdit;
begin
   NewEditBox := TEdit.Create(Self); {object now exists!}
   NewEditBox.Parent := Self;  (Self is better than the
Form--especially in an OnCreate event)
   end;
```

Note: After the line TEdit.Create(Self); the component exists so you should set properties like Left, Top, Visible, and so on. You should set properties before the parent is set so that the changes won't appear on the screen.

7

What follows are short discussions of the methods and keywords I used in this example.

Self

Every component you create must be owned by another component. The general syntax for the Create method reflects this:

Create(*AOwner*: TComponent)

Most of the time, you use the keyword **self**, which means that the component is owned by the class that the method is contained in—which is usually a Delphi form. On the other hand, if you make another component the owner of your new component, then you are making that component responsible for disposing of the object when it is destroyed.

Note: As with nonvisual objects, be sure to reclaim the memory used by your objects if they are owned by themselves. (Use the Free method, as described earlier in the chapter.)

Parent Property

The Parent property is the component that another component is contained in, such as a TForm, TPanel, or a TGroupBox.

Visual Basic Tip: If you need to create a structure analogous to a Visual Basic control array, declare an array of object variables and then use the techniques described above to create them individually.

The ObjectBrowser

Occasionally it is useful to see the hierarchy of Delphi objects directly. This is done through the ObjectBrowser that is available by choosing View | Browser. The ObjectBrowser can do much more than look at the object hierarchy. It can help you analyze the units and global variables in your code. It even allows you to move quickly to things like the code declarations for global variables. The ObjectBrowser for Delphi 32 is shown in Figure 7-2. (The one for Delphi 16 looks the same except for the Windows 95 title bar elements.)

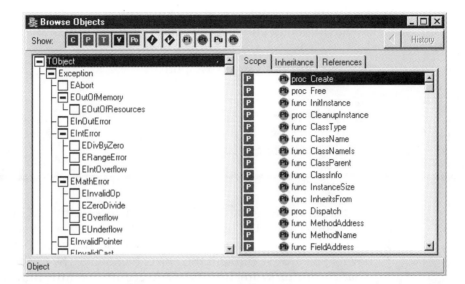

The
ObjectBrowser
window
Figure 7-2.

Note: You must have compiled your program at least once to use the ObjectBrowser. You do not have to be in break mode to work with the browser however.

Note: Like most Delphi objects, the ObjectBrowser also has a speedmenu that enables you to access the most common parts of the browser.

Since the ObjectBrowser is the gateway to all of Delphi's internal workings, it is very easy to be overwhelmed by the information it presents. You only occasionally need to work with the browser and when you do, you will want to filter out unnecessary information. For example, you can choose to look only at the variables or only at the constants in an object. Filters are controlled by the icons that appear on the Show bar at the top of the ObjectBrowser. You can use three different methods to set a filter:

◆ Click the filter's associated button. (For example, the C button is for constants, the P button is for Functions and Procedures.)

7

♦ Select (or deselect) the symbol filter from the Browser page of the Environment Options dialog box by working with the check boxes on this page.

♦ Press the filter's keyboard shortcut.

Tip: If you find yourself mostly using the ObjectBrowser to look at one type of object, use the Browser page on the Environment Options dialog box to make that the default.

As you can see in Figure 7-2, the ObjectBrowser is divided into two (resizeable) panes. The left one is called the Inspector pane and the right one the Details pane. When you first use the ObjectBrowser, Delphi defaults to having you browse through the object hierarchy. The easiest way to change what you are browsing is to use the speedmenu for the browser. A click on the appropriate item in the speedmenu lets you browse through not only the objects but also the units, globals, or symbol information in your project.

Tip: The ObjectBrowser has a neat search feature that works incrementally. This makes it easy to move around the ObjectBrowser. As you enter characters, the ObjectBrowser moves to whatever symbol matches the text you entered. As you enter characters, you see them displayed between the filter buttons on the Show bar and the History button. (To clear the search, press ESC; to find the next match, press CTRL-N.)

Compiler Options and their Effects on the ObjectBrowser

Although you can only use the ObjectBrowser on compiled code, how you compile your project affects what you can see. When you use the ObjectBrowser as a debugging tool, you will need to change some compiler options. (If you don't do this, then you can only use the ObjectBrowser to inspect symbols that were declared in the Interface part of the unit.) Table 7-1 summarizes what you can do.

Compiler Option	Effect on ObjectBrowser
Debug Information	Adds the ability to browse symbols defined in the Implementation part of the module.
Local Symbols	Adds line number references for use in the References page of the Details pane.
Symbol Info	Adds all the identifiers that you declared within a given procedure or function.

Tip: Since having these compiler options on both slows and bloats the compiled code, be sure to turn them off when you do the final compile.

The Inspector Pane

When you are looking at the object hierarchy, the Inspector pane displays an inheritance tree of the objects; when you are looking at units, it gives you a list of all units. (This includes the ones you have added as well as the ones that Delphi adds itself, like System.) The idea is you can see where the objects descend from graphically. (Notice how in Figure 7-2 that TObject is the ultimate ancestor.) Objects that descend from a common ancestor are branches off of a limb that starts at that object. You can actually expand or contract the tree by clicking on the little box to the left of the name. A plus sign in the box indicates that you can expand it; a minus sign indicates it is already expanded.

Tip: If you decide to work a lot with the ObjectBrowser, there are quite a few keyboard shortcuts available. For these consult the "ObjectBrowser Keyboard Shortcuts" topic in the online help.

7

When you select an object in the Inspector pane, Delphi updates the Details pane, which I describe next.

The Details Pane

This pane has three pages for Scope, Inheritance, and References, respectively. The Scope page gives you a list of all the symbols declared in the object currently selected in the Inspector pane. The Inheritance page gives an inheritance tree for the object, and the References page gives you the filenames and line numbers where the symbol appears in your code.

In-Depth Inspection

If you need to look further at an object, double-click on the object in the Inspector pane. Delphi moves the contents of the Details pane to the Inspector pane, and gives the declarations for the object you selected in the Details pane. If you want to actually look at the code for the object, select the object you want to work with and press CTRL-ENTER. Delphi moves the focus to the Code Editor window and moves the cursor to the place where the object was declared. In general, when you have selected a function or procedure, Delphi gives you the code; when the object is a constant, property, variable, or type, Delphi shows you the declaration.

Chapter 8

Error and Exception Handling

Regardless of how carefully you debug your program, it will be impossible to anticipate ordinary mishaps or the crazy things an inexperienced user will do. A program that rolls over and dies when the printer runs out of paper or if the user tries to open a nonexistent file is not going to be very useful. If you want your program to be robust (sometimes called "having the ability to degrade gracefully") and not just roll over, you'll want to prevent fatal errors. Both versions of Delphi use the idea of "protecting" blocks of code that comes from C++, as opposed to the more old-fashioned On Error GoTo that Visual Basic uses. This means that if an error results from processing statements in a code block, the program can deal with it.

Whenever an error results from processing a line of code, Delphi creates ("raises" is the technical term) an object descended from a TObject called the Exception object. As you will see later in this chapter, you can analyze properties of this object to determine what caused the error. (This information may give you the ability to resume where the code bombed—without triggering the error again. For example, you can tell the user to put paper in the printer or some such thing!)

 Note: When building a program with exception handling, you may not want Delphi to Break on Exceptions. This is a great feature if you want Delphi to show where an exception has occurred; however, it can be bothersome when you test your own exception handling. Since this is the default, you may want to uncheck this option. (The check box for it may be found by choosing the Tools | Options | Preferences page in Delphi 32, or by choosing the Options | Environment | Preferences page in Delphi 16.)

Protected Blocks

The way to activate (enable) exception/error trapping within a given code block is to surround the block with the **try/except** combination of keywords. The general code looks something like this:

```
try
    {code to do something};
except
    on...do {handle specified exceptions};
else {default handling code};
end;
```

Since you do not want Delphi to inadvertently "fall into" the error-trapping code, the **try/except** block helps maintain cleaner code by keeping the exception handler out of the normal program flow.

Occasionally you need to make sure that Delphi processes certain code regardless of which block is protected. (This is quite common when dealing with code that allocates memory or Windows resources—you really want to reclaim such things!) In this case, the syntax uses the **finally** keyword and looks like this:

```
    {code to allocate resources would go here}
try
    {memory allocation should occur prior to the try...finally block in
    case the allocation fails}  try
    {code to do something}
```

```
  except
    on ...do {handle specified exceptions};
    else {default handling code};
  end;
finally
    {code to free resources and anything else that needs to be ultimately
    cleaned up}
end;
```

Here the keyword **finally** starts a block of code that allows your code to clean up after itself. It will always be processed.

You can nest exception handlers by surrounding larger and larger blocks of code with more of the **try/except** or **try/finally** combinations. If you do not have an exception handler in a block of code, then Delphi will look at larger and larger surrounding blocks until it finds a protected block. For example, suppose you have protected the outer loop of a nested For Next loop, and the exception occurs in an unprotected inner loop. Since Delphi can't find an exception handler in the inner loop, it uses the one in the outer loop.

Finally, if your application doesn't handle the error that caused the exception, then Delphi will use its default exception handler—which just pops up a message box with what it thinks is the error. It then tries to continue the program. If it can't, then the program dies. However, once you start exception handling (error trapping) with a **try/except** block, exceptions will no longer bomb the program.

Tip: Because you rarely want Delphi to just use its default event handler, you may want to consider writing code in the OnException event for the TApplication object. This is triggered by any exception—before the default event handler is invoked.

In any case, the **try/except** block should include (or transfer control to) a code that identifies the problem and, if possible, fixes it. If the error cannot be corrected, then Delphi executes the default error handler in the **else** part of the **except** block. When Delphi handles the exception, the protected block ends.

8

Visual Basic Tip: Delphi does not return control to the next statement following the line of code that caused the exception, but continues processing code after the appropriate **on...do** statement.

However, you can't correct an error if you don't know why it happened. You identify the problem by means of the exception handler's **on...do** statement. This gives you the ability to handle specific exceptions. For example, if you write in a user-defined function

```
except
on EDivByZero do Result := 0;
```

then you have handled the problem of code that tries to divide by zero by setting the value of the function to be zero in this case.

The Exception Hierarchy

Figure 8-1 shows you the Exception hierarchy in Delphi 32. (It is basically the same in Delphi 16.) As you can see, all exceptions descend from the generic Exception object. Many of them, such as EIntError (discussed shortly) have descendants (subclasses) of more specific exceptions. Since there are dozens of exceptions, we can't cover them all here. Look at the online help for descriptions of the exceptions that we do not cover.

Tip: Delphi can identify many kinds of run-time library (RTL) errors. Look up "exceptions," and then select "Handling RTL Exceptions." You can even jump to short explanations of what might have caused any specific error.

Components will raise exceptions to indicate a problem—the challenge is to identify what caused it. Most component exceptions result from a programming error, such as accessing an invalid index in an array. The following is a short discussion of the most common run-time library exceptions.

Input/Output Exceptions

Input/output (I/O) exceptions usually occur when the run-time library tries to access files or I/O devices. The "I/O checking" box on the Compiler page (or equivalently, the I+ option) must be on in order for Delphi to be able to raise this exception. (The default is on.)

Most I/O exceptions derive from problems DOS and Windows encounter when trying to access a file or external device. The two subclasses of the Exception object that handle I/O errors derive from the EInOutError and EStreamError. You can analyze the ErrorCode property of these objects to determine which error happened. (See Chapter 10 for an example of how to use these exceptions when handling files—the most common place these exceptions are raised.)

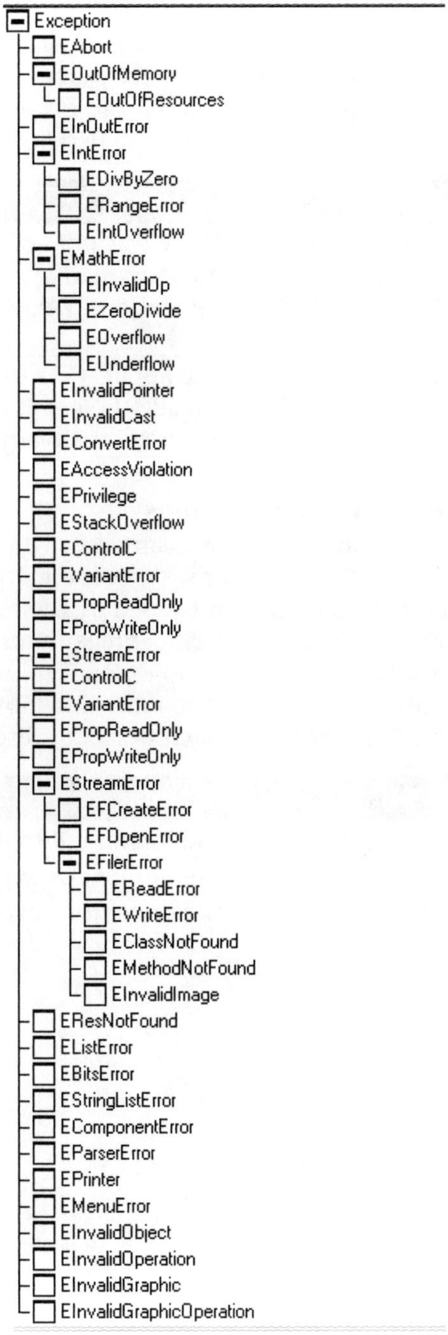

The Exception hierarchy
Figure 8-1.

Heap Exceptions

Heap exceptions can occur when you try to allocate or access dynamic memory. Heap errors caused by lack of memory are almost unheard of in the 32-bit version of Delphi, but can occur occasionally in the 16-bit version. The following table shows the two possible heap exceptions:

Exception	Meaning
EOutOfMemory	There was not enough space on the heap to complete the requested operation. EOutOfMemory has a descendant, EOutOfResources, that can be raised as well.
EInvalidPointer	The application tried to dispose of a pointer that points outside the heap. Usually, this means the pointer was disposed of already.

Integer Math Exceptions

Integer math exceptions can occur when you perform operations on integer-type expressions. The generic integer math exception, called EIntError, is usually not raised by the run-time library, but it provides a base from which all the specific integer math exceptions descend. However, you can, of course, use it in an exception handler if you do not need more specific information. The following table shows the specific integer math exceptions, each of which descends directly from EIntError:

Exception	Meaning
EDivByZero	You attempted to divide by zero.
ERangeError	The number or expression was out of range.
EIntOverflow	The operation involving integers overflowed.

For example:

```
begin
  try
    foo := A div B;   (div is for integer division)
  except
   on EDivByZero do
     begin
       MessageDlg('Can't divide by zero!', mtError, [mbOK], 0);
     end;
```

Floating-Point Math Exceptions

Floating-point math exceptions can occur when you perform operations on expressions involving floating-point types such as Real. The generic floating-point math exception is called EMathError. As with EIntError, this exception provides a base from which all the specific floating-point math exceptions descend. The following table shows the specific floating-point math exceptions, each of which descends directly from EMathError:

Exception	Meaning
EInvalidOp	The processor encountered an undefined instruction.
EZeroDivide	You attempted to divide by zero.
EOverflow	The floating-point operation overflowed.
EUnderflow	The floating-point operation underflowed.

Typecast Exceptions

Typecast exceptions can occur when you attempt to typecast an object into another type using the as operator. There is only one exception—EInvalidCast—for typecasting.

Conversion Exceptions

Conversion exceptions can occur when you convert data from one form to another using functions such as IntToStr, StrToInt, StrToFloat, and so on. The one exception is called EConvertError.

Hardware Exceptions in Delphi 16

Hardware exceptions can occur in two kinds of situations: either the processor detects a fault it can't handle, or the application intentionally calls a hardware interrupt in order to break execution. Hardware exception-handling is not compiled into DLLs—only into stand-alone applications. The generic hardware exception is called EProcessorException, but it is never raised by the run-time library. EProcessorException provides the base object from which all the specific hardware exceptions descend. The following table shows the specific hardware exceptions.

Note: The following exceptions are only applicable to Delphi 16. The new hardware exceptions in Delphi 32 are EAccessViolation, EPrivilege, and EStackOverflow, which are all derived from the Exception class.

8

Exception	Meaning
EFault	This is the base Exception object from which all fault objects descend.
EGPFault	This is a general-protection fault, usually caused by an uninitialized pointer or object.
EStackFault	The program made an illegal access to the processor's stack segment.
EPageFault	The Windows memory manager was unable to correctly use the swap file.
EInvalidOpCode	The processor encountered an undefined instruction. This usually means the processor was trying to execute data or uninitialized memory.
EBreakpoint	The application generated a breakpoint interrupt.
ESingleStep	The application generated a single-step interrupt.

Handling Classes of Exceptions

As mentioned at the beginning of this chapter, you can specify exception handlers around any blocks of code, or even nest exception handlers within other exception handlers. You can also specify an exception handler for a specific exception class. For example:

```
try
   { statements performing integer math }
except
   on ERangeError do { out-of-range handling };
   on EIntError do { handling for other integer math errors };
end;
```

The previous code will handle any integer math or range error. Remember that if Delphi triggers the exception handler for EIntError before an ERangeError occurs, the ERangeError handler is never triggered.

Reraising an Exception

Sometimes when you handle an exception in a protected block, you'll want to handle the exception and then pass it on to a larger protected block. The problem is that when your local handler finishes handling the exception, it destroys the exception instance, so the enclosing block's exception handler has nothing to work with. You can, however, prevent an exception handler from destroying the exception. This gives the enclosing handler a chance to respond. For this you use the keyword **raise**.

As an example of where you might want to do this if an exception occurs, you might want to display some sort of message to the user, then let the enclosing exception handler deal with the problem. The syntax looks like this:

```
try
  { initial statements }
  try
    { special statements }
  except
    on ESomeError do
    begin
      { handling for only the special statements }
      raise;      {this will reraise the exception }
    end;
  end;
except
  on ESomeError do ...;{ handling you want in all cases }
end;
```

If code in the first ("initial statements") part causes an exception, Delphi executes only the exception handler for the outer part (the one marked "handling you want in all cases"). However, if code in the block marked "special statements" causes an exception, Delphi will, of course, execute the inner exception handling. *But because of the use of **raise** in the inner exception handler, Delphi will also execute the outer exception handler.*

Tip: By reraising exceptions, you can easily provide special handling for special cases without losing (or duplicating) the existing handlers.

Protecting Resource Allocations

Any well-behaved application should include error handling that frees system resources.

Note: Anytime you allocate memory (for example, by using something like a GetMem or New) for pointers, create an object, or use files, you are probably using up scarce Windows resources.

8

If your application has encountered a severe error and your code has to close the application, it's a good idea to free up the file handles and any memory allocations that you generated inside your application. (The alternative is that your user *will* be frustrated by the diminishing performance of his or her system as Windows' resources vanish. The program may even crash.)

As an example, the following code allocates some memory for a pointer and a string list, catches a divide by zero error, and frees the previously allocated memory.

```
procedure TForm1.Button1Click(Sender: TComponent);
var
  APtr: PChar;
  AnInt, BadToDivide: Integer;
  MyStringList: TStringList;
begin
  BadToDivide := 0;
  MyStringList := TStringList.Create;
  GetMem(APtr, 50000);   { allocate 50000 bytes of memory }

{Note: If the GetMem fails (raising an EOutOfMemory exception)
then MyStringList won't get freed}
  try
  AnInt := 10 div BadToDivide;  { this generates an error }
  finally
    FreeMem(APtr, 500000);  {this code always gets processed}
    MyStringList.Free;
end;
```

User-Defined Exceptions

As with any Delphi object, Delphi allows you to add subclasses to the Exception object. Since these objects will be descendants of the Exception object, you can use then in exception handlers just like the built-in descendants of Exception. In particular, you can use them in the same exception-handling scheme as that used by the run-time library exceptions.

Two things need to be done to use your own exceptions. First you have to declare an exception object, and then you have to *raise* the exception.

Declaring an Exception Object

An exception is like any other Delphi object, so it has to be declared before you can use it. Only an object of the object type Exception will be handled by the standard exception handlers. For example:

```
type
  EMyError = class(Exception);
```

If you now raise your custom EMyError exception but haven't created a specific exception handler for EMyError, then Delphi's default exception handler will handle your exceptions. All this (default) exception handler does is display a message box with text about your exception.

On the other hand, the whole point of creating your own exceptions is to use this information inside your application. Once you have declared your own exception, you use the keyword **raise** to raise your exception, as in the following example:

```
type
  EMyError = class(Exception);
....
if Something <> Anotherthing then
  raise EMyError.Create('Raising my exception');
```

When Delphi finishes with an exception handler, the exception instance is automatically destroyed. This means you don't need to destroy your exception object in order to reclaim the memory it used up.

Note: The System unit contains a variable called ErrorAddr which, as its name implies, contains the address where your application raised the exception. Also the ExceptionObject function here returns a pointer to the currently raised exception object.

Silent Exceptions

As you have seen, Delphi handles any exception that you do not write code for by raising the default exception handler—which only makes Delphi display a message box. Occasionally (for example, with a program for new users), you may want to create an exception that does not display a message box. This is called a *silent* exception. Use of the Abort procedure is the simplest way to do this. The Abort automatically raises the EAbort exception (although you can raise EAbort directly).

8

Note: Except for EAbort, all of the other exception types display a message box.

Using the Abort procedure forces Delphi to break out of the current block, but does not halt execution of your code. (It gives you another way to break out of blocks other than the GoTo, for example.)

Note: The EAbort exception (Abort procedure) is a frequently used exception in database programming. For example, when the posting of a record is to be aborted for some reason, the Abort procedure is the one to use.

Chapter 9

Tools and Techniques for Testing and Debugging

Once a program becomes in any way complex, no matter how carefully you outline your program or how carefully you plan it, it probably won't do what you expect—at first. This is one lesson programmers are forced to painfully relearn over and over again. It seems that no matter how robust you try to make a program, someone, somehow, will find a way to crash it. A realistic goal is not a perfect program, but one that is as bulletproof (or robust) as possible—one that, even while crashing, tries to save the user's work before fading away.

While exception handlers (see the previous chapter) can help a lot, after you write a program, you will still need to test it for bugs. Once the testing process convinces you that there are bugs lurking, you need to find them and then eradicate them. Delphi has integrated many tools into the development environment to assist with this task, and this chapter will show you how to use them.

Of course, before trying to test and debug a program, you should first make a hard copy of the program source code. You might also want a copy of the specifications of the forms in ASCII format (see Chapter 4) so that you can quickly check whether the initial properties of a form and its components match what you expect.

Finally, this chapter gives you techniques for speeding up your programs that do the job but are unlikely to introduce new bugs (trying to over-optimize code is one of the most common sources of programming bugs). The chapter concludes with some words on good programming style.

The Debugging Tools and What They Do

The Run menu in both versions of Delphi contains most of the tools needed for testing and debugging. Most of the tools needed for testing and debugging can be found on the SpeedBar as well. Typically, the debugging tools are used when the program is temporarily suspended (in Stopped mode). Table 9-1 lists the debugging tools you can use on the Run menu.

The View menu contains a dialog box for working with breakpoints, as well as windows for call stacks and watches. (See the section "Watch" later in this chapter.)

Tip: The Code Editor's speedmenu gives you access to many of the debugging tools listed in Table 9-1. Click the right mouse button in a code page to display its speedmenu.

Designing Programs to Make Testing Easier

Long and complex programs are never easy to test, but writing the programs in certain ways will make your job easier. (These methods also make programming in general easier.) By breaking the program into manageable pieces each of which ideally does a single task alone, you can make testing your programs much, much easier. After you finish each object, procedure, or function, you can test it thoroughly to see whether it can handle all possible parameters that may be passed to it. Using thoroughly debugged

Tool	Keyboard Equivalent	Function
Run	ALT-R-R (F9)	Starts/Restarts the program.
Parameters	ALT-R-P	Sets command-line parameters.
Step Over	ALT-R-S (F8)	Performs like the Trace Into tool except procedure and function calls are treated as one step.
Trace Into	ALT-R-T (F7)	Moves through the program one statement at a time.
Run to Cursor	ALT-R-C (F4)	Executes the program up to the location of the cursor.
Show Execution Point	ALT-R-H	Shows you what line will be processed next.
Program Pause	ALT-R-G	Interrupts the program.
Program Reset	ALT-R-E (CTRL-F2)	Ends the program.
Add Watch	ALT-R-W (CTRL-F5)	Displays the Watch Properties dialog box, where you can create and edit watches.
Add Breakpoint	ALT-R-B	Stops the program immediately before the line is executed.
Evaluate/Modify	ALT-R-V (CTRL-F7)	Displays the Evaluate/Modify dialog box, where you can evaluate or modify an existing expression.

The Run
Menu
Debugging
Tools
Table 9-1.

(reusable) objects that encapsulate the properties and methods that you need (see Chapter 7) can save you a lot of work.

Next, combine all the procedures and objects you've checked and test everything again. In some cases, a procedure or function may need results from a piece not yet written in order to run. In this case, the best technique, often called *stub programming,* substitutes constants, where necessary, for the results of as-yet-unwritten procedures or functions. (The point is to always have a program that does something—even if it is just telling you what it is *going to do*.) Define the procedure or function, but fill it with constants instead of having it do anything. The procedure calls will still work the same, but they will receive only the constants from the stubs. You can then change the constants to vary the tests.

Now suppose you have eliminated the obvious syntax errors and can get the program to run—after a fashion. But testing the program has told you that it doesn't work as it's supposed to; it contains bugs that you need to isolate and eradicate. Don't be surprised or dismayed; bugs come with the territory. You have to find them and determine what kind they are.

There are essentially two kinds of bugs: run-time and logical. An example of a *run-time error* is trying to open a nonexistent file.

T ip: When first debugging a program for run-time errors, you may want to comment out the exception handlers. Another possibility is to use the "Break on exception" feature to find out what line caused the exception.

Logical bugs are a vast family that encompasses all errors resulting from a misunderstanding of how a program works. This includes procedures that don't communicate properly and internal errors of logic inside code.

Logical Bugs

To get rid of subtle logical bugs, you have to isolate them—that is, find the part of the program that's causing the problem. If you've followed the modular approach, your task is a lot easier. The pieces are more manageable, so finding the bug means the haystack isn't too big. Similarly, if you try to encapsulate commonly occurring behavior into a custom object, you can focus your attention on that object when debugging.

If you've been testing the program as you develop it, then you should already know in what object, procedure, or function the problem lies. Pinpointing the problematic object, procedure, or function is usually easier if you developed the program yourself, mostly because you start off with a good idea of the logic of the program. If the program is not yours or you've waited until the program is "finished," you can use the following techniques to check the pieces one at a time.

Assume that you've chosen a faulty object procedure or function to test. There are only three possibilities:

♦ What's going *in* is wrong—what you've fed to the object, procedure, or function is confusing it.

♦ What's coming *out* is wrong—the object, procedure, or function is sending incorrect information to other parts of the program (for example, it may be causing unplanned side effects).

♦ Something *inside* the object, procedure, or function is wrong (for example, it's performing an operation too many times, or it's not clearing the screen at the right time).

In the first two cases, the fault can be traced to any or all of the following: the parameters you send to the procedure or function (or to the methods of the object), what you've assigned to the parameters or to the properties, or the unit (form)-level or global variables modified within the function or procedure.

How do you decide which situation you're dealing with? First, it's hard to imagine a correctly written *short* object, procedure, or function that you can't analyze on a piece of paper to determine what should happen in most cases. Work through the procedure or function by hand, "playing computer." (This means don't make any assumptions other than what the computer would know at that point; don't assume variables have certain values unless you can convince yourself that they do.) You now need to check that the functions, objects, and procedures are doing what they are supposed to.

Adding Debugging Information

In order to use the integrated debugger you must compile your program so that there is a way for the debugger to connect the executable with your source code. This is usually called symbolic debug information. *Symbolic debug information* is a symbol table that links your program's source code to the machine code generated by the compiler. By default, Delphi generates debugging information. You can turn debugging information on/off by checking the debugging options in the Options | Project Compiler page.

If you want to use Turbo Debugger for Windows, you will need to include TDW symbolic debug information in your final .EXE file. Check the Include TDW Debug info check box in the Options | Project Linker page. However, adding symbolic debug information will greatly increase the size of your executable file and make the application run slower, so remember to make your final compile with symbolic debug information turned off.

Note: Turbo Debugger for Windows is a stand-alone product that adds many specialized debugging features to Delphi's built-in debugging facilities (such as hardware breakpoints). It is not covered in this book. For more on this product, please consult the online help or the documentation supplied for Turbo Debugger. You can get Turbo Debugger for Windows with the Delphi RAD pack or in the higher end versions of Delphi. You need Turbo Debugger in order to debug Delphi-created DLL's.

The Evaluate/Modify Dialog Box

Most programming languages have a way to test program statements, variables, and expressions, and Delphi is no exception. This is typically used after setting a breakpoint or while tracing through the program. Delphi uses the Evaluate/Modify dialog box, shown in the following illustration.

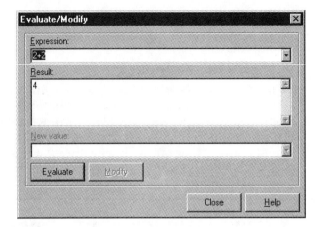

To bring the Evaluate/Modify dialog box to the foreground, use the Run menu. The Evaluate/Modify dialog box is modal (you must close the dialog box to go back to working in the design environment) and moveable. If you type 2 + 2 in the Evaluate/Modify dialog box and press ENTER, Delphi quickly responds with a 4. You can use the ordinary Microsoft Windows editing commands to modify the contents of a line in the Evaluate/Modify dialog box. You can also cut and paste between lines. Keep in mind, though, that the moment you press ENTER, Delphi attempts to process the line.

Also keep in mind that you can always re-execute previous lines in the Evaluate/Modify dialog box by selecting the line from the Expression drop-down combo box and pressing ENTER.

More on Debugging in the Evaluate/Modify Dialog Box

The Evaluate / Modify dialog box makes it easy to test a variable or an expression for its effects on certain values (for example, to see whether the results match with your hand calculations). You most commonly will use the Evaluate/Modify dialog box to examine the current value of constants, variables, or expressions. To look at the value of a variable, simply enter an expression in the edit portion of the Expression drop-down combo box. If you highlight a variable in the editor, it will automatically show up in the Evaluate / Modify dialog box.

To change the value of a variable after clicking Evaluate, place the cursor in the New Value drop-down combo box (the one below the Result box) and enter the new value. (It will be disabled, as shown in the illustration, if you cannot enter a new value.) Of course, caution is necessary when modifying values in order to avoid undesirable side effects.

Note: Any changes you make in the Evaluate/Modify dialog box affect neither the source code nor the compiled program. (But if it's the value of a variable or property, it will, of course, affect the running program.)

If you want to make the changes in your project that you made in the Evaluate/Modify dialog box, go back to the Code Editor and change the source code accordingly. Then recompile the project.

Trace Into

Often, when you have worked through a program by hand, you will want to have the computer walk through the same example, one line of code at a time. Delphi lets you execute one statement in your program at a time—a process called *single-stepping*—by repeatedly pressing F7 or the icon for the Trace Into tool on the SpeedBar. (Of course, if Delphi is waiting for an event to happen, there won't be any statements to execute.) If the execution point is located on a call to a function that was not compiled with debugging information, then Trace Into treats the code block as one statement and highlights the statement following the function call.

When single-stepping is first used, the first executable statement of the program is highlighted in the Code Editor window. (Usually, the first statement will be in the form's OnCreate handler, if there is one.) Each subsequent press of F7 or the Trace Into tool executes the highlighted statement and highlights the next statement to be executed. As you can imagine, single-stepping through a program is ideal for tracing the logical flow of a program through decision structures and procedures.

Whenever a procedure is called during single-stepping, the code fills the Code Editor window. After its statements have been highlighted and executed (one at a time), the routine that called it reappears in the Code Editor window.

Besides the F7 key or single-step tool from the toolbar, you can also use F8 (or the Step Over tool) to single-step through a program. With this tool, each procedure is processed as if it were a single statement. In many cases, this is preferable to single-stepping through a complex function that you already know works.

Stopping Programs Temporarily

More often than not, though, you'll need to stop your program temporarily and look at a snapshot of the values of many of the variables. For example, suppose you want to know why a variable seems not to have the value you want. You need to pinpoint the location where the value starts behaving strangely. Just printing the values to the Evaluate/Modify dialog may not be enough.

There are two ways to stop a program temporarily. One is to choose the Program Pause item from the Run menu. The other is to use breakpoints; these are places at which the program will stop as Delphi gets to them. Breakpoints are toggled off or on by pressing F5 or using the Code Editor's speedmenu. (You can also select Add Breakpoint from the Run menu.) Breakpoints are usually shown in red in your code. You have several options when creating a breakpoint with the Edit Breakpoint dialog box. The Condition edit box can contain an expression to trigger the breakpoint. A value in the Pass Count edit box will trigger the breakpoint after a specified number of passes. When you run the program and Delphi encounters a breakpoint, Delphi stops the code just before it executes the statement with the breakpoint and enters stopped mode.

You can set multiple breakpoints. To remove a breakpoint, position the cursor on the breakpoint and press F5. To clear all breakpoints from a program choose the Breakpoints option on the View menu. Finally you can click on the right mouse button in the Breakpoint List window and select the Disable All Breakpoints option.

Note: You can also use the View / Run to Cursor (F4) to stop a program at a specific place.

Tip: Use Run | Run to continue a stopped program. Use F8 or the Step Over tool on the SpeedBar to treat a call to a procedure or function procedure as a single step. This way, you don't have to step through all the lines in all the functions and procedures in your project when you know there's no need to. Combine this with the Call Stack option on the View menu to see which procedure called the one you are in or to look at the entire chain of procedure calls if need be.

Watch

Whenever you are debugging, the goal is to eventually wind your way down to an object, procedure, or function that just doesn't work. You now know that you have an error internal to an object, procedure, or function. Although the Evaluate/Modify dialog box can be used to examine the values of expressions while single-stepping through a program, using Delphi's Watch features is more efficient. You can specify the items you want to watch either before you start the program or while the program is running and you have temporarily stopped it. Delphi lets you watch any variables, expressions, or conditions in your code. One way to do this is to bring up the Watch Properties dialog box. This dialog box pops up when you choose Run | Add Watch. It looks like this:

As you can see above, the Expression box starts out blank. You enter the expression that you want to watch in this area. After that, the option buttons let you specify the format that Delphi should use to display the expression.

Note: You can watch only global variables or expressions attached to the current form or unit. If you try to use other kinds of expressions, you will see a "process not accessible" message.

Delphi actually displays the item it's watching in the Watch List window. As Delphi executes the program, the values of the Watch items will be updated in the Watch List window. To remove an item from the Watch List window, press CTRL-D or use the Watch List window's speedmenu.

Instant Watch
An Add Watch at Cursor item on the Code Editor's speedmenu (CTRL-F5) lets you look at the value of the variable or expression where the cursor is currently located. This capability, usually called Instant Watch, complements the feature in Delphi that lets you use the Evaluate/Modify dialog box to look at the value of any variables inside a procedure when a program is stopped within the procedure.

To use Instant Watch:

1. Select the variable or expression you want to watch by moving the cursor to the item or highlighting the expression using SHIFT-arrow key combinations.
2. Choose Add Watch at Cursor from the speedmenu (ALT-F10-A or CTRL-F5).

If the value isn't currently available, Delphi will tell you. At this point, you can close the box with the ESC key or choose to add this variable as a Watch item.

Some Final Remarks on Debugging

Feeding a procedure or function specific numbers and using the debugging techniques described here are not cure-alls. No technique can help unless you have a good grip on what the procedure or function should do. If you are using an if-then statement, are you testing for the right quantity? Should a >= be a = ? Use the Watch feature to check the value (True or False) of any Boolean relations that seem to be off (it is perfectly legal to enter x = 19 as a Watch value). Check any loops in the routine; loops are a common source of problems. Are counters initialized correctly (is there an off-by-one error)? Are you testing your indeterminate loops at the top when you should be testing them at the bottom?

Tip: When a Repeat or While loop seems to be running too long, add a temporary counter to the Repeat loop. Then use the counter in a watch at some (fairly) large value. When the program stops, examine the state of the expression tested in the loop to help determine why your loops are running too long.

Event-Driven Bugs and Problems

When you debug an event-driven program, you have to be aware of certain problems that could never come up in older programming languages. *Event cascades* are perhaps the most common. These are bugs caused by an infinite sequence of one event procedure calling itself or another event procedure, with no way to break the chain. The most likely time such bugs are introduced is when you make a change in the OnChange event handler for a control. The OnChange procedure is called again, which in turn is called again, and so on—theoretically forever, but in practice you'll get an error message.

Other special problems occur when you stop a program during an OnMouseDown or OnKeyDown event handler. In both situations, during the debugging process you'll naturally release the mouse button or lift the key that invoked the event handler. However, when Delphi resumes the program, it assumes the mouse button or the key is still pressed down, and so the relevant OnMouseUp and OnKeyUp handlers will never be called.

Programming Style

Although you can remember the logic of a complicated program for a while, you can't remember it forever. Good documentation is the key that can open the lock. Some people include the pseudocode or outline for the program as multiple comment statements. Along with meaningful variable names, this is obviously the best form of documentation. Set up conventions for global, form, or local variables and stick to them. Try to avoid tricky code; if you need to do something extraordinarily clever, make sure it's extensively commented. (Most of the time, you'll find that the clever piece of code wasn't really needed.) Nothing is harder to change six months down the line than "cute" code.

The point is that when you start thinking of tricks to speed up your programs, you can too easily lose sight of the fundamental issue: making sure your programs run robustly in the first place. In fact, dramatic speedups usually come from shifts in the algorithms in the program, not from little "tweaks." Roughly speaking, an algorithm is the method you use to solve a problem.

This is not to say that after a program is running robustly, you might not want to consider ways of making it run faster. Making sure that variables are integers whenever possible is an obvious and nondangerous change. Don't use "memory-hog" variant variables unless you need their special properties.

Try the following additional techniques to increase the speed of your program if necessary (obviously it also helps to have as much RAM and as fast a hard disk as possible):

- ◆ Preload DLLs when possible.
- ◆ Unload forms when no longer needed.
- ◆ Delete code if it is no longer used in your project. In particular, do the final compilation without symbolic debug information.
- ◆ Use local variables whenever possible.
- ◆ Use constant parameters whenever possible.

In any case, it's extremely difficult to modify or debug a program (even one that you, long ago, wrote yourself) that has few or no remark statements, little accompanying documentation, and uninformative variable names. A procedure called MakeMartini(Shaken,ButNot,Stirred) should be in a program about James Bond (and perhaps not even there), not in a program about trigonometric functions. In addition, since Delphi allows long variable names, don't make your programs a morass of variables named X, X13, X17, X39, and so on. If you strive for clarity in your programs rather than worrying about efficiency at first, you'll be a lot better off.

Finally, if an object, procedure, or function works well, remember to save it for reuse in other programs. One of the main points of the Pascal unit is to allow you to reuse a toolbox that you have either created or bought. Complicated programs will often have many procedures and functions. These procedures and functions may often have come up before in a slightly different context. This means that after you design the interface, sometimes all you have to do is modify and connect parts of a thoroughly debugged library of procedures and functions to the event procedures for the interface. (This is one reason why commercial toolkits for Delphi may be so useful. The time saved is worth the small cost.)

Chapter 10

Working with Files

This chapter shows you how, within a Delphi application, to handle disks and files. We start with the commands in Delphi that interact with DOS—for example, you can rename files, change the current drive, or switch directories using Delphi code. Then you'll see the commands in Delphi that make dealing with files easier—for example, how to find out how much space is left on a disk. Next, you'll see how to use the file system components that may be found on the System page of the Component palette in both versions of Delphi. Next, there's an introduction to file handling in Delphi. Delphi has the ability to handle both ASCII files and files that hold binary data, and you will see the techniques for working with both types of files. (It is worth noting that although Delphi contains many features for handling databases, as discussed in Chapter 14, you will still need to know how to set up and work with files directly.) Finally, file handling in both versions of Delphi works essentially the same. The main difference is, of course, that Delphi 32 supports the long filenames that Windows 95 and Windows NT allow.

Note: When working with files, you will often want to use the common dialog boxes that come with Delphi. These are covered in Chapter 13. Remember—Windows users expect to see these dialog boxes when working with files!

Directory and File Management Commands

Delphi has five procedures and two functions, summarized in Table 10-1, that interact directly with the operating system and mimic the usual operating system commands.

Note: Any function or procedure that accesses a disk will generate a run-time library exception if the underlying operating system cannot perform the task. See Chapter 8 for more on dealing with these types of run-time library exceptions.

The first three of these commands are used simply by following them with a string or string expression. For example:

```
MkDir('TESTDIR');
```

would add a subdirectory called TESTDIR to the current directory. The line

```
MkDir('C:\TESTDIR');
```

would add the subdirectory to the root directory of the C drive and the line

```
MkDir('C:\Gary Program Files\');
```

would create a long directory name in Delphi 32.

Delphi
Commands for
DOS Tasks
Table 10-1.

Command	Function
ChDir	Changes the default directory and the logged drive for DOS.
MkDir	Makes a new directory.
RmDir	Removes a directory.
Rename	Changes the name of a file. (There is also a RenameFile function that returns True if the renaming was successful.)
Erase	Deletes a file from a disk. (There's also a DeleteFile function that works similarly, except it returns True if the delete was successful.)

10

The commands Rename and Erase require that you first assign a variable of a special *File* type to the name of the file. For example, if you want to rename a file named GOODFILE to OLDFILE, you would use code that looks like this:

```
var
  FileName : File;
begin
  AssignFile(FileName, 'GOODFILE');
  Rename(FileName, 'OLDFILE');
  CloseFile(FileName);
end;
```

Note: This example was to show off the AssignFile procedure. In practice you would be more likely to use the RenameFile function, which returns a Boolean depending on the success or failure of the renaming.

In general, the AssignFile procedure links an external filename to a previously declared file variable of a File type. The link remains intact until you close the file.

Pascal Tip: You can still use the older Assign procedure, although the designers of Delphi recommend using the newer AssignFile procedure because Assign conflicts with the Assign method.

The value of a file variable must be a legal filename in the operating system you are working with. The rules for filenames are the rules that DOS imposes for the 16-bit version of Delphi and the much more generous rules that Windows 95 and Windows NT allow for Delphi 32.

♦   In Delphi 16: The standard eight characters plus a three-character extension (separated by a period).

♦   In Delphi 32: Up to 255 characters and spaces are allowed.

♦   Regardless of which operating system you use, the only characters allowed are

   A-Z, 0-9 (<Nl) { } @ # $ % & ! - _' / ~

Note: The commands that handle files will often accept the normal DOS wildcards. For example, Erase('*.*') deletes all the files in the current directory (not to be done casually).

Other File and I/O Functions

Certain tasks are so common that the designers of Delphi decided to add them to the language itself rather than make you use Windows' API calls or shell to DOS. (For those who know DOS, many of these replace functions that use Int21H.)

For example, the DiskFree function lets you find out how much disk space is free on a drive. The syntax for this function in Delphi 16 is

function DiskFree(*Drive*: Byte): Longint {returns an integer in Delphi 32}

Use 0 for the default drive, 1 for A, 2 for B, 3 for C, and so on. When you use this function, the long integer returned is the amount of disk space available.

As another example, the GetDir procedure returns a string that gives the current directory for a specific drive. For example, if you have set up a string variable called Drive, then after a line of code like

```
GetDir(3, Drive);
```

the value of the Drive string parameter would be the current directory on the C drive. The general syntax for this procedure is

procedure GetDir(*D*: Byte; var *S*: String)

If the drive is invalid, then the procedure sets the value of the *S* string parameter to be the string X:\.

What follows are short discussions of the most important of these functions (consult the online help for more details and for the remaining functions).

ChangeFileExt This function lets you change the file extension (for example, to indicate a backup). The syntax is

function ChangeFileExt(const *FileName, Extension*: string): string;

The string given by the *Extension* parameter becomes the new extension of the filename given by the *FileName* parameter.

10

DiskSize   This function returns a long integer that is the size (in bytes) of the specified drive. The syntax in Delphi 16 is

> function DiskSize(*Drive*: Byte): Longint; {returns an integer in Delphi 32}

where, as usual, the *Drive* parameter is 0 for the current drive, 1 for the A drive, and so on.

ExpandFileName   This very useful function returns a string that gives you the full path name of a file. The syntax is

> function ExpandFileName(const *FileName*: string): string;

ExtractFileExt, ExtractFileName   As you would expect from their names, these functions take a filename and return the file extension or the name without an extension.

ExtractFilePath   You often need to know the path for a specific file. This function takes a filename and returns the drive letter and directories that lead to the file.

FileAge, FileGetDate, FileDateToDateTime   The FileAge function gives the age of the file; the FileGetDate function gives the DOS time stamp. However, both functions return long integers. Use the FileDateToDateTime function to convert this long integer to the TDateTime type (and so make it usable by Delphi's date and time routines).

FileExists   This very useful Boolean function returns True if the file exists, and False otherwise. The syntax is

> function FileExists(const *FileName*: string): Boolean;

The FileGetAttr Function   The FileGetAttr function returns an integer. Using bit-masking techniques on the returned value with the "fa" constants (faReadOnly, faHidden, and so on) lets you determine how the various attributes are set. The syntax for this function is

> function FileGetAttr(const *FileName:* string): Integer;

FileSearch   This function lets you search through specified directories for a file. The syntax is

> function FileSearch(const *Name, DirList*: string): string;

where the *Name* parameter is the filename and the *DirList* parameter is a list of directories (separate them by a semicolon). The string returned is either the empty string or the full path name. For example:

```
if FileSearch('CH1', 'C:\; D:\') = '' then
  ShowMessage('Uh Oh file is lost!');
```

The FileSetAttr Function   The FileSetAttr function sets attribute information for files. The same "fa" constants for the various possible attributes that were used with FileGetAttr let you change the various attributes of a file. The syntax for this function is

function FileSetAttr(*FileName*: string, *AttributeValue*: Byte);

For example:

```
FileSetAttr(FileName, faReadOnly + faHidden);
```

would both hide the file and set it to be read-only.

Tip: Use the FileSetAttr function to hide files that you don't want casual users to know about.

For example, putting an encrypted password in a hidden file and then examining that file is a common (and reasonably secure) method of making sure that a program is being used by the right person.

FindFirst, FindNext   These two functions search a directory for a specified filename with a specified set of attributes.

The syntax for FindFirst is

function FindFirst(const *Path*: string; *Attr*: Word; var SearchRec: TSearchRec): Integer;

The *Path* parameter is the path name (it can include wildcards). The *Attr* parameter uses any combinations of the "fa" constants that you have seen earlier. The SearchRec parameter uses the built-in TSearchRec record type that will hold the results of the search. This type is defined as follows in Delphi 16:

10

```
TSearchRec = record
  Fill: array[1..21] of Byte;
  Attr: Byte;
  Time: LongInt;
  Size: LongInt;
  Name: string[12];
end;
```

In Delphi 32 this type is defined as:

```
TSearchRec = record
  Time: Integer;
  Size: Integer;
  Attr: Integer;
  Name: TFileName;   {This type is actually a string}
  ExcludeAttr: Integer;
  FindHandle; THandle;
  FindData: TWin32FindData;
end;
```

When you analyze this record then, for example, the Size field gives the file's size, and the Name field gives its name.

The syntax for FindNext is

function FindNext(var *F*: TSearchRec): Integer;

The FindNext function uses the information contained in the previous call to FindFirst.

The File System Components

The file system components in both versions of Delphi allow users to select a new drive, see the hierarchical directory structure of a disk, or see the names of the files in a given directory. As with all Delphi components, you need to write code to take full advantage of the power of the file system components. In addition, if you want to tell DOS to change drives or directories as the result of a mouse click by a user, you need to write code that uses the commands given in the first section in this chapter.

Note: The file system components complement the common dialog boxes that you will see in Chapter 13.

Here's the system tab on the Component palette with the file system components marked from the 32-bit version of Delphi. (They look the same in the16-bit version.).

FileListBox   FilterComboBox

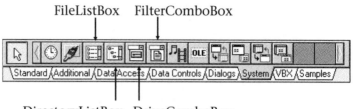

DirectoryListBox   DriveComboBox

The file system components are designed to work together. For example, your code checks what the user has done to, say, a DriveComboBox and then passes this information on to a DirectoryListBox. The changes in a DirectoryListBox are then passed on to a FileListBox.

The FileListBox Component

A FileListBox defaults to displaying the files in the current directory. As with any list box, you can control the position, size, color, and font characteristic at design time or with code. Most of the properties of a FileListBox are identical to those of ordinary list boxes. For example, as with any list box, when the number of items doesn't fit the current size of the component, Delphi automatically adds vertical scroll bars. This lets the user move through the list of files using the scroll bars.

Similarly, a FileListBox can respond to all the events that list boxes can detect. In addition, you can write event handlers for a keypress or a mouse movement. Remember that the Windows convention is to have a double-click, not a single click, choose the file. This is especially important to remember when you work with a FileListBox, because using an arrow key to move through a FileListBox would call any OnClick handler that you have written. (Recall that arrow movements are functionally equivalent to a single mouse click for a list box.)

Tip: It is quite common to use the Items and ItemIndex properties of a FileListBox rather than use the GetDir command.

Special Properties of the FileListBox Component

You can use a FileListBox's FileType property to display only the files that are read-only (which is good for novice users) or only those that have the Archive bit turned on or off (that is, to indicate whether the files have been backed up since the last change). The FileType property that controls this is a set made up of one or more of seven Boolean (True, False) values. This set property controls what type of files are shown in a FileListBox. They are ftArchive, ftHidden, ftNormal, ftReadOnly, ftSystem, ftVolumeID, and ftDirectory. The default setting is True for the ftNormal value and False for the remaining values.

The most important other properties for a FileListBox are Mask, FileName, and Directory. The Mask property determines which files are displayed in the FileListBox. The Mask property accepts the ordinary DOS wildcards: * (match any) and ? (match a single character). The default mask is set to *.* to display all files. (Of course, the Mask property looks at the settings of the various attribute properties before Delphi displays the files.)

The Directory and FileName properties set or return the current path for the FileListBox, but not for DOS. To tell DOS to change the current path from within Delphi, you need the ChDir command. On the other hand, you may just need to accumulate this information for use by your program without disturbing the default path. When you change the Directory or FileName property, Delphi looks to see if you have written an OnChange event handler for the FileListBox and, if so, activates it.

The DirectoryListBox Component

A DirectoryListBox displays the directory structure of the current drive. The current directory is represented by an open file folder. Subdirectories are shown as closed folders, and directories above the current directory are shown as nonshaded open folders.

 Note: When the user clicks on an item or moves through the list, that item is highlighted. When he or she double-clicks, Delphi automatically updates the directory list box.

The DriveComboBox Component

Unlike FileComboBoxes and DirectoryListBoxes, DriveComboBoxes are pull-down boxes. A DriveComboBox begins by displaying the current drive, and then, when the user clicks on the arrow, Delphi pulls down a list of all valid drives.

The key property for a DriveComboBox is the Drive property, which can be used to return or reset the current drive. For example, to synchronize a DriveComboBox with a DirectoryListBox, all you need is to link the drive and directory components via the DirList property. Here is all the code it takes to link a DriveComboBox to a DirectoryListBox:

```
DriveComboBox1.DirList := DirectoryListBox1;
```

The FilterComboBox Component

The FilterComboBox component is used to control the type of files that Delphi displays in a FileListBox. After setting the FilterComboBox's FileList property to the name of a FileListBox, set the Filter property to the file types that you want to display. Here is a code sample:

```
FilterComboBox1.Filter := 'Doc files (*.doc) | *.doc | Text files (*.txt) |
*.txt';
```

Tying All the File Components Together

When you have all the file system components on a form, you merely have to set the DriveComboBox.DirList and the DirectoryListBox.FileList properties in order to communicate any changes among the components. Delphi will then show what the user wants to see.

You can also write code to communicate the changes among the file system components. For example, if the user selects a new drive, Delphi activates the DriveComboBox OnChange event handler. After that, do the following:

1. In the DriveComboBox OnChange event handler, assign the DriveComboBox.Drive property to the DirectoryListBox.Drive property. This changes the display in the DirectoryListBox by activating its OnChange event handler.

2. In the DirectoryListBox OnChange event handler, assign the DirectoryListBox.Directory property to the FileListBox.Directory property. This updates the FileListBox.

Text Files

Text files contain readable ASCII characters and are exactly the ones you can use DOS' TYPE command to read—without having garbage fill your screen. Think of working with a text file in Delphi as analogous to recording information on a cassette tape. Operations on text files that are analogous to easy tasks for a cassette recorder, such as recording an album on a blank tape, will be easy to do. Those analogous to more difficult tasks, such as splicing tapes together or making a change within a tape, will be more difficult.

To avoid unnecessary work, use a text file only when you know that you are working with ordinary text and you will

♦ Rarely make changes within the file

♦ Massage (process) the file contents from start to finish, without needing to constantly jump around

♦ Usually add to the file at the end of the file

It *is* possible to make changes within the file, jump around when processing information, or add to the file other than at the end; it's just that these procedures are a bit cumbersome.

Note: Every line in a text file ends with a carriage return/line feed combination.

As with some of the file-handling functions, such as the Erase function that you have already seen, you must first use the AssignFile procedure in order to associate a file on disk with a file variable. This time, however, the declaration looks like this:

```
var
 FileIdentifier: TextFile;
begin
 AssignFile(FileIdentifier, filename);
```

where the keyword **TextFile** tells Delphi you will be working with a text file. Unless the filename is in the current directory, you need to provide enough information to identify its path. Also, the value of a text variable must be a legal filename.

Pascal Tip: If you want to use the older Text keyword, you must use it in the form of System.Text, but it is best not to use it at all.

Here's a table of some common operations on a cassette tape and the analogous operations on a sequential text file that has been assigned to a text variable named TxtFile:

Operation	Delphi Equivalent
Put the machine in playback mode and press Pause.	Reset(TxtFile);
Put the machine in record mode and press Pause.	Rewrite(TxtFile);
Press Stop.	CloseFile(TxtFile);
Start recording at the end of the recorded portion of the tape.	Append(TxtFile);

Each time Delphi processes a Reset, Rewrite, or Append command, it gets ready to send information into or take information out of the file. (The jargon is that it "sets up a channel" to communicate with the file.) What follows the Reset, Rewrite, or Append command is the name of the file variable you are working with.

The CloseFile command empties the buffer and tells DOS to update the file allocation table (FAT). But because of Windows' own buffering techniques, this may not happen precisely when Delphi processes the CloseFile command. For this reason, a sudden power outage when you have a file open almost inevitably leads to lost information and occasionally even to a corrupted disk. (Use of the CHKDSK/f command or SCANDISK is often necessary when this happens.)

Note: The Flush procedure allows you to force Delphi to save the output buffer to disk before it is filled.

When you process large files, the default buffer is only 128 bytes. This often causes your application to slow down noticeably. Delpi provides the SetrTextBuf procedure to change the size of a text file's buffer. (A larger size will probably speed up disk-intensive programs appreciably.)

Sending Information to a File

The Writeln command is probably the most common way to send individual pieces of information to a file. Here is an example of a fragment that sends one piece of information to a file named TEST.DAT:

10

```
{Writing to a file}
var:
  TxtFile: TextFile;
begin
  AssignFile(TxtFile, 'TEST.DAT');
  Rewrite(TxtFile);
  Writeln(TxtFile, 'TESTING, 1 2 3');
  CloseFile(TxtFile);
end;
```

After the usual comment statement, the variable declaration tells Delphi that you are going to set up a text file variable named TxtFile. The AssignFile statement associates this file variable to the file named TEST.DAT. The Rewrite statement opens the file for output and sets the file pointer to the beginning of the file. The Writeln statement actually sends the information to the file. What appears in the file are the characters inside the quotes—the file does not contain quotation marks. The Writeln command also sends a carriage return/line feed combination—a CR (carriage return), ASCII code 13, and an LF (line feed), ASCII code 10, to the file. This means the file will contain the word "TESTING", followed by a comma, followed by a space, followed by the numeral 1, followed by another space, followed by the numeral 2, followed by a space, followed by the numeral 3, and then an ASCII 13 followed by an ASCII 10.

Note: On rare occasions you will want to send data to a text file without adding a CR/LF combination. For this, use the Write procedure instead of Writeln.

On the other hand, if you need to send the contents of any string list (such as the Lines property of a memo box) directly to a file, Delphi lets you do this with a single line of code. Use the SaveToFile method of the TStrings object as follows:

```
StringListName.SaveToFile(FileName);
```

Reading Back Information from a Text File

If you want to read back the contents of a file into a string list, then your task is easy—one line of code is again enough.

```
StringListName.LoadFromFile(FileName);
```

On the other hand, to read back information from a file item by item, you must open the file for input by using the Reset procedure. The syntax is

Reset(*file variable*);

Once a file is reset, you can read information from the file with the Readln or Read procedures. Here's an example using Readln:

```
{Reading from a file}
var:
  TxtFile: TextFile;
  S: String[80];
begin
  AssignFile(TxtFile, 'TEST.DAT');
  Reset(TxtFile);
  Readln(TxtFile, S);
  CloseFile(TxtFile);
end;
```

Readln will read the specified number of characters (based on the size of the string variable) or up to a CR/LF combination—whichever comes first. It also moves the file pointer to the beginning of the following line when it finishes. If the line that Delphi is reading contains more than the specified number of characters (80 in our example), then the remaining characters are ignored and the file pointer is set to the beginning of the next line anyway.

Read, on the other hand, works just like Readln, *except* it does not move the pointer to the next line—it leaves the pointer where it was. This means that as an alternative to our example file, you could have used the following:

```
{Reading from a file}
var:
  TxtFile: TextFile;
  S1, S2, S3: String[5];
begin
  AssignFile(TxtFile, 'TEST.DAT');
  Reset(TxtFile);
  Read(TxtFile, S1, S2, S3);
  CloseFile(TxtFile);
end;
```

Note: As the previous example shows, you can use multiple variables in each Read (or Readln) statement.

10

Doing I/O Checking When Working with Files

In general, you would *never* use programs like the ones given in the previous section. You should *always* use exception handling to take into account that I/O can be prone to problems. *Always* have the CloseFile command in a **finally** block to avoid even the possibility of corrupting a user's FAT (file allocation table). Even the simplest programs of the previous section should be rewritten as follows:

```
{Reading from a file with Exception handling!}
var:
  TxtFile: TextFile;
  S: String[80];
begin
AssignFile(TxtFile, 'TEST.DAT');
try
  Reset(TxtFile); Readln(TxtFile, S);
finally
  CloseFile(TxtFile);
end;
```

Tip: The EInOutError exception is the one to trap.

Reading Numbers from Text Files

Besides storing strings, text files can also store numbers. What happens is that when you use a numeric variable in the Read or Readln statement, Delphi will automatically convert a string of numerals into the appropriate number. More precisely, Delphi

♦ Skips over blanks

♦ Reads in any numerals until it gets to a blank, a nondigit, or a second period

♦ Converts the resulting string of digits into the appropriate numeric type and assigns it to the numeric variable

Note: If the conversion is unsuccessful, Delphi generates an exception.

The Eof Function

If you know exactly how much information is contained in a file, you can use a For loop to read back the information. Most of the time, however, this is not practical—you simply don't know what limits to use for the loop. What you really need is a way to implement the following outline:

    While there's information left in the file
      Get next piece of information
    Loop

To do this, you need a way to test when you're at the end of a file. The function in Delphi that lets you do this is called the Eof (End of file) function. Its syntax looks like this:

    function Eof (var *TextFileID*: Text): Boolean;

This function returns True when you have read beyond the last character in the file, and False otherwise. This means you can write a While loop that looks like this:

```
var
  StringVariable: String;
  TextFileID: TextFile;
begin
  AssignFile(TextFileID, 'TEST.DAT');
try
  Reset(TextFileID);
  while not Eof(TextFileID) do
   begin
    Readln(TextFileId, StringVariable);
    ShowMessage(StringVariable);
   end;
finally
  CloseFile(TextFileID);
end;
```

This will display the contents of the file in message boxes—one line at a time.

Notice that you use a While loop rather than an Until loop to take into account the unlikely possibility that the file exists but doesn't contain any information—that is, it was opened for output but nothing was actually sent to the file. This fragment is a more or less direct translation of the outline. It picks up a line of data (that is, up to 255 characters or to the next carriage return/line feed pair), and it continues doing this until it gets to the end of the file.

Typed Files

Typed files are files that only contain data of a particular type, such as Integer, Real, or a previously defined Record type. Since typed files have a structure defined by the type of data they hold, you can read and write information back and forth from them very efficiently. For example, reading numbers back from a typed file is much faster than from a text file, because no conversions are necessary—typed files store numbers and strings in the same format in which they are stored by the program. Strings in a typed file are stored with the first byte containing the string's length; the following bytes store the actual characters. (There also might be some garbage characters used for filler if the string variable was not filled to its declared length.)

The extra speed requires some extra programming, of course. Here's an example of what you need to work with a typed file:

```
var
  RealFile: file of Double; {the Real type is for backward compatibility
                             it shouldn't be used }
  RealNumber: Double;
begin
  AssignFile(RealFile,'NUMBER.DAT');
try
  Rewrite(RealFile);
  RealNumber := Pi;
  Write(RealFile, RealNumber);
  RealNumber := Exp(1);
  Write(RealFile, RealNumber);
finally
  CloseFile(RealFile);
end;
try
  Reset(RealFile);
  Read(RealFile, RealNumber);
```

```
  ShowMessage('The value of pi is' + FloatToStr(RealNumber));
finally
  CloseFile(RealFile);
end;
```

In general, you use the Write command to write information to a typed file and the Read command to get it back (most commonly with an Eof loop as you saw earlier).

Records in Typed Files

Typed files can also hold user-defined data types. For example, suppose you have a record of type BookInfo:

```
type
  BookInfo = record
    Author: String[20];
    Title: String[30];
    Subject: String[15];
    Publisher: String[20];
    Miscellaneous: String[13];
  end;
var
  BookData: BookInfo;
  BookFile: file of BookInfo;
```

Now you can use the Read and Write commands to read or write back a whole record at a time.

Untyped Files

Untyped files are used when you have to (or want to) impose the least possible structure on a file. While text files consist of lines terminated with a CR/LF combination, and typed files consist of data taken from a particular type of data structure, untyped files have no structure whatsoever.

You can read information from an untyped file into any data type. Of course, this can lead to some really strange behavior on the part of your program if you try to read incompatible data into your variables. On the other hand, untyped files give you the fastest way to transfer data from a disk to your program.

The following code fragment reads in a file and writes it back out to a second file. This sample illustrates the use of the **file** keyword for untyped files, and two new procedures—BlockRead and BlockWrite:

10

```
var
  SrcFile: File;
  DestFile: File;
  RecsRead: Integer;
  Buffer: array [1..2048] of Byte;

begin
  AssignFile(SrcFile, 'file.in');
try
  Reset(SrcFile, 1);    {note:  the second argument indicates the
record size}
  AssignFile(DestFile, 'file.out');
  Rewrite(DestFile, 1);    {note:  the second argument indicates
the record size}
  BlockRead(SrcFile, Buffer, SizeOf(Buffer), RecsRead);
  while RecsRead > 0 do
     BlockWrite(DestFile, Buffer, SizeOf(Buffer));
     BlockRead(SrcFile, Buffer, SizeOf(Buffer), RecsRead);
  end;
finally
  CloseFile(SrcFile);
  CloseFile(DestFile);
end;
```

The preceding code sample uses several new features that are worth going over. When used with untyped files, Reset and Rewrite have a second argument that defines the record size. In our example, we chose a record size of 1 byte, since we set our buffer to be an array of bytes—the most primitive data structure possible.

You always use the BlockRead and BlockWrite procedures when using untyped files. The parameters for both these procedures are similar. The first parameter is the filename, the second is the name of the data structure, the third is the number of records to read. The fourth parameter is the actual number of records to read or write.

Sometimes you will want to position the file pointer to a specific record in a file. The Seek procedure takes the file variable as the first argument and uses the second argument for the file position you wish to point to. This is the Seek procedure syntax:

```
Seek(SrcFile, 0);
```

Tip: Two more file I/O functions that you may need for working with untyped files are FileSize and FilePos. FileSize returns the size of the file in bytes. FilePos returns the current position of the file pointer.

Command-line Information

Most professional programs allow (or require) the user to type in additional information when he or she invokes the program. This extra information is usually called *command-line information*. For example, when you write

```
COPY A:*.* B:
```

the command-line information is the string "A:*.* B:". The utility program COPY uses this information to know what to do. Delphi makes it easy to read this information. When you run any program from the File Manager, and for example, and use the form

```
FileExeName info1 info2 info3
```

the value of the function ParamCount is the number of parameters in the command line (three in this example), whereas the list ParamStr( ) gives the actual command-line parameters. ParamStr(0) is the path and filename of the executable. ParamStr(1) is the first string (info1), and so on.

Note: Obviously, you need a way to create sample pieces of command-line information while developing the program; otherwise, you wouldn't have any test data with which to debug the program. You do this with the Parameters option on the Run menu.

Chapter

11

Communicating with Other Windows Applications

Both Windows 3.X and Windows 95 can *multitask,* that is, run several applications at once. (For this to be really effective under Windows 3.X, and occasionally under Windows 95 or Windows NT, however, applications must cooperate by releasing the CPU. Recall that you do this with the ProcessMessages method of the Application Object.) Multitasking becomes even more useful if the various applications running on the Windows desktop can work with each other. For example, suppose you could write a Delphi program that monitors what a spreadsheet like Excel or Lotus 1-2-3 for Windows is doing. This would make it possible to use Delphi to add a feature that isn't built into the spreadsheet. For example, you might want to notify the user if a crucial quantity has changed or reached a target. Perhaps you want to write a program that analyzes a document being written in a Windows word processor, like Word for Windows, in real time, notifying the user when he or she has written a certain number of words.

Note: Delphi 32 has a TThread component that allows multiple threads to run concurrently. We do not cover this component in this book, but it is worth noting that multithreading is quite different from multitasking. In multithreading, you have a program that can do things simultaneously such as printing and accepting keyboard input; in multitasking you have simultaneous programs.

The most primitive way to communicate between Windows applications is via dynamic data exchange (DDE). DDE seems mysterious at first, but if you think of it as automated use of the Windows Clipboard, the mystery should disappear. The first section of this chapter covers the Clipboard. If you haven't spent much time using the Clipboard, you'll see that it is much more than a passive place to store objects for cutting and pasting. In DDE, your Delphi program essentially tells the other applications what to put into or take out of the Clipboard.

Note: Although you must use a registered Clipboard format, DDE doesn't use the Clipboard the way an ordinary cut-and-paste operation does. Any data already there does not get overwritten, and you can have multiple simultaneous DDE conversations.

OLE in Delphi is potentially an even more powerful way to have Windows applications communicate through Delphi. OLE lets you build your own integrated Windows applications as a single Delphi project.

Note: You can use the ShellExecute API call to start another program from within Delphi (check the online help for its syntax). In Delphi 32 you can still use this call, but you are better off using the CreateProcess call that is the Win 32 API.

Visual Basic Tip: Since Delphi, unlike Visual Basic, has no equivalent of the SendKeys function, communicating keystrokes from Delphi to another application requires some very tricky uses of the Windows API and cannot be recommended for most situations.

The Clipboard

The Windows Clipboard lets you exchange both graphics and text between Windows applications, and is often used for cut-and-paste operations inside a specific Windows application. In particular, Delphi uses the Clipboard for its cut-and-paste editing feature, and you can use the Clipboard together with the properties given in the section of this chapter called "Clipboard Formats and Graphical Transfers" to implement similar features in your projects.

Note: You must add the ClipBrd unit to the **uses** clause of any project that uses the Clipboard except when you restrict cutting and pasting to the components—TEDit, TMemo, TOLEContainer, TDDEServerItem, TDBEdit, TDBImage, and TDBMemo—that already have built in support for cut and paste methods via the Clipboard.

However, users of Microsoft Windows rarely think of the Clipboard at all, and if they do, they usually think of it as a passive feature of Windows. Yet the Clipboard viewer is an independent program, usually available in the Windows Main program group under Windows 3.X and in the Accessories folder in Windows 95.

You can use the File menu on the Clipboard viewer to view graphical files or to save the contents of the Clipboard as an independent file. Moreover, the Clipboard viewer program is often smart enough to convert images from one format to another. This is why you can use the Clipboard to transfer text to Delphi from a non-ASCII word processor like Word for Windows.

Since much of this section is about automating Clipboard operations, you may want to have the Clipboard viewer up and running while working through it. That way you can look at the contents of the Clipboard to check that what you think you've put there (automatically) really is there.

The Clipboard can hold only one piece of data for cut, copy, and paste at one time. In general it can hold only one piece of the same kind of data at a time. If you send new information of the same format to the Clipboard, you wipe out what was there before. Sometimes, however, you will want to make sure that the Clipboard is completely free before working with it. To do this, add a line of code inside your project that looks like this:

```
{Note: the Clipboard object is created in the ClipBrd unit}
begin
  Clipboard.Clear;
end;
```

As you might expect, this applies the Clear method to the predefined Clipboard object. If you need to send text to and from the Clipboard, use its AsText method, described next.

The AsText Method of the Clipboard

The AsText method is usually used in the following form to get text from the Clipboard:

    StringData := Clipboard.AsText;

Use AsText in the following form to send text to the Clipboard:

    Clipboard.AsText := StringData;

This sends the string information contained in the variable or string expression StringData to the Clipboard, wiping out whatever text was there.

Clipboard Formats and Graphical Transfers

To retrieve graphical images from the Clipboard, Delphi must know what type of image is stored there. Similarly, to transfer images to the Clipboard, the program must tell the Clipboard what type of graphics it is sending. The following table summarizes this information. The second column of the table gives the name of the constant that Delphi uses for the format.

Format	Symbolic Constant
Text (.TXT)	CF_TEXT
Ordinary bitmap (.BMP)	CF_BITMAP
Windows metafile (.WMF)	CF_METAFILEPICT
Object of type TPicture	CF_PICTURE
Any persistent object	CF_COMPONENT

The HasFormat Method

You ask the Clipboard what type of image it is currently storing by using the HasFormat method. The syntax for this method is

    Clipboard.HasFormat(*Format*)

where Format is one of the values given in the previous table. This method returns True if the image in the Clipboard has the right format. For example:

```
if Clipboard.HasFormat(CF_BITMAP) then ShowMessage ('Clipboard
has a bitmap');
```

To assign (send) an image to the Clipboard, you use the Assign method. The syntax for this method looks like this:

Clipboard.Assign(*Bitmap*);

where Bitmap is an object of type TGraphic, TBitmap, TMetaFile, or TPicture. Remember, you use the AsText method to retrieve text data from the Clipboard. To retrieve an image from the Clipboard:

1. Verify the format of the current contents of the Clipboard.
2. Use the Assign method of the target component.

11

For example:

```
   if Clipboard.HasFormat(CF_BITMAP) then
Image1.Picture.Bitmap.Assign(Clipboard);
```

Dynamic Data Exchange (DDE)

The way DDE works is that one Windows application (called the client) tells another Windows application (called the server) that it wants information. Technically, a DDE conversation is between two windows, and from the point of view of Microsoft Windows, most components, including forms, *are* windows.

What you need to do is called setting up a DDE *conversation,* or DDE *link.* For Delphi, the DDEServerConv component can be used to create a DDE server. Although technically only the DDEServerConv component can be a server, the other components on the form will probably be providing the information via their properties, so this isn't usually much of a problem. Information generally flows from the server to the client, although the client can, if necessary, send information back to the server.

Windows allows an application to engage in many DDE conversations at the same time. An application can even play the role of server and client simultaneously. For example, your Delphi project can send information to Word for Windows while receiving it from Excel. However, only one piece of information may be sent at any one time.

You must know the name of the application you want to talk to. If an application supports DDE, the DDE name will be given in the documentation. For example, as far as DDE is concerned, the name for Word for Windows is "WinWord." The DDE name for Excel is still "Excel." The DDE name for any Delphi form acting as a DDE server is the name you chose when you made it into an executable file. If you are running the project within the Delphi development environment, the DDE name is the name of the project, without any extension. Once you know the name of the application you want to talk to, this will be the value of the DDEService property of the DDEClientConv component.

Next, you need to know the *topic* of the DDE conversation. Usually this is a specific filename. For example, Excel recognizes a full filename (a path name) ending in .XLS or .XLC as a suitable topic. Finally, you need to know what you are currently talking about. This is called the *item* of the DDE conversation. For example, if Excel is the DDE server, the item for a DDE conversation could be a cell or range of cells. If the TDDEServerConv component is used, the Name property of the TDDEServerConv component is the topic. If no TDDEServerConv component is used, the caption of the form is the topic. The component name of the DDEServerItem is the item for a DDE conversation.

The TDDEClient component can have two kinds of DDE conversations (links). A TDDEClient.ConnectMode of Automatic means that the link is automatically established when the form with the TDDEClient component is created at run time. The Manual choice for ConnectMode means that the link is only established when the OpenLink method is called.

Creating DDE Links at Design Time

This section uses Microsoft Excel for its examples. If you do not have Excel, you should still be able to follow the discussion. All you need to know is that spreadsheets like Excel are organized into rows and columns, and that Excel, like Delphi, has a Copy menu on its main menu bar with similar items.

For the following discussion, start up a new project, and add a DDEClientConv and DDEClientItem component from the System component page. Set the DDEConv property of DDEClientItem1 to DDEClientConv1. Next, start up Excel (or imagine that you are starting it).

To set up a client link with Excel as the DDE server, and the contents of the first row and column as the item for this DDE conversation, do the following:

1. Move to the Excel window and highlight (select) the contents of the cell in the first row and first column.
2. From the Edit menu in Excel, choose the Copy command.
3. Move to the Delphi window, select the DDEClientConv component, and click the Ellipsis (...) button for either the DDEService or DDETopic property in the Object Inspector.

4. Choose Paste Link. (If you followed steps 1 through 3, this option should be enabled, and the Clipboard will contain our DDE information.) Then choose OK.

5. Select the DDEClientItem component. In the Object Inspector, choose the DDEItem property, and choose the item from its drop-down list (Clipboard contents must remain unchanged).

6. If Excel is not in your path, set the DDEClientConv.ServiceApplication property to point to Excel. Do not include the extension (.EXE). For example, use C:\EXCEL\EXCEL and not C:\EXCEL\EXCEL.EXE for the value of this property.

11

Note: To create a manually updated DDE Client, add only the DDEClientConv component to the form. Your application will execute code that calls the RequestData method of this component.

Now you can test whether the link was successfully made. For this, move back to the Excel window, type something in the cell in the first row and first column, and press ENTER. Whatever you type should appear in the DDEClientItem component and become the value of its Text property, because links made at design time are automatic links. In addition, every time the DDE server updates the information for a Delphi DDEClientItem component, Delphi generates the OnChange event. This lets you act on the information in real time as well.

Note that when you switch from designing a Delphi project to running it within the development environment, Delphi must break the DDE link. Many applications will automatically attempt to reestablish the DDE link, but you may find that server links, especially, need to be established by code. (See the next section, "Links via Code.")

This link is permanent. If you save the project, Delphi preserves the information about the link as the value of certain properties. You'll see these properties in the next section. In particular, try the following for the DDE link set up previously:

1. Close Excel and save the Delphi project.

2. Start up a new project temporarily.

3. Open the Delphi project with the DDE link and press F9 to run the project.

Delphi will always attempt to start up the application that was the server for a DDE conversation set up at design time.

As you might expect, DDE conversations—at least as far as Delphi is concerned—are determined by the value of certain properties. Manipulating the values of these properties via code will make your DDE conversations far more flexible than DDE links made at design time can ever be.

Links via Code

As an example of putting all the link properties and methods together, consider the Delphi 16 DEMOS\DDEDEMO\DDECLI.DPR project. The user supplies the name of the application that is acting as the DDE server (i.e. the DDEService property), the topic, and the item. After opening the DDECLI project, notice that there are buttons, labels, edit boxes, groupings, a DDEClientConv, a DDEClientItem, and a menu component to start the link, as well as one to paste a link.

Here are the doNewLink and DDEClientItemChange event handlers that set up the link:

```
procedure TFormD.doNewLink(Sender: Tobject);
begin
  DDEClient.SetLink (AppName.Text, TopicName.Text);
  DDEClientItem.DDEConv := DDEClient;
  DDEClientItem.DDEItem := ItemName.Text;
 end;


procedure TFormD.DDEClientItemChange(Sender: Tobject);
begin
  DDEDat.Lines := DDEClientItem.Lines;
end;
```

The idea behind these events is simple. The SetLink method establishes the link with a specified server and topic. The DDEClientItem is then linked to the DDEClient conversation setup with the SetLink. The DDEClientItem. DDEItem is then set to the edit box containing the item. The DDECLI demo also provides sample code for poking data and executing macro commands.

DDE Component Properties, Methods, and Events

There are lots of properties that can be set when dealing with DDE. This section goes over the most important of them. For more information, please consult the online help.

DDEServerItem Properties

First, let's go over the properties used to set up a DDE server.

ServerConv   The ServerConv property specifies the DDE server conversation component to associate with the DDE server item component. The value of ServerConv is the name of the DDE server conversation component that defines the DDE conversation.

Lines   The Lines property contains the text data for the DDE client. The Lines and Text properties are similar, except that the Text property can only hold 255 characters.

11

Text   The Text property contains the text data for the DDE client, as does the Lines property. The Text property can only hold 255 characters, whereas the Lines property can hold larger strings because it is a string list. See the section in Chapter 5 on string lists for more on them.

DDEServerItem Method

Now we will go over the most important methods used to set up a DDE server.

CopyToClipboard   The CopyToClipboard method copies the text data specified in the Text property of a DDE server item component to the Windows Clipboard. You can then create a link by activating the DDE client application, selecting the topic and item of the DDE conversation, and executing an Edit | Paste Link command, or its equivalent in the command structure of the DDE client application.

DDEServerItem Events

What follows is a short discussion of the most important events for a DDE server.

OnChange   If the value stored in a DDE server item component changes, your application can change the Text property of the DDE server item component by assigning a new value to it. The DDE client can change the value by poking data (transferring data from the DDE client to the DDE server).

OnPokeData   If the DDE client application pokes data to the server, the OnPokeData event is triggered.

DDEServerConv Events

What follows is a short discussion of the most important events that the DDE components can recognize.

Note: Other than the Name property of course, there are no key DDEServerConv properties. There are no DDEServerConv methods.

OnClose   An OnClose event occurs when a form or DDE conversation is closed.

OnExecuteMacro   The OnExecuteMacro event occurs when a DDE client application sends a macro to a DDE server conversation component. Write code to process the macro in the OnExecuteMacro event handler.

OnOpen   An OnOpen event occurs when a DDE conversation is opened.

DDEClientConv Properties
We now cover the properties for using Delphi as a DDE client.

ConnectMode   The value of the ConnectMode property determines the type of connection to establish with a DDE server. If you use DDEAutomatic, this establishes a link when the form is created at run time. If you choose DDEManual, this establishes a link only after Delphi processes the OpenLink method.

DDEService   The value of the DDEService property specifies the DDE server name. See the application's documentation for the information about how to specify the DDEService property.

DDETopic   The value of the DDETopic property specifies the topic of a DDE link. DDETopic is typically a filename used by the application linked in DDEService. See the application's documentation for specific information about specifying DDETopic.

FormatChars   If the value of the FormatChars property is False, then all text characters of the linked data from the DDE server appear in the linked data in the DDE client. If True, ASCII characters 8 (backspace), 9 (tab), 10 (linefeed), and 13 (carriage return) are filtered out and won't appear in the DDE client data.

ServiceApplication   The ServiceApplication property specifies the main executable filename (and path, if necessary) of a DDE server application, without the .EXE extension. Typically, this is the same value as the DDEService property. Sometimes, however, DDEService is a value other than the DDE server application's executable filename. In either case, ServiceApplication must be specified for Delphi to run an inactive DDE server to establish a DDE conversation and won't appear in the DDE client data.

DDEClientConv Events

When you set up a DDE client, many events can be triggered. Here are discussions of the most important of them.

11

OnClose   An OnClose event occurs when a form or DDE conversation is closed.

OnOpen   An OnOpen event occurs when a DDE conversation is opened.

DDEClientConv Methods

What follows are short discussions of the methods used to set up a DDE client conversation.

CloseLink   The CloseLink method terminates an ongoing DDE conversation.

ExecuteMacro   The ExecuteMacro method attempts to send a macro command string to a DDE server application.

ExecuteMacroLines   The ExecuteMacroLines method attempts to send a macro command string list to a DDE server application.

OpenLink   The OpenLink method initiates a new DDE conversation.

PokeData   The PokeData method sends data to a DDE server application. It is used to send a string of up to 255 characters.

PokeDataLines   The PokeDataLines method sends data to a DDE server application. It is used to send a string greater than 255 characters.

RequestData   The RequestData method requests data from a DDE server.

SetLink   The SetLink method specifies the service and topic of a DDE conversation and attempts to open the link if ConnectMode is DDEAutomatic. The Service parameter defines the DDE service and is assigned to the DDEService property. The Topic parameter defines the DDE topic and is assigned to the DDETopic property.

DDEClientItem Properties

When you set up a DDE client, there are quite a few properties that you may need to set. Here are discussions of the most important of them.

DDEConv The value of the DDEConv property specifies the name of a DDE client conversation component to associate with the DDE client item component.

DDEItem The value of the DDEItem property specifies the item (that is, what data is actually going to be passed from server to client) in a DDE conversation. See the application's documentation for specific information about specifying DDEItem.

Lines, Text Both the Lines and Text properties contain the text data from the DDE server. The difference is that the Text property can only hold 255 characters, and the Lines property is actually a string list, so it can hold thousands of lines of text.

Note: The DDEClientItem component has no methods.

DDEClientItem Event

When you set up a DDE client, many events can be triggered. There is only one event, OnChange, which we discuss next.

OnChange Delphi triggers an OnChange event when the value of the Text property of a DDE client item component changes. The DDE server application continuously updates the Text property of the DDE client item component.

OLE

OLE, which originally stood for "object linking and embedding," is a technology that started out by complementing and extending dynamic data exchange. Now it is just called OLE and stands for nothing. For example, OLE goes beyond DDE in that, instead of merely transferring information, information will now be presented in the same way it would appear in the originating application.

There are two versions of OLE. OLE 1.0 allows the user to activate an OLE object that was created with an OLE 1.0 server application. Then the server

11

application opens its own window in the foreground and takes over the focus. The OLE container application exists in a separate window in the background. (This is usually called *out-of-place activation.*)

OLE 2.0 allows the user to activate an OLE object that was created with an OLE 2.0 server application. In this case, the server's menu and toolbar replace the ones in the OLE container. The OLE object could now be edited from within the OLE container window, but all the processing is handled by the OLE server. This is usually called *in-place activation*. In OLE 2.0, spreadsheets appear as spreadsheets, word processor documents appear as they would in the word processor, and so on. When you add an OLE container (TOleContainer) component to your Delphi project, you give the user a bridge to another Windows application. Delphi does not let you create OLE 2.0 servers, only OLE containers.

Note: To enable in-place OLE support in a Delphi application, you must connect to an OLE server that supports in-place activation. Your main form must have a MainMenu and the code needed to handle menu negotiation.

There are three parts to OLE. The *objects* are the data supplied by the Windows applications that support OLE—for example, an Excel worksheet (or, more likely, part of an Excel worksheet).

To understand *linking,* imagine that you are part of the group working on this book. Besides the author, there are a technical editor, a copy editor, a proofreader, and others involved. The most efficient work method for your group would be to maintain a single copy of the document and to have each person involved be able to link to it and make changes. There would still be only one copy of the document (on a central server) involved; that way your group doesn't have to worry about important changes being missed. In other words, it allows work in a "parallel" rather than a "serial" way. With a linked object, the data stays in the application that created it. Think of linking as attaching a chain to preexisting data—as with any chained objects, you can effect changes by jerking on the chain. Technically, what linking does is insert a placeholder into the Delphi application and store an image of the data in the TOleContainer component.

The idea of the *embedding* part of OLE is that you create documents that integrate various Windows applications under one roof. Embedding in OLE 2 allows the component to maintain the data in the object inside itself. When Delphi activates the OLE container component, control switches back to the application that created the data, and you can use that application's power to modify the data in place.

Note: There is now a new kind of OLE—Microsoft calls it OLE Automation. OLE Automation allows you to use another application's underlying language to control it. Delphi 16 does not support OLE Automation, Delphi 32 does. (For an example of OLE automation, check out the DEMOS directory.)

One of the main ideas behind the introduction of OLE was that Microsoft wanted users to stop thinking of applications as being paramount. Instead, they want users to think of the document itself as central. For example, suppose you are preparing a complicated report that uses spreadsheet data and a graphical package. You want parts of the document to be under the control of the word processor, and parts to be under the control of the spreadsheet. In OLE 2, the other application temporarily takes over to work with the data embedded in the control. When you embed an object in an OLE client control, then no other application can access the data (as opposed to linking it where they can). Moreover, the application that created the embedded data is automatically started up whenever the user works with the embedded data.

Note: The trouble is that all this takes gobs of RAM. Think long and hard about running an OLE application on a machine with less than 16 megabytes of RAM!

Using OLE

When you add a TOleContainer component to your Delphi projects, you create what is called an *OLE compound document*. An OLE container component is one of the tools supplied with Delphi. The component, located in the System page of the component toolbar, is the one labeled "OLE."

In Delphi 16 your Delphi project can only be the client (or container) application that receives the information from the server (source) application that sends it. With OLE, your Delphi project receives the information and serves as the client. (The OLE container component supplied with Delphi 1.0 is an OLE client component and does not allow a Delphi application to become an OLE server.)

Note: Delphi 32 does allow you to build a special type of OLE server, called an OLE automation server. For more on this, please consult the online help.

Some important terminology for dealing with OLE is explained in the following sections.

11

OLE Classes   OLE classes are the applications that produce the OLE object. Any application that supports OLE has a unique OLE class name. For example, "WordDocument" or "ExcelWorksheet." (Class names can be case sensitive.) You can get a list of the class names (the paste special OLE items) available by clicking on the ellipses for the ObjClass property in the Object Inspector window.

OLE Documents   OLE documents are the source files that contain the data for the OLE object. These can be a Word document or an Excel spreadsheet. You can get a list of the class names available by clicking on the ellipses for the ObjDoc property in the Object Inspector window.

OLE Items   OLE items are any data the OLE container component can work with. They can be a single graph, a range of cells in a spreadsheet, a whole spreadsheet, or part or all of a word processed document. You can get a list of the class names available by clicking on the ellipsis for the ObjItem property in the Object Inspector window.

Using OLE 2 at Design Time

Compared to OLE 1.0, creating links or embeddings at design time is easy in OLE 2. Essentially, you need only work with the dialog boxes that will be described in this section.

If you have added a TOleContainer component to a form, clicking on the ellipsis for the ObjClass property brings up the Insert Object dialog box as shown in Figure 11-1. (These are Delphi 16 dialog boxes, the Delphi 32 boxes look similar.)

Note: The more OLE-compliant applications you have, the more items will appear.

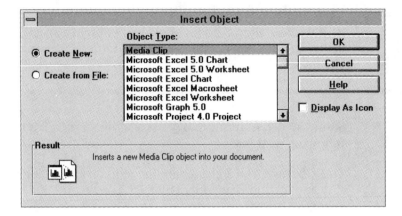

The OLE Insert
Object dialog
box with the
Create New
radio button
activated
Figure 11-1.

The OLE Insert Object box gives you the names of all the Windows applications you can hook into. You can have the object show up as an icon or with the data visible in the OLE component. The two radio buttons on the far left determine whether you will work with an existing file created by the application (a linked object) or want the other application to create one anew (an embedded object). If you choose to link the control by choosing the Create from File option, the dialog box looks like the one in Figure 11-2. You can click on the Browse button to open a dialog box that lets you pick the file. When you have done that, check the Link box. An example of this dialog box for Delphi 16 is shown in Figure 11-2.

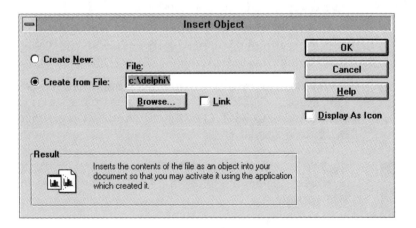

The OLE Insert
Object dialog
box with the
Create from
File radio
button
activated
Figure 11-2.

Note: You can click on the Cancel button if you want to set the OLE properties via code. You do not need to use this dialog box to work with OLE. In fact, if you create an executable file with an OLE connection made at design time, the file will be much larger than if you create the connection at run time with code.

Paste Special

Sometimes you want to create linked or embedded objects by using information stored in the Windows Clipboard to determine the ObjDoc and ObjItem properties. To do this, you first need to copy the data from the application to the Clipboard by using the Copy command in the application. You then need to use the Paste Special dialog box, which is available at design time, by clicking the ellipses for the ObjItem property when the focus is in the TOleContainer component. This dialog box automatically examines the contents of the Clipboard to determine the needed OLE properties. Figure 11-3 shows the Paste Special dialog box for Dephi 16. (Again it looks similar in Delphi 32.) If you want to create an embedded object, click the Paste radio button; for a linked object, choose Paste Link, and then click OK.

The TOleContainer Component Properties

As you might expect, the dialog box only makes it simpler to set the properties of the OLE component. You can always change them via the

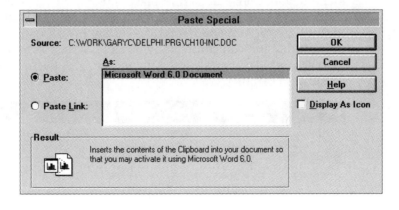

The Paste
Special dialog
box
Figure 11-3.

Object Inspector window or code (and, of course, you will have to do this to enable OLE at run time).

The AutoSize property allows you to change how the control looks at run time. If the value is False, then the control clips the data displayed at run time. Set the value of this property to True to have the control automatically resize the control.

The Insert Object dialog box that pops up is also setting the crucial ObjClass property, which specifies the application containing the data. For example:

```
OLEContainer1.ObjClass := 'Paintbrush.Picture';
```

The ObjDoc property gives the name of the linked object or the file to be used as a template for an embedded object. The ObjItem property is used for linked objects to specify what portion of the linked document the Delphi application can work with. For example:

```
OLEContainer1.ObjDoc := 'C:\WINDOWS\256COLOR.BMP';
```

As another example, a spreadsheet range might be indicated by setting this property to 'R1C1:R1C10'.

Creating OLE Connections via Code

Now that you are familiar with OLE terminology, let's use the DEMOS\OLE2\OLE2DEMO.DPR project supplied with Delphi 16 to examine linking to objects at run time. The OLE2DEMO project has a form named OLE2WIN with a MainMenu component, along with a button and OLE container component. The MainMenu component handles the needed menu negotiation, when an in-place activation occurs, by setting the GroupIndex property of certain menu items. The OLE server will merge up to three groups of menu items. Each group is distinguished by a unique group index and can contain any number of menu commands. The following table summarizes the menu item groups that the OLE server application can merge.

Group	Index	Description
Edit	1	Menu item(s) from the server for editing the active OLE object.
View	3	Menu item(s) from the server for modifying the view of the OLE object.
Help	5	Menu item(s) from the server for accessing the server's online help.

Any menu items in your container application that have a value of 1, 3, or 5 for their GroupIndex properties will be replaced by the menu items with corresponding index values from the OLE server application. The menu items from your OLE container that have a GroupIndex value other than 1, 3, or 5 won't be replaced by menus from the server.

Note: You can also merge an OLE Server's toolbar and status bar with your application. See the online help or Chapter 15 of the User's Guide supplied with Delphi for more details.

Once the OLE2DEMO is running, you can choose the New item from the File menu to create a new instance of the form and make the form visible using the following code:

```
procedure TMainWindow.NewOleWin1Click(Sender: TObject);
var
  Child : TOLEWin;
begin
  Child := TOLEWin.Create(Self);
  Child.Visible := True;
end;
```

Click the Reset Object item from the Object menu, and the Insert Object dialog box is displayed:

```
procedure TOLEWin.ResetBtnClick(Sender: TObject);
var
  InitInfo: Pointer;
begin
  if ActiveControl.InheritsFrom (TOleContainer) then
  begin
    if InsertOleObjectDlg (Self, 0, InitInfo) = True then
    begin
      TOleContainer(ActiveControl).PInitInfo := InitInfo;
      ReleaseOleInitInfo (InitInfo);
    end;
  end;
end;
```

You can now choose to link or embed an object. The above code also initializes the OLE container with the information that the InitInfo pointer points to, and then frees the memory used by the InitInfo pointer. It is always a good practice to clean up memory when you are done.

When the user closes the OLE Container form, the OLE container is deactivated in the Form.OnClose event:

```
procedure TOLEChild.FormClose(Sender: TObject; var Action:
TCloseAction);
begin
    OLEContainer1.Active := False;
end;
```

OLE Automation

Delphi is extendible—that's one of its greatest strengths. However, you may not want to spend your time creating custom components or DLLs that duplicate functionality found in other applications such as Excel, Visio, or Word. The key to tapping other (OLE-compliant) applications is OLE Automation. You can use Delphi 32 to write programs that let you manipulate the data and the objects in these applications.

 Note: OLE Automation is the one place where everyone must use variants—regardless of philosophical prejudices.

Some objects that support OLE Automation also support linking and embedding. If an object in an OLE container control supports OLE Automation, then you can access its properties and methods directly. A full discussion of OLE Automation is beyond the scope of this section. If what you read here whets your appetite, refer to your Delphi manuals for more information. The first step in using OLE Automation is to add the **uses OleAuto** unit to the implementation clause of the unit. Then you have to use a variant variable to manage the communication process.

You also have to be aware that OLE Automation starts up the other application. You therefore have to catch the error when this doesn't succeed. For example, if you are controlling WordBasic you would use

```
var
  MSWordBasic: Variant;
begin
   try
    MSWordBasic := CreateOleObject('Word.Basic');
   except
    ShowMessage('Word wouldn't start up-program ending');
```

```
      Application.Terminate;
end;
end;
```

A few points worth noting before you go head over heels into a love affair with OLE automation:

♦ OLE Automation requires being familiar with the object you want to program. The syntax for the commands is always going to be tricky. For example, to actually program the WordBasic object created in the previous program requires familiarity with WordBasic's extremely quirky syntax. Here is the code needed to write out the contents of a memo box to a new Word document, print it, save it, and then close it.

```
implementation

{$R *.DFM}

uses OleAuto;
var
   WordBasicOleAutoObject : Variant;

procedure TForm1.Button1Click(Sender: TObject);
var
  LineNo : Word;
begin
  {The methods FileNewDefault, Insert, FilePrintDefault,
  FileSaveAs and FileClose all came out of the Word 6
  on-line documentation on Word Basic}
  try
    WordBasicOleAutoObject := CreateOleObject('Word.Basic');
    WordBasicOleAutoObject.FileNewDefault;
    for LineNo := 0 to Memo1.Lines.Count - 1 do
       WordBasicOleAutoObject.Insert(Memo1.Lines[LineNo] + #13);
    WordBasicOleAutoObject.FilePrintDefault;
    WordBasicOleAutoObject.FileSaveAs('C:\TEST.DOC');
    WordBasicOleAutoObject.FileClose;
   except
    on E: EOleError do ShowMessage(E.Message);
   end;
end;

end.
```

♦ If you try to use OLE automation on programs like Word or Excel, be prepared for sloth. The bigger the application you are trying to control, the more memory you will need and the worse the performance will be. Word and Excel are *big*.

In sum, think long and hard before using OLE Automation in an application that is destined to run on anything less than state-of-the-art machinery. The amount of RAM seems to be even more important than the speed of the CPU. Don't try to use OLE Automation with 4 megabytes of RAM; think hard before using it when you have 8MB. OLE will start getting usable when you have 16MB of RAM, but 32MB (!) seems to be the "sweet spot."

On the other hand, we may be seeing the beginnings of smaller and tighter OLE servers based on the OCX model. For example, a company like AlphaBlox has small (often less than 300K) OLE servers that do useful things. When Microsoft (or Lotus) gets around to exposing only the spelling checker from their humongous word processing programs, they will be small enough to be very useful. OLE automation for servers this small will run effectively on any machine running Windows 95.

Tip: You can use Windows API calls to detect the kind of hardware a user has.

Chapter 12

Graphics

This chapter shows you the basics of graphics in both versions of Delphi. (The methods are the same regardless of which version of Delphi you are using.) You can draw on forms, with a printer, or on a TImage component. The TShape component, on the other hand, gives you a quick way to draw shapes like circles or rectangles. Using Delphi's graphical methods will often require writing a fair amount of code, but in return for the extra work, these methods allow you to control every dot that appears on your screen or that prints on your printer. Because Microsoft Windows is a graphically based environment, the graphics powers of Delphi can be astonishing.

Note: The TPictureBox component (which we do not discuss here) lets you display bitmaps, icons, or Windows metafiles. Consult the online help for more on this component.

Traditional programming languages usually distinguish graphics from text; this distinction is much less important with Windows and, therefore, with Delphi. This is why you can create forms that display text with such varied fonts, and why you are able to use the TextOut method to position text accurately on the screen. Nonetheless, *all* the graphical methods such as TextOut actually belong to the Canvas object and not to the screen or form. This means that in addition to the Form, ImageBox, or Printer, any component you buy or make that has a Canvas object can be used for drawing.

In general, after processing a graphical method, Delphi tells Windows what to display. Windows, in turn, tells the display adapter how to display the image. This means that what you can do with Delphi's graphical statements ultimately depends on the driver programs that Windows uses to control the screen and printer. However, using these driver programs is automatic. You do not have to worry about all the possible hardware combinations a user may have. This is different from what MS-DOS programmers are used to. When you program graphics under DOS, a part of the program must check what kind of graphic board is installed (or whether *any* graphic board is installed), and then adjust the program accordingly.

The TShape Component

The TShape component, which is available on the Additional page of the Component palette (it looks like a landscape), lets you quickly display a shape on a form without tying up many Windows resources. As you might expect, you use the Height and Width properties to control the size of the shape component on a form.

The key to using the TShape component is its Shape property, which has six possible values. For example, stCircle gives you a circle, and stRectangle gives you a rectangle. Exactly how Delphi displays the shape is controlled by the Color and Style properties that are nested below the Brush property. The Color property uses the standard Delphi constants for its values, such as clWhite, clBlack, and so on. The Style property has eight possible values, which are also described using built-in constants, as shown in Table 12-1.

Value of Style Property	What It Looks Like
bsSolid	
bsClear	
bsBDiagonal	
bsFDiagonal	
bsCross	
bsDiagCross	
bsHorizontal	
bsVertical	

12

Possible
Values of the
Style Property
for the TShape
Component
Table 12-1.

Basics of Graphics

You can draw on a form, a TImage component, or the printer. You saw the TImage component at work back in Chapter 1. The TImage component is on the Additional page of the Component palette. As you will soon see, you draw on all three of these objects in the same way, by using the Canvas object that you saw back in Chapter 5.

Images displayed on a TImage component are *persistent,* meaning that if the window is covered and then uncovered, the picture is not erased. Images displayed in a form are not. This always involves a trade-off between memory and speed. Because they have persistent graphics, TImage components can use a lot of memory (Delphi must tell Windows to allocate enough memory to hold the entire image so that it can re-create it). Painting on a form uses less memory, but requires more code and often more processing time. For example, if you minimize a form that contains something that you drew on it, and later restore it, the image will be gone.

Note: Since Delphi activates the OnPaint event each time a part of the form is newly exposed, you can write the necessary code in the OnPaint procedure whenever you want to redraw part of a form.

Therefore, the least memory-intensive way to handle the problem of graphics disappearing because a user covered a form is to redraw the image in the form's OnPaint event handler.

Caution: Be very careful about including in the OnPaint event handler any commands that move or resize the object. If you do, Delphi will just call the OnPaint procedure again, and you will be stuck in an infinite regression.

You will occasionally need to use the Refresh method when working with graphics. This method applies to both forms and components. It forces an immediate refresh of the form or component. If you use the Refresh method, Delphi will also call any OnPaint event handler you have written for the object. This method is commonly used in the form's OnResize event handler to redisplay any graphics. Also, while Delphi handles refreshing the screen during idle time, occasionally you will want to control this process yourself. Whenever Delphi processes a Component.Refresh statement, it will redraw the object immediately and generate the OnPaint event (if the component recognizes this event).

More on the TImage Component

The most important properties of the TImage component are summarized next.

AutoSize   When this property of the TImage component is True *before you load the picture*, the image control resizes to fit the image placed in it. The default is False, so the picture may be clipped or may not fill up the TImage component.

Center   This Boolean property determines if the image is centered inside the TImage component. The default is True.

Stretch If you set the AutoSize property to False and the Stretch property to True, then Delphi allows bitmaps and metafiles to grow to fill the TImage component. Icons remain unchanged.

Picture This property determines what image appears in the component. It is usually used with the LoadFromFile method. The way to use this method might look like this:

```
Image1.Picture.LoadFromFile('BTFLY.BMP');
```

Fundamentals of Canvas Graphics

The Canvas object, which is a property of the TForm and TImage component as well as the TPrinter object, is the key to drawing in Delphi. You work with properties and methods of the Canvas object to do everything from coloring a specific dot to drawing a rounded rectangle.

12

Colors

If you do not specify a color for your drawing, Delphi uses the foreground color of the object for all the graphical methods. (Note: This is not true for TextOut, TextRect, and so on, which require the use of the API functions SetColor and SetBkColor to change the color of text output.) You must specify the color before using the actual graphics method. There are three ways to specify colors:

♦ Use the predefined color constants such as clBlack or clGreen.

♦ Use the Color dialog box to select a color, and then use the value within the Color property and assign it to the Color property of another control.

♦ Use the ColorToRGB function. The syntax for this function in Delphi 1.0 is

ColorToRGB(Color: TColor) : Longint;

where the color is a component's color property.

Pixel Control

Now that you know how colors are assigned, how do you turn on a pixel? For this, use the Canvas object's Pixels property. The syntax for this method is

FormName.Canvas.Pixels(*Col, Row*) := *color code*;

for a form, or

> *ImageBoxName*.Canvas.Pixels(*Col, Row*) := *color code*;

for a TImage component.

If you are lucky enough to have a color printer with a good Windows driver, you can add the Printers unit to the **uses** clause and then use

> *Printer*.Canvas.Pixels(*Col, Row*) := *color code*;

In general, all you need to do is replace the parameters with the values you want and *color code* with the appropriate built-in constant. The value of the first entry determines the column, and the second determines the row. After Delphi processes this statement, the pixel associated with that point lights up.

Drawing Shapes

Obviously, if you had to draw everything by plotting individual points, programming graphics would be too time-consuming to be practical. In addition to the Shape component, Delphi comes with a rich supply of graphical features, called *graphics primitives*. These allow you to plot such geometric figures as lines, boxes, circles, ellipses, and wedges with a single statement. For example, here's the code needed to draw a line from the top left corner of the form to wherever the user clicked the mouse:

```
procedure TForm1.FormMouseDown(Sender: TObject; Button: TMouseButton;
  Shift: TShiftState; X, Y: Integer);
begin
  Canvas.MoveTo(0, 0);
  Canvas.LineTo(X, Y);
end;
```

The first statement moves the starting point of the line to 0,0—the top left corner. The second statement gives you a line starting at the top left corner and going to the point where the user clicked the mouse button. (The line uses the color currently specified by the value of the Canvas.Brush.Color property of the form.)

Normally, to describe a circle or ellipse in Delphi, you give the coordinates of its bounding rectangle as parameters to the Ellipse method. For example, the following fragment draws a circle that fills the entire client area of the form:

```
Canvas.Ellipse(0, 0, ClientWidth, ClientHeight);
```

You can also add a color code to the Circle method. For example:

```
Canvas.Brush.Color := clRed;
Canvas.Ellipse(0, 0, ClientWidth, ClientHeight);
```

would draw a red circle.

Note: The Canvas object also provides properties for the following graphic objects: arcs, chords, pies, polygons, and rectangles—check the online help for more on these.

Last Point Referenced

Delphi keeps track of where it stopped plotting. This location is usually called the *last point referenced (LPR),* and the value of the PenPos property stores this information.

12

Note: Use the MoveTo method to change the PenPos property, rather than doing it directly.

Pens

The Pen property of a Canvas object controls how lines or shapes are drawn. The pen has five properties: Color, Handle, Mode, Style, and Width. A pen's default width is 1 pixel. The following code sample shows how to change a pen's width to 2 pixels:

```
Canvas.Pen.Width : = 2;
```

After you change the pen's width, Delphi draws all subsequent shapes using the new width for their boundaries.

If you do not want a solid line, all you need to do is change the pen's Style property. There are seven possible settings, as listed in Table 12-2.

You will occasionally need to use the Mode property, which determines how the pen interacts with pixels on the screen. For example, if you set the Mode property to pmNot, then Delphi uses the opposite color to the one on the screen when it draws the line or shape on the Canvas.

Value of Style Property	What the Pen Draws
psSolid(default)	A solid line
psDash	A line of a series of dashes
psDot	A line of a series of dots
psDashDot	A line of alternating dashes and dots
psDashDotDot	A line of a series of dash-dot-dot combinations
psClear	Lines of no visible marks
psInsideFrame	Lines within the frame of closed shapes that specify a bounding rectangle

Values of the
Pen's Style
Property
Table 12-2.

Note: The Handle property gives you the Windows GDI object handle for Delphi objects. This means that when a Windows API function requires an HDC as a parameter, pass it the value of the Canvas' Handle property. This lets you use Windows API calls for more sophisticated graphics.

Brushes

The Brush property of the Canvas object allows you to specify how Delphi fills an area. Boxes (and circles) are usually empty or solid, but Delphi allows you eight different patterns to fill boxes. To do this, you need to change the Style property of the form or picture box. The Style property for brushes works exactly the same as it does for the Shape control, so the values for the Style properties are the same. For example, bsSolid gives you a filled shape.

Saving Images to Disk

Delphi makes it easy to save the pictures you've drawn to a TImage component. The SaveToFile statement uses the following syntax:

ImageBoxName.Picture.SaveToFile(*FileName*);

The operating system uses the Picture property to identify the image in the component. If you originally loaded the picture from a file by assigning an image to the Picture property of the TImage component, Delphi saves the picture in the same format as the original file. For example, icon files remain as icon files. Otherwise, Delphi saves the picture as a bitmap (.BMP) file.

Chapter 13

Advanced User Interface Features

Now that you have learned most of the programming techniques needed in Delphi, it's time to turn to the user interface again. The first part of this chapter shows you techniques that will work no matter what the version of Delphi. For example, you'll see more about the common dialog boxes in this chapter. The look of a dialog box is slightly different in each version of Delphi; the techniques, luckily, are identical. The second half of this chapter briefly surveys the components that are available only in Delphi 32. In some cases there is overlap—there is a special component for status bars under Windows 95.

When you start adding many different components to a form, the way they overlap becomes more important. So this chapter has a section on the order that Delphi uses to display interface elements. This section explains what happens if you draw overlapping components—which ones appear on top and how this can be changed. (It's called

Z-Order. The "Z" stands for the z-axis, the conventional way to describe depth.)

There's also a section on MDI (multiple document interface) applications and a discussion on how to monitor what the user is doing with his or her mouse. We end the part of this chapter that will be of interest to users of both Delphi 16 and Delphi 32 with a short discussion of how to add a help system to your applications.

Then it's on to the Windows 95 controls supplied with Delphi 32. However, since it would take hundreds of pages to show off all their power, I will confine myself to showing you how the Windows 95 RichTextBox (in Delphi it is called a TRichEdit editor component) allows you to use multiple fonts, underlining, bold, etc., in a TMemo-like component. Finally, because I am one of the world's worst spellers, I can't resist showing you the basics of how to use the spell-checking OCX control supplied with Delphi 32.

Adding Toolbars and Status Bars to Projects

The TPanel component is the best way for building a toolbar or a status bar on a form in Delphi 16 and even in Delphi 32. This is because placing a panel on the bottom or top of a form is easy in Delphi by use of the Align property. The value of the Align property determines where the panel appears. The Align property's six values are described in Table 13-1.

Align Property Value	Action
alBottom	The value for a status bar. The panel is flush with the bottom of the form and also automatically is the correct width.
alClient	This value sizes the panel to fill the client area of the form.
alLeft	The panel is flush with the left of the form and also automatically is the correct height.
alNone	The default for ordinary forms. You can position the panel anywhere you want.
alRight	The panel is flush with the right of the form and also automatically is the correct height.
alTop	The value for a toolbar. The panel will appear flush against the top and will automatically have the same width as the form.

The Align Property Values and Actions **Table 13-1.**

Building a Toolbar or Status Bar

First, decide on the icons you want to use for your toolbar. Next, assign these icons to the Glyph property of the TSpeedButton components that will be on the toolbar. Now to actually build the toolbar, follow these steps:

1. Place a TPanel component on the form. (The TPanel component is the last one on the Standard page of the Component palette.)

2. Change the Height property of the panel to be large enough to encompass the icons that are used on the toolbar. (You can do this either via the Object Inspector or via the mouse.)

3. Set the Align property of the panel to alTop. (This will automatically set the width of the panel to be that of the form.)

4. Clear the Caption property of the form.

5. While the panel is still selected, place as many TSpeedButton components to the panel as are needed. (The "sticky click" method of adding components introduced in Chapter 3 is probably the easiest way to do this.)

6. Set the Glyph property of the button to the filename of the icons you want.

13

Tip: To give the toolbar a professional look, you should position the SpeedButton components sequentially with no space between them, and they should be centered inside the panel. For example, if the panel's height is 41 and the height of the buttons is 25, you will want to set the Height property of the SpeedButton to 8 so that the buttons are centered.

Note: When you add any component by double-clicking the Component icon on the Component palette, Delphi automatically centers it vertically and horizontally.

You might also want to consider adding help hints like Delphi uses. That way, if the user is unsure of what an icon does, he or she need only leave the mouse on the button for a specified amount of time before a textual description of the button pops up. Recall that you do this by setting the SpeedButton's ShowHint property to True. Set the Hint property to the text you want to pop up, and set the HintPause property to specify the time lag before it pops up.

Note: You may want the SpeedButtons to behave as a group; for example, you may only want one to be on at any one time. To do this, set the GroupIndex property appropriately.

Grouped buttons always give the impression of toggling between being pressed in and not. If you want a nongrouped SpeedButton to give the impression of toggling between being pressed in and not pressed, set the AllowAllUp to True and the GroupIndex property to be not zero. The Down property governs the initial state.

Status Bars

Status bars tend to be text-oriented. Often the only graphics used are shaded lines to separate the text items to give a nicer look to the bar. These lines can be created using the Canvas property. Unfortunately, the Canvas property of a Panel is not exposed (i.e., it is private). Thus you would need to make a descendent of a TPanel component that exposes this property for your use if you want to draw on a panel.

One possible method of updating the status bar is to write the code that sends the text to the status bar in whatever procedure necessitated updating the status bar. However, the cleanest choice is usually to call a subprogram that updates the status bar—it is always best to have procedures concentrate on what they are supposed to be doing, rather than having them update status bars as well! (For example, the general procedure that updates the status bar may need to call another procedure in order to parse the text.)

Tip: To give the status bar a more professional look with lowered rather than raised text and a nice frame, set the BevelInner property of the panel to bvLowered and the BorderWidth property to 2.

Common Dialog Boxes

While working with Windows and Delphi, you've become accustomed to seeing one of eight standard dialog boxes for opening or saving a file, printing, choosing fonts, or setting colors. These components take advantage of the standard dialog boxes located in a DLL in your \WINDOWS\SYSTEM directory. All versions of Windows include a version of this DLL. Common dialog boxes are easy to use in principle, but the number of possibilities is large, so this chapter can give you only a feeling for how to work with them.

All the common dialog box components are in the Dialogs page of the Component palette (see Chapter 2 for descriptions of the icons, or use the help hints). To use a common dialog box, you need to place the appropriate component or components on the form.

The common dialog box components are nonvisual and so are invisible to the user while the program is running. To actually pop up a specific common dialog box requires Delphi processing the Execute method of the common dialog box component while the program is running. For example, if you have an Open File item on the File menu and the associated Click event handler is in Open1 OnClick, the code to pop up a File Open dialog box using the default name of the component starts like this:

```
procedure TForm1.Open1Click(Sender: TObject);
begin
   if OpenDialog1.Execute then...
```

Table 13-2 lists the common dialog boxes available in Delphi.

Note: The common dialog box components take no actions; they accept information only. You will always need to write the code that tells Delphi what to do with the information entered, and then have this code processed when the user closes the common dialog box.

13

Working with Common Dialog Boxes

Before you pop up the box, you need to initialize the various properties that determine how the common dialog box looks. For example, you might want to make the Print dialog box default be that the Print Range is set to print only page 1. This is done by adjusting the value of the FromPage and ToPage properties of the common dialog component as follows:

```
PrintDialog1.FromPage := 1;
PrintDialog1.ToPage := 1;
```

All the common dialog boxes allow you to determine if the user clicks the Cancel button (or presses ESC). Setting up a trap for this is necessary in most (if not all) cases—think how fragile the bitmap viewer in Chapter 1 was. To trap a click on the Cancel button or a press on the ESC key that closes a dialog box, you'll need to include a code fragment like the following:

```
if OpenDialog1.Execute then
   begin
```

```
    {statements using OpenDialog1.Filename};
  end;
```

If the user clicks the Cancel button or presses ESC, then Delphi returns False as the value of the Execute method, so this code wouldn't be processed. For example, if we changed the code in the bitmap viewer in Chapter 1 by adding one more line so that it looks like:

```
procedure TForm1.FormActivate(Sender: Tobject)
begin
  if OpenDialog1. Execute then
  begin
      Image1.Picture.LoadFromFile(OpenDialog1.Filename);
  end;
end;
```

it would be quite a bit more robust.

The File Open (TOpenDialog) and File Save (TSaveDialog) Boxes

Table 13-3 describes the most important properties used for these dialog boxes.

Dialog Box Name	Description
TColorDialog	Shows available colors.
TFontDialog	Shows the fonts available. Includes point sizes and colors if appropriate.
TOpenDialog	Displays filenames. Can set filters for specific extensions, directories, and drives.
TSaveDialog	Displays filenames. Also can set filters for specific extensions, directories, and drives.
TPrintDialog	Displays the Windows standard Print dialog box for determining output. Can also be used to obtain information about installed printers.
TPrinterSetupDialog	Displays a list of available printers. Also lets you obtain information on how to set the paper orientation, size, and source. (Can be opened from the Print dialog box as well.)
TFindDialog	Displays an edit control so the user can enter a string to search for.
TReplaceDialog	Gives two edit controls for both the target and its replacement.

Common Dialog Boxes Available in Delphi
Table 13-2.

Property	Use
DefaultExt	Sets the default extension for files shown in the box.
Title	Sets the title bar. In particular, you do not need to use Open and Save if you are using these boxes in other contexts.
FileName	Gives the name and path of the file selected.
Filter	Affects the "List Files of Type" box. You can have multiple filters by separating them by a vertical bar (|), usually found above the backslash on the keyboard. The format is the description string, the vertical bar, the filter, another bar, and so on.
FilterIndex	This is used when you set up many filters using the Filter property.
Options	This property is used to set various possible options on how the box will look.
InitialDir	Specifies the initial directory.

Important Properties of the TOpenDialog and TSaveDialog Boxes
Table 13-3.

13

The Options properties are very important in determining the final look and feel of the box. For example, a line of code like:

```
With OpenDialog1 do
  Options := Options + [ofAllowMultiSelect];
```

allows the File Name list box to use the standard Windows techniques for multiple selections while keeping whatever options were already set.

You can combine more than one flag, as shown in the following example:

```
With OpenDialog1 do
  Options := Options + [ofNoChangeDir, ofHideReadOnly];
```

What this line of code does is keep the currently set options. Additionally, it prevents the user from changing the directory and also hides the read-only check box.

Once the user clicks the OK button in a dialog box, you have to read back the information that he or she entered, and then take appropriate actions. For example, OpenDialog1.FileName would contain the name of the file chosen.

The TColorDialog Dialog Box
Table 13-4 describes the important properties used for this dialog box.

Property	Use
Color	Shows or gets the color chosen by the user.
Options	As with OpenDialog and SaveDialog boxes, this specifies the form of the box.

The symbolic constants for this box begin with "cd". For example,
ColorDialog1.Options := ColorDialog1.Options + [cdFULLOPEN] would
display the whole dialog box (including the one for defining custom colors).
When the user clicks the OK button, the value of, for example,
ColorDialog1.Color is the long integer code for the color selected.

The TFontDialog (Font Choice) Dialog Box

Table 13-5 describes the important remaining properties used for this dialog
box.

You read back the value of the various font properties to see what the user
wants. For example, the value of FontDialog1.Font.Name is the name of the
font the user chose. Then have Delphi process the code to have the new
value go into effect. Here is an example of how to select a font for the entire
form:

```
begin
  if FontDialog1.Execute then
     Font.Assign(FontDialog1.Font);
end;
```

There are 15 Options property values for the Font dialog box, and they all
begin with "fd". They are a nested (set) property available in the Object
Inspector, or you can set them via code. The Option property controls what
the Font dialog box will display. For example, by setting the fdAnsiOnly
value, the user will not be able to choose any symbol fonts. As always with a

Property	Use
Font.Color	Used only for color printers.
Font.Name	Sets or returns the font name.
Font.Size	Sets or returns the size of the font in points.
Options	As with OpenDialog and SaveDialog boxes, this specifies the form of the box.

set property, when you use code, you enclose it with square brackets and separate it by commas. You might want to look at the online help to see what the other flags do.

The TPrint Dialog Box Component

The printer dialog box gives you the standard Windows Printer dialog box. As before, the Options property controls how the box appears. The symbolic constants for the Printer dialog box all begin with "pr" or "po". For example, if the PrintRange parameter is set to prALLPAGES, then the All option button in the Print Range panel is set. Check the online help for more details on the possible Options you can use.

Table 13-6 describes the key properties used for this dialog box.

MDI Forms

MDI stands for *multiple document interface,* which is Microsoft's term for a windowing environment like that of many word processors or spreadsheets—one window, usually called the MDI *container* or MDI *parent form,* contains many other windows, usually called *child forms.* For example, you can use an MDI container form to allow a user to work with two windows in the same application. You can have only one MDI container form to a project, and that form must, naturally enough, be the startup form.

13

To make an MDI container form, set the FormStyle property of the main form (the form that you want to be the MDI container) to be fsMDIForm. Next, create the additional forms from the File menu as well. These will be the child forms to your newly created MDI parent form after you set their FormStyle property to be fsMDIChild. You can also turn an existing form into an MDI child form by adjusting this property. At design time, child forms and the MDI parent form look similar—it's hard to tell the differences between them.

When you run the project, on the other hand, all the child forms must be explicitly shown (with the Visible method set to True) and are displayed within the MDI parent form's boundaries. Moreover, if the child form is

<table>
<tr><th>Property</th><th>Use</th></tr>
<tr><td>Copies</td><td>Sets or returns the number of copies the user wants.</td></tr>
<tr><td>FromPage, ToPage</td><td>Defines what pages are wanted.</td></tr>
<tr><td>MaxPage, MinPage</td><td>Specifies the maximum and minimum pages the user can put in the Print Range panel.</td></tr>
</table>

Important Properties of the Printer Dialog Box

Table 13-6.

minimized, its icon appears inside the MDI parent form, rather than in the Windows desktop. (If you maximize a child form, its caption replaces the caption of the parent form.) Finally, you can neither hide nor disable child forms without using the Windows API. (But you can destroy and re-create in order to give this effect in Delphi if need be.)

One of the nicest features of Delphi's MDI forms is that the menus of the container form change according to which child form has the focus. This lets you work with specific menus for each child form. What happens is that the menu for the child form that has the focus appears on the menu bar of the MDI container form—replacing whatever menu was previously there. In particular, the user only sees the menu for the child form when that child form is active.

The Window Menu and Arranging the Child Windows

Every MDI application should have a Window menu that allows the user to arrange or cascade the child windows—much like Windows 3.X does. The Window menu should also include a list of the MDI child windows. This is easy to do. Let's assume you have a menu item named MyWindows on an MDI form. To add the list of MDI child windows, set

```
Form.WindowMenu := MyWindows;
```

Delphi will automatically display the list of the MDI child form captions—and even put a check mark next to the one that most recently was active. To activate the Tile, Cascade, and Arrange items on the Windows menu, write code like this:

```
procedure TFrameForm.Tile1Click(Sender: TObject);
begin
  TileMode := tbHorizontal;
  Tile;
end;
```

The example uses the Tile method and TileMode property. The other two methods you will need are Cascade and ArrangeIcons, described next.

Cascade   The Cascade method rearranges the child windows so that they overlap, showing only the title bar of each window.

ArrangeIcons   When you have several child windows minimized, you can use this method to rearrange the icons so that they are evenly spaced inside the parent window.

More on How Delphi Displays Work: Z-Order

Delphi paints the parts of your application in three layers. The back (bottom) layer is where you draw information directly on the form using the graphical methods that you saw in Chapter 12. The middle layer contains the graphical components (lines, shapes, picture boxes, and the image component). The top layer contains the nongraphical components like buttons, list boxes, check boxes, and option buttons. Certain components such as labels have a transparent property that lets information from the layers below shine through.

Within each layer you can control the order in which components appear. For example, if you overlap two image controls or push buttons, can you specify which one appears on top? If you use an MDI form, can you control which child form is on top?

You can control the order in which components appear in this way. At design time you can use the Bring To Front and Send To Back options from the Edit menu to effect the initial ordering of what's on top. To change it dynamically while the program is running, you need the BringToFront or SendToBack method.

13

Remember that you cannot bring a nonwindowed component to the front when it is under a window component.

Monitoring Mouse Activity

Windows, and therefore Delphi, constantly monitors what the user is doing with the mouse. Up to this point, all you have used are the OnClick and OnDblClick events. These detect whether the user clicked the mouse once or twice in a form or component. This section shows you how to obtain and use more subtle information. Was a mouse button pressed? Which button was it? Is the mouse pointer over a component? Did the user release a button, and if so, which one? Did the user move the mouse out of one form and into another? Exactly where inside the form is the mouse? Delphi can detect all these events. Of course, as with all Delphi operations, you must write the event handlers that determine how Delphi will respond to the event. For example, if you want to pop up a menu after a click of the right mouse button, you'll need to write the necessary lines of code.

Finally, just as designing a Delphi application involves dragging components around a blank form, Delphi lets you write applications that allow the user to move components around by dragging and dropping. You'll see how to do this as well.

The Mouse Event Handlers

There are three fundamental mouse event handlers:

Event Name	Event That Caused It
OnMouseDown	User clicks one of the mouse buttons.
OnMouseUp	User releases a mouse button.
OnMouseMove	User moves the mouse pointer.

In many ways, these procedures are analogous to the OnKeyUp, OnKeyDown event handlers that you saw in Chapter 5. For example, as with those event handlers, Delphi lets you use a ShiftState parameter to determine if the user was holding down SHIFT, ALT, or CTRL at the same time he or she pressed or released a mouse button.

Components recognize a mouse event only when the mouse pointer is inside the component; the underlying form recognizes the mouse event in all other cases. However, if a mouse button is pressed and held while the mouse pointer is inside a component or form, that object captures the mouse. This means that no other Delphi object can react to mouse events until the user releases the mouse button, regardless of where the user moves the mouse.

The MouseUp and MouseDown event handlers take the same form and use the same parameters:

TForm1.FormMouseDown(*Sender*: TObject; *Button*: TMouseButton; *Shift*: TShiftState; *X, Y*: Integer);

The MouseMove event handler just lacks a parameter for the button:

TForm1.FormMouseMove(*Sender*: TObject; *Shift*: TShiftState; *X, Y*: Integer);

As the next sections show, you analyze the Button argument to determine which mouse button was pressed. Similarly, you can find out if the user was holding down any combination with SHIFT, CTRL, or ALT by analyzing the Shift parameter. Finally, X and Y give you the information you need to determine the position of the mouse pointer, using the internal coordinates of the object (forms and picture boxes) if they exist.

The OnMouseUp/OnMouseDown Events

To see the event handler given in this section at work, start up a new project. Go to the Object Inspector, and activate the Event page. Double-click to open the Code Editor window for the OnMouseDown event handler. Now enter the following:

```
procedure TForm1.FormMouseDown(Sender: TObject; Button:
TMouseButton;
  Shift: TShiftState; X, Y: Integer);
Canvas.Ellipse(X-50, Y-50, X+50, Y+50);
 end;
```

This simple event handler uses the positioning information passed by X and
Y. Each time you click a mouse button, a small circle is centered exactly
where you clicked. If you add an OnMouseUp event handler that looks like:

```
procedure TForm1.FormMouseUp(Sender: TObject; Button:
TMouseButton;
  Shift: TShiftState; X, Y: Integer);
begin
  with Canvas do
  begin
    Brush.Style := bsSolid; {note: this change will persist!}
    Brush.Color := clRed;   {this change too will persist}
    Ellipse(X-50, Y-50, X+50, Y+50);
  end;
end;
```

13

then each time you release the same button, Delphi fills the circle with red.
And, when you move the mouse even slightly, you get a new circle. On the
other hand, even though you may have two or even three mouse buttons,
Delphi will not generate another OnMouseDown event until you release the
original mouse button. This prevents you from making some circles filled
and others empty when using these two procedures.

Suppose, however, you wanted to make some circles filled and some empty.
One way to do this is to use the added information given by the Button
argument. For example, suppose the user has a two-button mouse. You can
easily write code so that if the user presses the right mouse button, he or she
gets a filled circle, and otherwise all he or she gets is a colored circular
outline. The Button argument has three predefined constants to determine
which button was pressed, mbLeft, mbRight, and mbCenter. You can rewrite
the OnMouseUp event handler to allow both filled and empty circles using
the left/right buttons as follows:

```
procedure TForm1.FormMouseUp(Sender: TObject; Button:
TMouseButton;
  Shift: TShiftState; X, Y: Integer);
begin
  with Canvas do
  begin
    Brush.Style := bsSolid;
```

```
    case Button of
    mbRight: Brush.Color := clRed;
    mbLeft: Brush.Color := ClWhite;
    end;
    Ellipse(X-50, Y-50, X+50, Y+50);
  end;
end;
```

You can also let the user combine the keyboard with a mouse. For example, you can have the SHIFT-right mouse button combination drop down a special menu. To do this, analyze the ShiftState argument in the mouse movement event handler. The possible values for this set are described in Table 13-7.

Note: Microsoft Windows programs (for example, Delphi itself!) have begun to adopt the convention that pressing the right mouse button pops up a context-sensitive menu. This is usually controlled via the Object Inspector by setting the AutoPopup method of the popup menu to be True.

The OnMouseMove Event

Delphi calls the OnMouseMove event handler whenever the user moves the mouse. You should not get into the habit of thinking that the OnMouseMove event is generated continuously as the mouse pointer moves across objects. In fact, a combination of the user's software and hardware determines how often the OnMouseMove event is generated.

Nonetheless, since the OnMouseMove event handler will be called relatively frequently, any code inside this event handler will be executed often. For this reason, you will want to tighten the code inside the OnMouseMove

Value of ShiftState Type	What It Does
ssShift	SHIFT was pressed with the mouse button.
ssAlt	ALT was pressed with the mouse button.
ssCtrl	CTRL was pressed with the mouse button.
ssRight	The right mouse button was pressed.
ssLeft	The left mouse button was pressed.
ssMiddle	The middle mouse button was pressed (usually needs a three-button mouse, but pressing both mouse buttons on a two-button mouse will often generate this).
ssDouble	Both mouse buttons were pressed.

Values and Actions of TShiftState Parameters

Table 13-7.

event handler as much as possible, or provide a flag to prevent repetitive processing. For example, use integer variables for counters, and do not recompute the value of variables inside this event unless the new value depends on the parameters for the event. Always remember that accessing object properties is much slower than using a variable.

Dragging and Dropping Operations

To move a component as you are designing the interface in your Delphi project, you hold down a mouse button (the left one) and then move the mouse pointer to where you want the component to end up. An outline of the component moves with the mouse pointer. When you are happy with the location, you release the mouse button. The Microsoft Windows documentation calls moving an object with the mouse button depressed *dragging,* and calls what happens when you end dragging by releasing the mouse button *dropping.* Delphi makes it easy to program this potential into your projects. You can even drag and drop from one form to another if your project uses multiple forms.

Components permit two types of dragging: manual and automatic. These correspond to two different values of the DragMode property. The default is to not allow you to drag components around except under special circumstances. (As always, you'll need to write the code for these special circumstances; see the next section.) This is called manual dragging, and the DragMode property will have the value dmManual. Changing the value of this property to dmAutomatic means that the user may drag the component around the project. Regardless of the setting for the DragMode property, the component will actually move only if you write the code to reposition it, as shown in the next example.

13

For this example, start up a new project, and add a single button to it. Set the DragMode property of that button to dmAutomatic. The event that recognizes dragging and dropping operations is called the OnDragDrop event, and it is associated with the component or form where the "drop" occurs. Thus, if you want to drag a component to a new location on a form, you write code for the form's OnDragDrop event handler. For example, to allow dragging and dropping to move the single button around the form in this example, set the Accept parameter in the FormDragOver event to be True as in the following:

```
procedure TForm1.FormDragOver(Sender, Source: TObject, X,Y
Integer, State: TDragState; var Accept: Boolean);
begin
  Accept := (Source is TButton);
end;
```

Now you can use this code to move the button around:

```
procedure TForm1.FormDragDrop(Sender, Source: TObject;
X, Y: Integer);
begin
  if Source is TButton then
  begin
    TButton(Source).Left := X;
    TButton(Source).Top := Y;
end;
end;
```

Since the type of the Source parameter is a TObject, you must first cast it to the correct component type in order to access any of its properties and methods. Then you can refer to its properties and methods by using the dot notation, as in the preceding example. If you need to know more information about what type of component is being dragged before applying a method or setting a property, use the name of the source component in an "if TypeOfComponent is" statement. You saw these in Chapter 7.

If you run this example, you will notice that the object remains visible in its original location while the drag mouse pointer moves. You cannot use the OnDragDrop event to make a component invisible while the dragging/dropping operation takes place. This is because this event handler is called only after the user drops the object. In fact, the OnDragDrop event need not move the component at all. You often use this event to allow the user just to initiate some action. This is especially common when dragging from one form to another.

If you get tired of the drag mouse pointer that Delphi uses during a drag operation, you can change it. The easiest way is to set the DragCursor property of the component at design time. To do this, select the DragCursor property from the Object Inspector. Now choose a setting. The other possibility is to create your own custom cursor. If you design a custom icon, a common practice is to reverse the colors for the drag icon.

Table 13-8 summarizes the events, methods, and properties used for dragging and dropping.

Manual and Automatic Dragging

If you have left the value of the DragMode property at its default value of
dmManual, then you must use the BeginDrag/EndDrag method to allow
dragging of the component. The syntax for this method is

> *component*.BeginDrag(*Immediate*);

The Immediate is a Boolean value, True or False, as described here:

component.BeginDrag(True);	Dragging begins immediately.
component.BeginDrag(False);	Dragging begins after the mouse moves 5 pixels.

One way to use the flexibility this method gives you is to allow expert users
to drag and drop components, but to make the default that users cannot do
this. For example, use the CTRL-OnMouseDown combination to allow
dragging to take place. You can do this by beginning the OnMouseDown
event handler with the following:

```
procedure TForm1.Button1MouseDown(Sender: TObject;
Button: TMouseButton;
  Shift: TShiftState; X, Y: Integer);
begin
  if  ssCtrl in Shift then
    Button1.BeginDrag(True);
end;
```

13

Item	Description
DragMode property	Allows automatic dragging (value = dmAutomatic) or manual dragging (value = dmManual).
DragCursor property	Set this to change the mouse pointer to a custom cursor when dragging.
OnDragDrop event	Associated with the target of the operation; generated when the source component is dropped on the target component.
OnDragOver event	Associated with any component the source component passes over during dragging. Must have the Accept parameter set to True in order for the Drop to occur.
OnEndDrag event	When the dragging operation is over.
BeginDrag method	Starts dragging when DragMode is set to manual.
EndDrag method	Stops dragging when DragMode is set to manual.

Events, Methods, and Properties Used for Dragging and Dropping
Table 13-8.

Another example of where you might want to use this method is in self-running demonstration programs. You can use the BeginDrag method to start the dragging operation and the EndDrag method to drop the component. This lets you show off dragging and dropping operations.

 Note: If you set the DragMode property to dmAutomatic, then the user can drag components without you needing to write any code to allow this.

The OnDragOver Event

All Delphi objects except menus and timers will detect if a component is passing over them. You can use the OnDragOver event to allow even greater flexibility for your projects. This event lets you monitor the path a component takes while being dragged. You might consider changing the background color of the component being passed over.

The event handler template for forms is

```
procedure TForm1.FormDragOver(Sender, Source: TObject;
X, Y: Integer; State: TDragState; var Accept: Boolean);
begin

end;
```

For components, this event handler template takes the form of

```
procedure TForm1.Button1DragOver(Sender, Source: TObject;
X, Y: Integer; State: TDragState; var Accept: Boolean);
begin

end;
```

The Source is the component being dragged, but the event handler is associated with the component being passed over. The X and Y parameters give you the Left and Top values of where the component being dragged is currently located. This is given in terms of the scale of the object you pass over for forms and the underlying form for all other components. The State parameter has three possible values:

Value of State Parameter	Description
dsDragEnter	Source is now inside target.
dsDragLeave	Source is just left of target.
dsDragMove	Source moved inside target.

Note: Unless the Accept parameter is set to True, the control cannot be dropped onto the target control. If the Accept parameter of the form is not set to be True, you can do dragging and dropping on the form.

Help Systems

A professional Windows application needs a help system that does what Windows users expect. If your online help doesn't have the look and feel of a Windows help system, users will have to learn too much (and you'll probably be working too hard to teach them). Delphi comes with the Windows Help compiler to make it possible to create a help system for your applications.

13

Roughly speaking, the way you use the Help compiler is simple: you write a text file containing certain formatting codes that the Help compiler translates into jumps, definitions, and so on. The text file must be written with a word processor that supports what Microsoft calls RTF (rich text format). Many full-featured word processors support this format. Obviously, you're best off using a Windows word processor when preparing the text files to feed to the Help compiler. This way you can work with the Help compiler in one window and the word processor in the other.

However, I don't recommend doing it this way. (If you insist, Delphi's online help has a discussion of the mark-up techniques needed.) This is because it is *much* easier to create a help system using one of the many third-party tools out there—I guarantee that you will find the money well spent.

Tip: My favorite commercial tool for building help systems is RoboHelp from Blue Sky Software, which comes in both Windows 3.X and Windows 95 versions. There are also a couple of tools—WHAT (Windows Help Authoring Templates) and WHPE (Windows Help Project Editor)—on the Microsoft Software Developers CD-ROM that can make writing help files easier. Check out the WinHelp Lib of the WINSDK forum on CompuServe for additional tools.

In any case, a help system should also include the standard menu that users are accustomed to. The Help menu should certainly have Contents, Search, and About items. The Search item should lead to the list of keywords the user can search through. These keywords will connect to the topics that you write. Various parts of your application (like Delphi itself) should have context-sensitive help. This way all users know that if they press F1, they can get help about a specific item on a form.

You use the HelpFile property of the TApplication object to associate a (compiled) Help file with your application. You create context-sensitive help by setting the HelpContext of the form or component. Once you assign the value of the HelpContext property, you have to tell the Help compiler how to map the HelpContext property to specific topics.

The Help project file contains the information needed for the Help compiler to do its job. The Help project file must be an ordinary ASCII file. The custom is to use .HPJ as the extension on all Help project files. The Help compiler changes this to .HLP for the compiled version. The Help project file lists all the topic files and can optionally add bitmaps or a map between context strings and context numbers. You can also assign two context strings to the same topic by modifying the project file.

To map Help context numbers to specific topics for context-sensitive help, place the topic after the keyword [MAP], followed by white space (press the SPACEBAR or TAB), followed by the Help context numbers. Here's a sample of what you might have in the [MAP] section of the Help project file if you are doing it by hand instead of using one of the third-party tools.

```
[MAP]
FILE_MENU      5     ;5 is context number
                     ;Comments follow semicolons
EDIT_MENU     10     ;10 is context number
VIEW_MENU     15     ;15 is context number
```

Now when you call the Windows help engine (see the next section for more on ways to do this) with a HelpContext property value of 5, you would get the Help page for the FILE_MENU screen, and so on. The point is that the context number is passed by the Delphi program as the value of the HelpContext property.

Tip: If you want a Help button to appear in a common dialog box, set the ShowHelp value of the Options property of the dialog box.

Calling the Windows Help Engine

The TApplication object has three methods that you can use to call the Windows Help engine. All three methods call the correct version of the WinHelp API function for your operating system. (You can also use the WinHelp API directly.) They all theoretically return Booleans that tell you whether the call to the WinHelp Engine was successful.

HelpCommand   This method is essentially equivalent to the WinHelp API call. As such it needs the same parameters as the WinHelp API function. (You can look these up in the online help.) Its syntax is

> function HelpCommand(*Command*: Word; *Data* Longint): Boolean;

The Data parameter is a Longint in Delphi 16 and an Integer parameter in Delphi 32. The Command parameter is the same as the wCommand parameter in the WinHelp API function that may be found in the User or User 32 library (USER.EXE and USER.32.DLL). For example:

```
Application.HelpCommand(HELP_HELPONHELP, 0);   {'or use 4 }
```

13

will display the "Help on Help" page.

Caution: The HelpCommand method only works if a help file has been assigned to the Application.HelpFile property.

HelpContext   The syntax for this function method is simply:

> function HelpContext(Context: THelpContext): Boolean;

You give it the help context number, and you see the help screen for that number. (Since in theory, context ID's can be negative, THelpContext is a type that allows both positive and negative numbers up to the range of Longint in Delphi 16 and Integer in Delphi 32.)

HelpJump   As you might expect, this goes to the specified jump. The syntax is

> function HelpJump(const JumpId: string) : Boolean;

where now you give the string that gives the name of the jump, rather than the ID.

The Win 95 Controls

Windows 95 comes with a set of so-called "common controls" that Delphi lets you get access to. They are described in the following table.

 Note: Delphi 16 already went far in implementing controls that have the look and feel of the Win 95 common controls. For this reason, many Delphi programmers prefer to use the components common to both versions of Delphi whenever possible.

TTabControl	Very similar to the TTabSet component—and for that reason, it's rarely used.
TPageControl	This lets you make multiple page dialog boxes (like Delphi itself).
TTreeView	To display outlines.
TListView	To display multiple column lists.
TImageList	This component stores the images for the TTreeView control. (The TTreeView control's Images property will automatically show as well as the TImageList components on the form associated with it.)
TTrackBar	For sliders or tick bars.
TProgressBar	This also tracks progress visually. The TGauge component works similarly and is more flexible, so there is often no reason to use this component.
THeaderControl	For movable headers, similar to a THeader component.
TStatusBar	For building status bars at the bottom of the screen.
TRichEdit	A component that allows text to be entered in multiple fonts.
TUpDown	Up and down arrow (or left and right) buttons to increase or decrease values.
THotKey	This appears as a special edit box that can be used in setup-type dialog boxes to determine key mappings for programs. The HotKey property returns the hot key as the value of a TShortcut type.

The TRichEdit Component

This is one of the most useful Win 95 controls. The idea is that you often want to go beyond the limited functionality supported by an edit or memo component and display multiple fonts simultaneously. When this happens, turn to the TRichEdit (often called a "RichTextBox") component.

Many of the properties of the TRichEdit component are similar to those of a TMemo component. For example, Lines is a TString object that contains the lines of text.

Note: Most formatting in a TRichEdit component is done to the currently selected text. As with the other edit controls, this can be read off (or changed) by working with the SelText property. The other key properties are SelLength and SelStart.

The following table summarizes the most important new properties of a TRichEdit component:

Property	Description
DefaultText	Specifies how text defaults appear.
PlainText	This Boolean property controls whether the text is ordinary text or rich text.
SelAttributes	This is the key property for the component. It contains a description of how the text should appear. This is an object in its own right with properties such as Color, Name, Pitch, Size, Style, and Height. These properties work just like they do for TFont. You can assign fonts to selected text and vice versa.

For example, to change the currently selected text to italic:

```
RichEdit1.SelAttributes.Style := [fsItalic];
```

Tip: The RichEdit sample project supplied with Delphi 32 is a very good example to study if you need to go further with the TRichEdit component. It gives a fully functional mini-word processor in only a couple of hundred lines of code.

The SpellChecker OCX

Just for fun, I want to show you how to check the spelling of a single word in an edit box by using the spell-checking OCX component. This control can do far more, of course—it can easily check the entire contents of a memo box, for example. Checking (and then replacing) a single misspelled word (assuming the box contains only one word) requires only two lines of code!

For this project:

1. Place an edit box on a form.
2. Place the OCX spell-checking control on the form. (It may be found, naturally enough, on the OCX tab of the Component palette.)
3. Place a button on the form.

Then use the following code in the click event procedure of the button:

```
procedure TForm1.Button1Click(Sender: TObject)
begin
  VCSPeller1.CheckText :=Edit1.Text;
  If VCSpeller1.ResultCode = 0 Then
     Edit1.Text :=VCSpeller1.ReplacementWord;
end;
```

Of course, this only corrects (and replaces) a single word; use it on anything larger in the edit box and it won't work. If you want to actually correct all the words in an edit box, memo, or RichEdit component, you will be happy to know that this control can even separate the text into distinct words without your having to write the code that parses it. It will then check them sequentially. See the online help for more information.

T ip: You may need to look in the VSpell subdirectory to get at the needed VSOCX.HLP help file.

Chapter 14

A Survey of Database Features

In this chapter, we briefly survey some of Delphi's
database powers, emphasizing the role of the data aware
components. *Data aware components* are ones that (after
Delphi connects to a database) can be used to retrieve or
send data to or from the database. This chapter can only be
an introduction, because you will quickly discover that if
you want to do any serious work with databases using
either version of Delphi, you will need and want the extra
power that database programming will give you. And you
will then discover just as quickly that you need to consult
more specialized books. Database programming, whether
done from Delphi or from a full-fledged database manager
like Borland's Paradox, is not trivial. It would take a book
at least twice as large as this one to explain any substantial
part of the database programming power available to you
with either version of Delphi.

Note: If you have a client/server edition of Delphi, you will have even more power at your disposal—we won't cover the client/server features of Delphi in this book.

Note: The Database Desktop choice under the Tool menu is a handy tool for maintaining and creating databases. The Database Desktop allows you to create, restructure, index, modify, copy, and query database tables. You can also use the Database Desktop to copy data and structure information from one database format to another database format.

Some Words About Modern Databases

Before you start working with databases using Delphi, it is a good idea to get a feel for what modern databases are all about. This section tries, without getting too technical, to explain what is usually called the *relational model* for a database. This is the model used by Delphi, Paradox, Microsoft Access, and many other programmable PC databases, such as dBASE and FoxPro.

But first, before we describe the more sophisticated relational model, let's start with simpler databases. A Rolodex is a good example of this kind of simpler database, called a *flat file* database. This kind of database is merely an indexed set of "cards." To build this kind of database, typed files are ideal because they are easy to set up and manipulate and don't require massive resources. Notice that in these databases the data exists in a set form. Indexes are added as a way of quickly getting to specific records, but are not essential—especially for small sets of data.

The trouble with using only typed files for all database applications is that they are too limited. Suppose, for example, you are running a business. This business maintains a list of customers in one indexed system and a list of bills in another. When someone's address changes, you want the address to change in both places automatically. This is possible only with a lot of work, as long as data for each list is kept in separate databases.

More sophisticated databases, like the ones you can build with the Database Desktop (and build completely with Paradox or the database power of Delphi), don't fit the indexed card model. This makes it easy to avoid the update problem just described. They have many other advantages as well, although the extra power usually requires more powerful computers and more code.

There really is no convenient way to describe the underlying structure of the databases that you can build using the various versions of the Borland Database Engine (BDE) supplied with Delphi; that is, what actually lies on the user's hard disk. In fact, for now, think of a database as a large amount of data that exists in no fixed form; it is merely "out there" in some sort of nebulous glob. However, the data is controlled by an oracle with great powers. These powers let the oracle bring order out of chaos.

For example, suppose the database contained data on all computer books published, or even all books published. You want to ask this oracle a specific question about computer books. There are a lot of computer books out there, often many on the same subject with the same title. There are also a lot of authors out there. It's a lot of information to sort through. The oracle, being very powerful with lots of storage space, has all possible information about computer books stored away in some form or other and, moreover, knows everything that's out there. So the oracle knows the authors, the titles, the page counts, the publishers, and lots more. The information kept by the oracle could be used in many ways. You might need all books by a specific author, all books with a specific string in the title, all books by a specific publisher, or all books that satisfy the three conditions.

Now imagine that you ask the oracle to list all books published by Osborne/McGraw-Hill in 1995, including the title, the author, and the page count. The oracle works through all its data and then presents you with a gridlike arrangement of the books satisfying your request. You probably neither know nor care how the oracle does this or how the information is actually stored and processed by the oracle. You end up with a grid, and you can manipulate it easily.

14

Next, notice that a typed file really can't handle this type of situation. If you had a single record associated with each author, you would simply have no way of knowing how many fields to add to allow for all of an author's books. He or she might continue to write and write and write. Of course, you could have a separate record for each book, but this forces a lot of duplication—the vital statistics of the author would need to be repeated each time, for example.

But, if the data were simply out there in some vague formless mass, the oracle could use lots of internal bookkeeping tricks to avoid redundancies, to compress the data, to search through the data, and so on.

Note: In modern database terminology, the questions you ask are called *queries* and the resulting data you are presented with is either a *table* or a *view*.

The difference between a table and a view is that a table is built into the database structures, and a view is a way of looking at information that might span many tables. The oracle (in Delphi, it's the BDE) will respond to different queries with different tables (views), although there is still only one (potentially huge) database out there.

The usual language for asking queries of a relational database is called SQL. "SQL" stands for *structured query language* and is usually pronounced either "seekel" or "sequel" (some say "S-Q-L"). Essentially, this language is built in to Delphi.

In real life, oracles don't exist and data can't be nebulous. So, as you'll see in the next section, data is essentially stored in overlapping tables (grids) that are joined together as needed by the database engine. The columns of these tables (grids) are called *fields* and the rows are called *records*.

Delphi's Database Architecture

Delphi can access many types of databases. Using forms and reports that you create, the BDE can access local databases, like Paradox and dBASE, network SQL server databases, like InterBase and Sybase, and any data source accessible through ODBC (open database connectivity).

Just as in nondatabase applications, Delphi has components to create database applications. Database components have properties that can be set at design time or via code at run time. Delphi also has two pages of database tools available on the Component palette. The ones on the Data Access page let you connect to databases; the ones on the Data Controls page are used to actually display the information. When you need to refer to both types together, it is common to say "data aware controls."

The Data Access Components

The components on the Data Access page let you connect to databases. These components simplify the process of pointing to a database, table, and records. None of the Data Access components is visible at run time.

To build a database application, you place Data Access components on a form and set properties to specify the database, table, and records to use. They provide the link between the Data Aware components and the data source. Table 14-1 lists the Data Access components and their purpose. Except for the addition of the session component, the palettes are the same in both versions of Delphi.

The TTable and TQuery components are the most commonly used Data Access components that you place on a form in order to create a link with a database. You establish the link from the TTable and TQuery components to

Icon	Component	Purpose
	TDataSource	Connects the TTable, TQuery, TStoredProc, and Data Aware Controls components.
	TTable	Retrieves data from a table and sends it to data aware components through a TDataSource component. Sends data from data aware components to the database.
	TQuery	Uses SQL statements to retrieve data from a table and sends it to data aware components through a TDataSource component. Sends data from data aware components to the database.
	TStoredProc	Allows access to server-stored procedures. Sends data from data aware components to the database.
	TDatabase	Used primarily with remote databases. Creates a persistent connection to a database.
	TSession	Nonvisible component only available in Delphi 32. Lets you have global control over the various database connections.
	TBatchMove	Moves and copies table structures and data from one database to another.
	TUpdateSQL	Lets you update an SQL query.
	TReport	Used for printing and viewing of reports through ReportSmith.

Data Access
Components
Table 14-1.

14

data aware components through the TDataSource component. The data aware components display the data to the user. What follows is a short discussion of the most important of these components.

The TTable Component

The TTable component is a fast and easy way to establish a link with a data source. To use the TTable component, do the following:

1. Place a TTable component on the form.
2. Set the DatabaseName property to the directory of the database.
3. Set the TableName property to the table in the database.

4. Double-click the TTable component on the form in order to format the table's output to the data aware components.

5. Set the Active property to True to open the table.

(You can use the speedmenu of the TTable component to add specific fields to the table.)

Note: Double-clicking on a TTable, TQuery, or a TStoredProc component on your form will display the Fields Editor window. Normally, double-clicking a component on a form will display the Code Editor window and a default event procedure. The TDataSource component is the only Data Access component that acts in this manner.

The TQuery Component

The TQuery component allows SQL access, such as a SELECT statement, to return a subset of data from a data source. To use the TQuery component:

1. Place a TQuery component on the form.

2. Set the DatabaseName property to the directory of the database.

3. Set the SQL property to the SQL statements desired. Click the list button to open the String Editor dialog box. For example: 'SELECT * FROM CUSTOMER.DB'

4. Double-click the TQuery component on the form to format the TQuery component's output to the data aware components.

5. Set the Active property to True to open the query.

The TDataSource Component

The TDataSource component provides a conduit for data from a TTable, TQuery, or TStoredProc component to a data aware component. To use the TDataSource component:

1. Place a TDataSource component on the form.

2. Set the DataSet property to the name of a TTable, TQuery, or TStoredProc component. If any Data Access component exists on the form, it will be displayed in DataSet's drop-down list box.

The Components on the Data Controls Page

The Data aware components on the Data Controls page help you display, edit, and send data back to a database. Many of these components are simply data aware versions of standard components. All of the Data Controls components are visible at run time.

Part of building a database application is displaying the data a TTable or TQuery component will return to the program. The database engine built into Delphi pipes the data through a TDataSource component to the data aware components that you place on a form. Data aware components provide the visual link between the data source and the user. Table 14-2 lists the Data Controls components common to both versions of Delphi and their purpose. Table 14-3 lists the ones in Delphi 32 only, and Table 14-4 lists the ones available in Delphi 16 only.

14

Icon	Component	Purpose
	TDBGrid	Spreadsheet-type component that allows viewing and editing data in a tabular form.
	TDBNavigator	VCR-type button bar used to navigate within a table. Can move the current record pointer forward or backward, insert or edit a record, cancel an edit, or refresh the displayed data.
	TDBText	Label component for displaying data the user cannot directly edit.
	TDBEdit	Edit box component to allow the user to edit data from the current record.
	TDBMemo	Memo component for editing text BLOB from the current record. (BLOB stands for "binary large object" and is usually used for graphics.)
	TDBImage	Image box component to display and edit bitmapped BLOB from the current record.
	TDBListBox	List box component that can display data from a table's column.
	TDBComboBox	Combo box component that can display or edit data from a table's column.
	TDBCheckBox	Check box component that can display or edit a Boolean field from the current record.
	TDBRadioGroup	Radio group component containing radio buttons to display or set column data in a table.

Data Controls
Components
Common to
Both Versions
of Delphi
Table 14-2.

Data Controls
Components
in 32-Bit
Version of
Delphi
Table 14-3.

Icon	Component	Purpose
	TDBLookupListBox	List box component that displays data mapped through another table at run time.
	TDBLookupComboBox	Combo box component that displays data mapped through another table at run time.
	TDBCtrlGrid	Multirecord grid.

Database Form Expert

The Database Form Expert (available on the Database menu in Delphi 32, and on the Help menu in Delphi 16) simplifies the steps needed to create a tabular or data-entry form by use of an existing database. Inexperienced as well as experienced database developers can benefit from the Database Form Expert. The Expert can create simple forms or master/detail forms that contain data from a master table, or it can create data from a detail table using the TTable and TQuery Data Access components.

To start the Database Form Expert, choose Database Form Expert from the appropriate menu. By asking questions, the Database Form Expert will let you:

♦ Make a master or detail form

♦ Get data from a TTable or TQuery component

♦ Determine where the data is

♦ Add fields and the format for displaying the data

In particular, the Database Form Expert will place the necessary database components on the form and connect the TDataSource component(s) to the

Data Controls
Components
in 16-Bit
Version of
Delphi
Table 14-4.

Icon	Component	Purpose
	TDBLookupList	List box component that displays data mapped through another table at run time.
	TDBLookupCombo	Combo box component that displays data mapped through another table at run time.

Data Access components (TTable, TQuery, or TStoredProc) and the data aware components. It will even set a tab order for the components.

A Final Note

This chapter has shown you only a very small part of Delphi's database tools and their capacities. Delphi's database component automates many tasks that would take a great deal of coding. Nonetheless, you will eventually need to write code to go beyond the simplest of database applications. When that time comes, Delphi will not disappoint you—its language contains an awesome amount of power just waiting for you to unleash it.

14

Index

Note: Page numbers in *italics* refer to illustrations and tables.

B

C